D0953341

DISCARD

Also by Bruce Jay Friedman

NOVELS

Stern
A Mother's Kisses
The Dick
About Harry Towns
The Current Climate
The Lonely Guy's Book of Life
Tokyo Woes
A Father's Kisses
Violencia

SHORT FICTION

Far From the City of Class
Black Angels
Let's Hear it for a Beautiful Guy
Black Humor(Anthology)
The Collected Short Fiction of Bruce Jay Friedman
Three Balconies: Stories and a Novella

SCREENPLAYS

Stir Crazy
Splash
Doctor Detroit
Fore Play
Steambath

PLAYS

Scuba Duba
Steambath
Have You Spoken to Any Jews Lately?

NON-FICTION

The Lonely Guy
The Slightly Older Guy
Even the Rhinos Were Nymphos
Sexual Pensées

LUCKY BRUCE
A LITERARY MEMOIR

Bruce Jay Friedman

Lucky Bruce

A Literary Memoir

Farmington Public Library
2101 Farmington Avenue
Farmington, NM 87401

BIBLIOASIS

002000351205

Copyright © Bruce Jay Friedman, 2011

All rights reserved. No part of this publication may be reproduced or
transmitted in any form or by any means, electronic or mechanical,
including photocopying, recording, or any information storage and
retrieval system, without permission in writing from the publisher.

FIRST EDITION

Library and Archives Canada Cataloguing in Publication

Friedman, Bruce Jay, 1930-
Lucky Bruce : a literary memoir / Bruce Jay Friedman.

ISBN 978-1-926845-31-9

1. Friedman, Bruce Jay, 1930-. 2. Authors, American—
20th century—Biography. I. Title.

PS3556.R5Z53 2011   813'.54   C2011-903416-6

PRINTED AND BOUND IN USA

In memory of Mario Puzo

and Joseph Heller

EXT. An apartment building in the Bronx. 1947.

Two mothers meet.

MRS. GIBSON: *I'm so excited. My son Richie is off to study medicine at Kentucky.*

MRS. FRIEDMAN: *Congratulations.*

MRS. GIBSON: *What about Bruce?*

MRS. FRIEDMAN: *He's going to be a writer.*

MRS. GIBSON: (considers, shrugs) *Oh well, we can't always get what we want.*

What concerned me most was the dry cleaning. When I dropped off my clothing, I'd made the mistake of announcing that I had written the film. There was a pretty girl in the store. I may have been trying to impress her. I was trying to impress her. Now I was afraid to leave the apartment. People on the street would stare at me.

"That turkey that just opened? There's the fellow who's responsible for it."

I asked my wife Pat if she would please pick up the dry cleaning.

Vincent Canby had enjoyed my books and plays. But writing in The N.Y. Times *he had described* Stir Crazy *as "an energetic mess."*

That takes care of that, I thought. Unless there are people who are chomping at the bit to see an energetic mess, I might as well bury the body.

Still, it occurred to me, as the day moved along, that a few friends, acting out of loyalty and compassion, might have braved a viewing of the movie.

I hailed a cab. The driver had just moved to the city from a trailer park in North Carolina. I congratulated her on the move and asked if she would drop me off at Cinema One and wait while I spoke to someone at the box office.

I asked the man in the booth if he had gotten rid of any tickets for the six o'clock show.

"It's sold out."

That was odd. Probably a benefit of some kind.

"What about the eight o'clock?"

"Not a ticket left."

That was strange as well. Must have been a lot of benefits that time of year.

I asked my trailer park friend to take me up to the Triplex on Eighty-Sixth Street. There, I saw a line down the street, stretching far off in the distance. Clearly they were there for another film.

I asked a young man what he was waiting to see.

"Stir Crazy, you fool. Why else would I be here?"

I called Josh, the eldest of my three sons, who lived in the Broadway area.

"Dad," he said. "I had to get away from the theater. The people who couldn't get tickets were rioting and breaking down the police barriers."

Stir Crazy became the biggest-grossing comedy – at the time – in Columbia Pictures history.

All of this puzzled me.

I asked a friend and veteran producer, Martin Ransohoff, to explain the phenomenon.

"They can smell it," he said.

1

"New Yukkeh, they tahd and Proustian. We goan be bold and Tolstoyan."

> From an inspirational speech to the author by Capt. George B. Leonard, editor of *Air Training* magazine.

It's been alleged by some – a few, and certainly not an entire horde of enthusiasts – that I've had a glittering career. For a writer, that is. If so, I never stopped to examine it. It was always on to the next story, the next adventure or, more than likely, the next mortgage payment. Now, with the lights dimming a bit, it might be time to consider that this career I've been cobbling together – none of it planned – might actually have had a touch of glitter to it.

It all began for me, in a literary sense, during the Korean War. We weren't quite part of the Great Generation, having missed out on World War II by a decade or so. Still, I thought of us as being a reasonably great generation. There was a war going on, albeit a dreary affair. The Korean War had very little panache to it. It was mostly about huddling on hillsides, blowing on your hands and losing toes to frostbite. There would be no heroic storming of the beaches at Anzio, with John Wayne egging us on. Still, it was a war, the only one we had. The country called, and off we went, with no thought of slipping across the border to hunker down in Ontario until it blew over. The questioning would come later, with the war that followed.

I was finishing up a degree in Journalism at the University of Missouri in 1951, awaiting the call to be drafted, then shipped across the Pacific and no doubt expected to shoot Koreans. I could barely find Korea on the map and had no wish to shoot at its inhabitants. On the contrary, my fantasy was that one of their finest sharpshooters would be lurking in a tree, prepared to pick me off the moment I stepped off the plane. Such ego. And that would be it for me, at twenty-one, the only vestige of my literary life being an essay I'd written for a freshman English class on Hemingway's Lost Generation.

"Were they really all that lost?" I'd asked, in a precociously revisionist spirit. "Or were they just swanning around, *pretending* to be lost?"

It was a glum time for me. In a devil-may-care spirit, I threw away what little money I had in all-night poker games and had a spiritless affair with a Stephens College history major. As we made love, or what passed for it, she said: "You don't really care much for this, do you?"

I took the last of my journalism classes, which required that I memorize the names of editors of turn-of-the-century farming weeklies. I was also expected to sprint through the halls carrying hot linotype from a printer to the editor of the local newspaper. As an elective, I'd taken a course in Serbo-Croatian cabals; here again, the cabals were carried off at the turn of the century. And thus would I go to my grave, fortified by a knowledge of turn-of-the-century farming weeklies and Serbo-Croatian cabals.

Sensing my desolate state, my mother arranged to meet me in Chicago and to see to it that I had a pleasant weekend before facing whatever darkness lay ahead.

"You need some fun in your system," is the way she put it.

"Fun" was the operative word in her life. As she lay dying, on a couch, in 1973, wearing a bathrobe and puffing on one of her beloved Chesterfield cigarettes, she said: "Don't have any sympathy for me, darling. I've had my fun."

There we were in 1951 Chicago, which might not be the coldest place on earth, but in my experience it might as well have been. Despite the best efforts of the Drake Hotel to keep us comfortable, I felt chilled to the bone for the entire weekend. Years later, on an assignment for *The Saturday Evening Post*, I almost froze to death standing alongside Lake Michigan, wearing a thin raincoat and waiting to investigate a murder with a pair of late-arriving homicide detectives.

Yet for all of what I found to be the unforgiving weather, Chicago, for Saul Bellow, was the *only* city. (No doubt the residents of Irkutsk have the same sense of local pride.) I met the Nobelist – and the pride of Chicago – only once, in the sixties, standing behind him in a movie-line in Manhattan. He recognized me. He later claimed to have *discovered* me, publishing my story "The All-American" in his magazine, *The Noble Savage*. None of this was true, although he'd read the story in my agent Candida Donadio's office, enjoyed it and may have *considered* publishing it.

His only words to me in the movie-line were: "How can you live in this hellhole?"

As for the Chicago visit, my mother meant well, although some might question her choice of activities to amuse me. We had dinner the first night at the Gold Coast apartment of a childhood friend of hers named Munko who had enriched himself by scalping tickets to hot Chicago musicals. As a demonstration of his new affluence, he carved off slices of rare roast beef, holding up each one to be admired.

"You must have made a lot of money, didn't you, Munko?" my mother said.

"Yes, I did, Molly," he said with satisfaction, then carved off a few more slices.

To be fair about it, he had grown up dirt poor on the streets of Manhattan's lower East Side and had every reason to take pride in being able to carve up slices of roast beef with flamboyance.

We spent the second evening of our visit at a nightclub, joining a group of paraplegics in listening to the music of the Tommy Dorsey orchestra. The wounded veterans kept time to the song selections by tapping their drink mixers on the arms of their wheelchairs. Dorsey, too, had been a Lower East Side friend of my mother's. Several times during his performance, she poked at me and said: "You know how long I know that sonofabitch?"

Such were the highlights of my trip. Still, as she often did, my mother had come to the rescue. I told her my spirits had been lifted – they hadn't. But thus assured, she kissed me on the cheek and off she went to keep an appointment in Manhattan with her corsetière. (She spent a great deal of time at corsetières. I spent many an afternoon with her. I would sit in a waiting room and snappishly page through corsetière industry magazines, which were maddeningly unarousing.)

Do I have a Proustian recollection of my mother's scent as we said goodbye in Chicago? Not particularly, but no doubt it was Shalimar, her signature perfume. For the Boise State academics who keep track of such things, I recorded an hallucinatory version of the weekend in a short story I wrote some years later. It was called – and how could it not be? – "The Good Time."

In a dark mood, I returned to my dorm and dreamed of Korea: the very name rang in my ears and began to sound like an urological disease.

"Stay away from him. He's got Korea."

To demonstrate that there is a great balance wheel to life, years later, I had a highly satisfying romance – to a point – with a lovely Korean woman. Not insignificantly, her pitch black hair, when released, touched the floor. She had also convinced me that she had taken a course on the penis at New York University. Had she? Did it matter? That she'd thought of such a course was enough.

Back at the Missouri dorm, in one of the Last-Minute-Reprieves that were emblematic of my life, the Air Force put out an emergency call for a dozen administrative officers; they were to be given two weeks of military training, then expected to hit the ground firing off memos at Scott Air Force Base in Illinois. I almost broke a leg dashing over to sign up for the program. Somebody Up There not only loved but adored me.

I reported to a campus military barracks and quickly got the hang of dealing with an M-l rifle. Though I demonstrated great skill at disassembling the weapon, I was all at sea when it came to putting it back together. At one point, before a weapons inspection, I got disgusted and kicked all the parts of it under my bed. I told the officer in charge I must have left it at a party. It was a lame excuse. Remarkably, he swallowed it.

Shaky as I was about military matters, I loved being in the Air Force and loved the uniform. I thought it was much more dashing than that of the other services, especially when the cap was worn at a rakish angle. And I loved being a second lieutenant, and the gold shoulder bars that were part of the package. I did a great deal of crisp saluting and continue the practice to this day, greeting the puzzled Chechnyan doormen in our Manhattan building as if they are superior officers. The wings pinned to the lapels of an administrative officer were virtually identical to those worn by heroic fighter pilots. At cocktail lounges in Illinois, when asked about aerial combat, I would look off in the distance with clenched teeth as if my experience was all too painful to recall. Years later, in the eighties, I became friends with the novelist James Salter. ("Brilliant" generally accompanies his name, and rightly so.) Salter had been an authentic air ace, having shot down enemy aircraft in the legendary MIG Alley. I always felt shamed in his presence. In thin defense of myself, I had taken a stab at being a fighter pilot and been laughed out of the examiner's office and told to buy a pair of glasses before I walked off a cliff. Evidently I'd been legally blind for four years at the university. This explained why I could never quite make out what was written on blackboards or understand why people made a fuss over football games when it was impossible to see the activity on the field. Or so it seemed to me. What exactly were they watching?

The Air Force didn't quite know what to do with me. I dashed off a few memos in the morning on behalf of a heavily decorated Captain who grew pale with fear at the idea of having to respond to written correspondence. My use of the word "hitherto" impressed him and made him feel he was in safe hands. I made sure to kick off each memo with a few "hithertos" and an occasional "aforesaid" while he went off to snap at the panties of Air Force secretaries. (Until, later in the day, his somber 300-pound Cherokee wife and four children came to fetch him and take him home.) In the afternoons, I took naps in a supply room. For a brief period and perhaps because of my allegedly rough upbringing in the Bronx, I was asked to put together a platoon and train it in how to deal with angry mobs. The commanding general was fearful that local electricians, dissatisfied with their contracts, would descend upon the base and there would be no one to fight them off. There were plenty of pilots on hand, of course, but it was felt that for all of their dashing appearance, they wouldn't be much good at beating up electricians. I found a surly-looking corporal in the supply room, and gave him a quick briefing ("A mob is not like any other gathering . . . It has to be dealt with gingerly before it flies out of control.")

Then I introduced him to the platoon.

"You'll find that José here is an expert in dealing with angry mobs."

Off I went then, once again, to take my treasured naps.

I think of my literary career as having officially begun soon afterward, with an invitation to join the staff of a new magazine called *Air Training*. It was headed up by a pilot named George B. Leonard, a tall and lanky Southern gentleman with a bookish background and a high sense of drama. (He was later to become an iconic figure in West Coast counter-culture.)

When I met him at his office, he fell back, as though in shock.

"This incredible," he said. "You old Tom Wolfe himself, back from the grave, ready to start kickin' and fussin', and preparin' to plant your big boots on the literary map of America. Why, Tom, you old hell-raiser, welcome back."

I found this flattering, though I assured Leonard that I was just a young man who had barely gotten out of the gate as a writer, my "Hemingway's Lost Generation" essay notwithstanding.

"You tebbly modest," said Leonard, "as befits a young man of your enormous capabilities."

Leonard was obsessed with *The New Yorker* magazine and had somehow taken it into his head that *Air Training* would be competitive with the legendary weekly.

"New Yukkeh, they tahd and Proustian." he said. "We goan be bold and Tolstoian."

Then, as if he was addressing the staff of the fabled magazine, he put an arm around my shoulder, raised a fist and cried out a challenge:

"Editors of the New Yukkeh, with your Toke (of the Town) and your long skinny columns of tahp, slahly desahned, of coase, to be phallic and sexual . . . *Heah mah voice*. Friedman and ah comin' for you, and we goan whip your tahd and pretentious ass."

Then he picked up a copy of the celebrated magazine and shook his head in puzzlement, as if he couldn't understand the appeal of such a publication.

"New Yukkeh," he said, holding his nose. "Pee yew."

As absurd as it sounds, I found all of this to be inspiring. With Leonard's supportive arm around my shoulder, I could hear "John Brown's Body" being chanted in the distance. I had no idea of how an obscure training magazine could hold its own, much less overtake, the iconic home of Ross and Benchley and Thurber – and now J.D. Salinger. But so inspiring was Capt. George B. Leonard that I was willing to give it a try.

I joined a staff made up of a former Chicago bridge tender named Jack O'Callaghan, the folksinger Will Holt, who was to become a famed cabaret performer, and a quartet of gays and lesbians who made up the art department. (With regard to homosexuals at the time, the policy of the Air Force was *Don't Even Think About It*.) The staff photographer was a career master sergeant of Mexican descent named Joe Colazzo. A short stocky man with wavy black hair and thick red lips, he had, after a struggle, fallen in love with the new Rolleiflex camera that had replaced his beloved, albeit cumbersome, Speed Graphic.

"I love m' little Rollei" he would say, stroking it in its leather case. "It will help me to take great fo-toes."

His main function was to track down women at the base and, for the purpose of morale, to take what were then called "cheese-cake" pictures of them. His style was a bit heavy-handed. Pointing his camera, he would say, "You're so darned cute. If you could just turn around slightly so I can get a better angle on them sweet little titties." Yet I don't recall a single one of the subjects objecting to his style. He had a 5-year-old son at home he referred to as "little Hendry." Often, in the middle of a photo shoot, he would lower his head in shame and say: "What is *wrong* with me? Little Hendry is home waitin' for me, and here I am talkin' titties."

My first effort for the magazine was a column called "Air Force Fables." In the opening episode, a serviceman appears in a barracks carrying a magic wand and announces: "I am your fairy sergeant." No sooner had the first issue been distributed than a cable came in from an infuriated colonel in Pyongyang saying: "What's gotten into you people? Don't you realize we're fighting a war over here? There are shells falling all about us. And this Fried-man of yours is giving us fairy sergeants. In the name of decency, STOP FABLES."

Stop them we did, though my literary education continued. The bridge-tending O'Callaghan instructed me in the sensory appeal of simple foods, often taken for granted.

"Toast" he would say," then close his eyes and lick his lips as if he'd just taken a bite of a slice. "Warm, crunchy, delicious *toast*. The cozy smell of it. *Ummmm*."

The exercise heightened my appreciation of toast, although I can't say that it was to make a dramatic alteration in my literary style. Leonard's contribution was substantial. He presented me with three novels which I recall reading (gobbling up) in a weekend: Thomas Wolfe's *Of Time and the River,* James Jones' *From Here to Eternity* and, grace be to God, J.D. Salinger's *Catcher in the Rye.* It was the Salinger book that got to me, as it had, of course, to so many others. I'd thought of literature as having to do with long, tortuous sentences dealing with infinity, the mysteries of the cosmos, the immutable hills of North Carolina (everything had to be immutable), the bitter (and existential?) fate of mankind. But here was a world, and a style, that I recognized. Not at the moment, but who knows, in the distant future I might be able to pull off a story or even a book in that spirit. What I experienced did not rise to the level of an epiphany. Boys from the Bronx tended not to have epiphanies. But I did stare off in the distance with the moist eyes that seemed obligatory. *A writer's life for me?* Could it be? My mother had always wanted me to pursue a career in theatrical public relations. ("They all have big homes in Rockaway.") I meant no disrespect to those in the field. But what if I were to soar beyond theatrical public relations itself and become a novelist, a real writer? Pinocchio becoming a real boy.

(Through difficult times, I often wondered if my mother hadn't been on to something.)

2

Feeling invincible, I headed for a lesbian bar I'd been visiting in Greenwich Village. It puzzled me that the unbearably beautiful women there tended to shy away from me.

The author, after selling his first short story to *The New Yorker*.

The Cold War, in the early fifties, was at its height. There were "Commies" lurking about at every turn, or so it was felt. More than one high-ranking officer felt a need to "lob a few into the Kremlin" and settle the whole business. George B. Leonard thought otherwise, and took our magazine in another direction. Though not a Commie himself, he had great respect for Soviet airmen in particular. Imagining a typical one, he wrote:

"Though he of peasant stock and obviously backward in Western skills, and though he little more than a rosy-cheeked boy – observe him as he joyously whips his MIG-23 about the Sahberian skahs, pullin' G-forces as if they so many blinis.

"He Mitya of the Soviet Air Force."

There was a fear that the Soviets would slip their Tupolev bombers beneath the radar screen at the Canadian border with the intention of savaging the American heartland. Civilian volunteers were called upon to peer at the skies and sound the alarm if they saw such aircraft coming our way. It fell to me to present an award to a man named Vince, who had set the record for hours spent peering at the skies over Ely, Minnesota. Though he had achieved nothing in the way of a result and had been rendered half-blind in the process, he graciously accepted an Air Force plaque in his honor.

"Even if you never spot a single bomber," I said, vamping a bit, "believe me, they know about you in the Kremlin."

Squinting at me with admiration, he insisted on giving a dinner in *my* honor, featuring the local specialty which was walleyed pike. Though the fish did not have a distinctive taste – it was a fish like any other – I was taken with its name. Thinking to impress my sister Dollie with my wartime derring-do, I fired off a postcard to her in New Jersey – as if I was Amundsen reporting in from the South Pole.

"I am in far-off Minnesota and I have just eaten walleyed pike."

Such was the nature of my experience in the armed forces. There was the magazine, of course, the presentation of congratulatory plaques, and for some unfathomable reason I was ordered to hang lighting fixtures for a night club in St. Louis. That was the sum of it. Try as I might, I could not, in the years to follow, whip these materials into a rousing wartime saga. As a result, novels went unfinished and actors were abandoned during rehearsals of at least one play with an Air Force theme (*Lawrence of America*) that lacked a single compelling moment.

It took me decades to realize that *absolutely nothing of consequence had happened to me in the Air Force.*

With an exception. To my great good fortune, an episode toward the end of my tour, in 1953, did set me off in a literary direction. The Air Force had built mock peasant villages in the desert at Gila Bend, Arizona, for jet fighters to use as target practice, the better to help them obliterate the real thing in Korea. In charge, essentially, of cleaning up the wreckage and having it built up again – was a bantam rooster of a major who had been dropped from the jet program because of a hearing disability. He flew me over the target ranges in a tiny propeller-driven aircraft, and became increasingly agitated as the jets whistled by overhead. Standing up in the cockpit, he shook his fists at them, cried out, "Oh, you bastardos," and underwent what appeared to be a total mental breakdown. A deranged Ahab of the skies, he twisted and contorted us along the side of a mountain, finally crash-landing our little aircraft into a supply shack. One wing was in flames. A ground crew awaited, and doused us with fire-resistant foam.

I was, predictably, shaken by the experience and had no idea of what to do about it. When I pulled myself together, I wrote a short story based on the experience. Writers tend to dance coyly around the question of whether their work is autobiographical.

"I've taken a few liberties. It sort of is . . . but not really."

My first attempt at a story was blatantly autobiographical.

In preparation for this maiden effort, I adhered strictly to Ernest Hemingway's dictum – that good writing can only be accomplished at First Light. Crawling out of bed at an ungodly hour, I staggered over to the typewriter, waited for the required glimpse of daylight and wearily wrote "The Man They Threw Out of Jets." I've come to feel that Hemingway's advisory was a hoax, designed to stunt the careers of young writers – and possible competitors – for generations to come. And that the great man himself would arise each day, well-rested, and begin his work day at noon.

On a whim, and not daring to mention a word to my commanding officer, I (rebelliously?) sent the story off to *The New Yorker* – George B. Leonard's *bête noire* – and promptly forgot about it.

I considered staying on in the Air Force. There was the beloved uniform, of course, but also the freedom, the camaraderie, the magnificent veal cutlets at the Officer's Club, being able to hitch a ride on an aircraft – the way one might hail a cab – and to have it take you to a destination of your choice (Las Vegas, being a favorite). I had a feeling, however, that there would always be a ceiling on the careers of Jewish boys from the Bronx. A great fuss had been made in the press over Hyman Rickover, a Jew who had become an admiral in the Navy. But he was a technical sort of fellow, and there was little that was hell-for-leather about him. Not the model I had in mind. I saw myself rising to the rank of major, held back at that point and becoming an *éminence grise*, consigned to whispering insights into the ear of a general with a more acceptable birthright. I wasn't entirely paranoid; it would be almost six decades before Obama arrived. I don't recall seeing a single black officer during my time in the Air Force. A single airman, for that matter. Jews in the higher ranks were nowhere in evidence. Then, too, there was a woman I'd met in St. Louis. I'd seen Ginger Howard at a dance at Missouri University four years before. I thought she was hopelessly beautiful. ("A gardenia that had been left out in the rain," was my fictional description of her.) I experienced what the novelist Mario Puzo was to describe as "the thunderbolt."

Lacking the courage to speak to her, I thought about her all through college. Four years later, I did manage to call, explaining that I had wanted to approach her at the dance, but couldn't think of a good opening remark.

"Do you have one now?" she was curious to know.

"No," I responded, "but I'm working on one."

Though we were never to have an actual conversation – there may have been an exchange about Sinatra – it was tacitly understood that I would return home, get a job and call for her to join me. Marriage would follow. This was the fifties, 1954, to be precise, and we had, after all, rolled around in my car a few times.

So off I went to New York in my beloved '46 Chevy, with its attention-getting white wall tires. On a used car lot in Belleville, Illinois, the vehicle had virtually winked at me like a puppy, begging me to buy it. An Israeli soldier hitched a ride. He had been sent to Scott Air Force base to train as a fighter pilot. "Small" doesn't quite describe him. A little slip of a man is what he was. The Arab nations and the Taiwanese had dispatched dozens of such trainees. The Israelis felt that this single little fellow – a Holocaust survivor – was enough. When we reached Manhattan I had to resist taking him home with me and fattening him up before releasing him to the wilds of Brooklyn. Further along, I learned that he had cleared the skies of Egyptian fighters in the 1967 war.

No sooner had I gotten comfortable in my mother's Bronx apartment than a letter arrived from a fellow named Hollis Alpert at *The New Yorker* magazine. His job was to poke through the tons of unsolicited manuscripts (the "slush pile") that arrived at the magazine and to fish out – and work with – two hopefuls per month who showed some promise. I was fished out along with John Sack, who was to have a strong career as a journalist and foreign correspondent. Alpert said that the esteemed William Maxwell had serious questions about my submission but that Alpert himself felt it had merit and wondered if I had anything else he might look at. There was my old "Hemingway's Lost Generation" essay, of course, but I didn't think it was suitable. So I sat down at my mother's kitchen table and dashed off a story called "Wonderful Golden Rule Days," about a childhood misadventure. Or at least it *seems* I dashed it off. I don't recall writhing in agony to get it right. There would be much writhing in the future. But not just then.

A letter arrived soon after – in the magazine's signature style – saying, "All of us here are delighted with your story and we would like to publish it in the magazine."

My response was: "All of us here in the Bronx are delighted that all of you there at *The New Yorker* are pleased with my story."

I was thrilled. How could I not be? It was as if I'd skipped the minor leagues and gone straight to the Yankees. Though the magazine has lost little of its gilded position, it seemed to have even more at the time. There was little interfering television in the early fifties. And certainly no iPods. J.D. Salinger fever was at its height. Word of a new story by The Master (or one from Roald Dahl, for that matter) would travel through the neighborhoods, as if spread by the French Underground. To be in that company. And that of the great Irwin Shaw. My father gazed at me in wonder, although it may have been a reaction to my height. He was a small man. I'd grown a bit in the Air Force and now towered over him. My mother seemed pleased. ("They're smart people. They must know what they're doing.") Still, there was a small area of doubt. How would this further the career she had planned for me in theatrical public relations? Only Ginger Howard in far-off St. Louis was clearly disappointed. The last of her girlfriends had gotten married. She was unthinkably old at twenty-one. If only I'd called and said I had a job and could come and fetch her. In truth, I was in no rush to get married. It nagged at me that we had yet to have a conversation, which did not bode well for the future. Still, there was her great Cyd Charisse imitation, which had to be considered.

Alpert invited me downtown for a visit to the magazine. A tall owlish looking man, he shushed me down as we walked through the hallowed corridors.

"Mr. Shawn is on the floor now. It upsets him to hear strange voices."

"Have you ever met J.D. Salinger?" I whispered.

"Many times," he said.

He pointed to a desk in an unoccupied office.

"That's where Jerry put the finishing touches on 'Bananafish.'"

Jerry. It was the first time I'd heard the iconic figure referred to in that homey manner. A result is that I experienced my first *frisson*. I now had an epiphany and a frisson under my belt. Not bad for a Bronx fellow. Decades would pass before I heard a second such reference. (A.E. Hotchner, author of *Papa Hemingway*, said to me years later, "Of course I knew Jerry. We played poker each week at Chumley's. He was dismissive of American writers, although he did feel that Melville had ability.")

Alpert advised me not to get married (he was to have five wives).

"They all turn out to be pack rats."

I was to get conflicting advice on the subject of marriage. Several years later, George B. Leonard, then a civilian, told me: "Do not get divosed." This, while he was halfway along in his own divorce.

Alpert explained that writers fell into two categories: "Good ones who are *New Yorker* writers and good ones who are not."

Though I was about to be published in the magazine, he may have been sending me a discreet signal. Indeed, it was to be fifteen years before I published a second story in the magazine.

Before I left his office, he made a remark that I felt was wounding and unnecessary.

"Keep sending us stories and let us fail to appreciate them."

Those poor wives. . . .

I met Alpert years later in Sag Harbor. He called out to me. "I discovered you, Friedman. Discover me back."

"The Man They Threw Out of Jets" was snapped up by *The Antioch Review* and published in 1955, several years after my meeting with Alpert. Not that I was idle in the years to come, but the review published a second story of mine fifty years later, almost to the day. I suggested to Robert Fogarty, the editor, that we pick up the pace, and we did. (Four more stories were published in the review in quick succession.)

For the moment, though, I had a perfect score and there was a part of me that was tempted to quit while I was ahead. Another treat was to follow. "Wonderful Golden Rule Days" appeared in the very same issue of *The New Yorker* as a story by Roald Dahl, another hero. This was long before Dahl entered his anti-Semitic/children's book phase, posing an intriguing question. Upon learning that Céline, as an example, has been unmasked as the author of anti-Semitic pamphlets for the Gestapo, does one go back and *dis*-enjoy his masterful *Journey to the End of the Night*?

For all the pleasure of having a first story published, there was something unsettling about seeing it in print. Truman Capote had said that the primary reason he enjoyed being published in *The*

New Yorker was the unmatched quality of the editing. My story had, indeed, been edited, but there was something manicured about the result. It was as if a strange barber had cut my hair to his (immaculate) specifications, not mine. What had happened to the rough edges? I liked my rough edges. In many ways, I was *all* rough edges.

Still, I was not to let this minor glitch spoil the experience. Feeling invincible, I headed for a lesbian bar I'd been visiting in the Village. It puzzled me that the women there tended to shy away from me. Perhaps if I produced (flashed?) a clipping of my story, it would turn things around. It didn't. A title for that particular episode – and perhaps for my life in general – might be *The Man Who Didn't Get It.*

Still, though the field of theatrical public relations might suffer – the fates had handed me a career, if not a magic wand. All I had to do is dream a little, dash off some stories (there he goes again, dashing off stories) – and someone would be on hand to throw money at me. Indeed, Brendan Gill at the magazine had called.

"Never fear," he said. "You will receive top dollar."

I knew nothing of the awful shipwrecks to come, the horrible ten-car collisions. Being pushed, unwillingly, out of a coveted apartment. Half a decade spent trying to pump life into the corpse of an unpublishable novel. But, setting aside the inconvenience of spending long hours tied to a chair, there were unexpected delights as well. A play (*Scuba Duba*) that seemed doomed became, magically, a hit. A novel (*Stern*) that caused me to hide away in shame was greeted by a warm critical welcome.

Still, what if I'd gone off in the wrong direction? There was still time for me to take a stab at theatrical public relations – my mother's plan for me. And what about singing with a band? My mother had once stopped a talent agent on Broadway and asked him to listen to my voice. With puzzled tourists passing by, I sang a few bars of "Careless" into the man's ear. (*Careless, now that you've got me loving you. You're careless. . . . careless in everything you do*")

"The kid's got good head tones," he'd said. Then he disappeared into a crowd.

There were so many other fields that lay unexplored. I'd heard there was a fortune to be made in seamless gutters.

But does a writer have a choice?

Mario Puzo, who later became a friend, had answered the question with the following scene.

INT. Living room. . . . Hell's Kitchen . . . 1935 . . .

PUZO, 15 years old, has returned from Fresh Air Camp in a state of high excitement. He had discovered classical literature and was especially taken with *The Three Musketeers* and *King Arthur and the Knights of the Round Table.*

PUZO: (to his mother): *Mom, I've decided to become a writer.*

MOTHER: (stunned) *Mario, are you crazy. Don't you want a real job . . . with the railroad . . . where you get a pension and health benefits?*

PUZO: (patiently) *Mom . . . can a hunchback lose his hump?*

3

A shrine should be built in honor of those fat little beauties.
The author, in appreciation of Big Little Books –
his early favorites.

A bar I liked called Eric's, which enjoyed some seedy prominence in the eighties and nineties, had a sign in the window that said "No sad stories." You'd think that someone born in the thick of the Great Depression would have a sad story to tell, but mine isn't one of them. In the thirties and forties, the four of us –my older sister and I and our parents – lived, or more correctly, were crammed into a small apartment in the Bronx. I slept in a chair in the kitchen and Dollie was put (stashed?) in a bookcase that concealed a small cot which was hauled out for her at night. My father worked in New York's garment center as a cutter of women's underwear and supported us on a salary of thirty dollars a week. I was self-conscious about his profession and took some teasing for it. ("Ha ha, your father makes ladies' underwear.") I fired back, saying: "It's only slips and petticoats," as if the making of a more intimate garment such as panties would establish us as a family of perverts.

It eased my embarrassment to know that Gottfried Underwear produced a "fine" (and expensive) line of garments. Now

31

and then, my mother would raise (hoist?) her skirt on Sheridan Avenue and demonstrate to a neighbor the superior quality of a Gottfried petticoat. My father would occasionally return from work with a manila envelope under his arm, whistling innocently – as if to conceal a crime, which, to an extent, he'd pulled off. (Gottfried employees were not permitted to take home "samples.") Each of the envelopes contained a "fine" slip or petticoat which was designated for the wife of Dr. Pasachoff, our family physician. It was my mother's feeling that the doctor's fee was insufficient compensation for a man of his eminence. ("His wife will faint when she sees what she's getting.")

Pasachoff indeed had been the first physician in the Bronx to discover and make use of the "wonder drug" penicillin. Massive doses of the drug saved my gangrenous right arm in 1945. His brother, a surgeon, had wanted to saw it off. He had served in the WWII Pacific and sawed off quite a few of them. My mother intervened. ("I have a better idea. I'll saw off your head.") Happily, the medicine did the trick. I recovered and was treated to a dinner I'd dreamed about – the chopped steak and creamed spinach at Lindy's restaurant on Broadway. For weeks, throughout my illness, I hadn't had much appetite. And I still prefer a chopped steak to the finest Porterhouse.

I had enough trouble with two arms. I'm not at all sure I would have gotten by with one.

It seemed to me that the Bronx, in the forties, was populated by short feisty dads who wore Fedoras, kept their chins thrust out challengingly and bounced along the streets to a Tin Pan Alley beat. (James Cagney and George Raft of the movies, both born on the lower East Side, would have been the prototypes.) My father was one of them. He did keep his chin thrust out, although a thin scar beneath his lip was evidence that he had thrust it out a bit too invitingly at the wrong individual. One of my earliest memories had to do with running a finger (tenderly?) along the scar. And "feisty" didn't quite describe him. "Jaunty" was more like it. His walk was distinctively light and easy; it was right on the edge of tap-dancing. I tried imitating the walk for years – until my knees gave out. My son Josh picked up the torch and for a decade has been jauntily dancing along through the streets of Dallas.

Judging from the looks thrown his way by admiring Bronx housewives, I would have to say my father was a handsome man – bald, before it became a fashion statement – but bald nonetheless. Handsome – and bald. This troubled me. I assumed I would lose my hair as well and spent years guarding each strand and feeling remorse when I lost one. I never did reach his level of baldness. From time to time, I'd run into a lesser player in Hollywood named Howard Himelstein. After an astonished look at my hairline, he"d say: "I can't believe it. I thought it would be all gone now, but somehow you've held the line."

For all of his slender means, my father was something of a fashion plate. There was only one man in our building who surpassed him in nattiness. As a buyer for the Saks Fifth Avenue menswear department, Mr. Sussman, with all sorts of apparel available to him, held a clear advantage. Passing each other in the street, the two men would exchange uneasy looks. My father wore only Hickey Freeman suits (he had four of them) and owned a variety of straw boaters. We were a hat family. I generally wear one. A fine moment came about for me not too long ago in a restaurant, when the actor Al Pacino said to me admiringly: "Some men can wear a hat." (And when will this man stop name-dropping?)

A fresh and virtually year-round suntan added to my father's appearance. Though he rarely left the city, he had the capability of lying on a park bench for no more than ten minutes, sticking his face up at the sun and coming away with a rich tan. (He did much the same in the bleachers at the Yankee Stadium. Rarely looked at the game, only the sun.) Inevitably, a neighbor would stop him, assume he'd been to Miami and say: "You look great. When'd you get back?"

The feisty Bronx dads of the time were all fiercely patriotic, many having been born in harrowing circumstances in Eastern

Europe. They loved this country as few others had; with hands over their hearts they wept openly at the playing of the National anthem in Yankee Stadium. In World War I, many could not wait to get "over there" in 1914 and teach that Kaiser a lesson. My father, born in the States, attempted to join the Navy at fifteen and was rejected for having a hernia. Or so the story went. I was enormously proud of an Uncle Dave who had been gassed at the Marne. ("My uncle was gassed at the Marne'" was a conversation-stopper in my little circle.) He received a full disability pension, never collected a dime of it and organized the "79 Club" which arranged for a small army of wounded veterans to attend the Friday night fights at the old Madison Square Garden. Uncle Sonny, another favorite, had been a motorcyle courier for General Pershing and had "gone in" after Pancho Villa in the Mexican war. Those were my heroes: Salinger, Uncle Dave and Uncle Sonny. Attention, of course, was paid to my father.

In his early twenties, he worked in the pit of a movie theater, playing the piano accompaniment to silent films. The only song he knew was "Whispering," but he finessed his way through by playing it in several different tempos, a speeded-up version for Westerns, a slow and melodic one for love stories. My 21-year-old mother (Molly Liebowitz) took a seat in the balcony one night. They looked at each other. The result was a marriage that lasted more than four decades. Years later, in her tiny Bronx apartment, she would sit on a sofa, drag on a cigarette and say, fatalistically: "I saw a smile and look what happened."

Smiles were terribly important in our family. Smiles – and outward appearance in general.

"That was our fate," my mother would say. "We were so gorgeous that no one ever believed we were in trouble."

I'm not much good at genealogical tables. Nor do I have much interest in them. You will never catch me writing a novel that leads off with one of those awful family tables that dates back several centuries, one that the reader, maddeningly, has to keep referring to. Or *reading* such a novel, for that matter. ("War and Peace" is an exception. Sort of.) My father's parents were from Romania, or, more than likely, Hungary. I know this only because my mother, when upset with him, would cry out: "You're a lousy Hungarian." And he did like goulash. There was something about his forebears making shoulder pads in "the old country." My maternal grandmother was a sweet and quiet woman who padded about in houseslippers in a neighboring aunt's apartment and always had a freshly baked cookie for me. She was in her eighties when I knew her and she spoke little English. I discovered later – my sister's research – that as a young woman she had run a notoriously rowdy, hell-for-leather tavern in Albania. She may very well have been the Elaine of Voskopoja.

My mother's background is a bit cloudy. I'd always assumed she was born on the lower East Side of Manhattan. A dark secret emerged recently – my sister's dogged research again. My mother had actually been born in Russia and "come over" on the boat when she was six months old. Who really cares – but had she known it would be revealed, it would have mattered to her. Her family founded Liebowitz Brothers, a good-sized department store on Canal Street, that was on its way to becoming a Bloomingdale's but the three brothers who managed the store went after each other with knives; the store shriveled away to nothing.

My mother was flame-haired – or at least I think she was flame-haired. Who has flame-hair in their seventies? There was very little schooling in her background and a great deal of dancing. She loved to dance, although in truth, her feet rarely moved and there was very little motion below the waist. What she did came closer to swaying, and making announcements about the effect the music had on her. ("That song . . . it goes right through me. . . .")

I thought she was quite pretty. The actress Myrna Loy comes to mind, although boys in the Bronx (and Kansas?) do get carried away in this area, more than one feeling that his poor, bedraggled mother is the image of Liz Taylor.

Rounding out the team was my sister, Dollie, who was seven years older than I was and not much of a player in my life. When I was born, she insisted that I be named "Bunny." When she failed at that, she more or less disappeared as a presence, showing up in 1945, when I was fifteen with a boy she'd fallen in love with named Irving Messing.

I hadn't realized how much she meant to me until her new crush was invited over for dinner one night. I suddenly got to my feet and cried out: "Boyfriend, boyfriend, boyfriend. That's all I ever hear around here is boyfriend." With that, I flew out of the apartment in tears and hid out in the local drugstore. Apparently, I hadn't been heard from much until that point.

After I'd left, my mother is reported to have said: "Who knew it had a voice."

I greatly misjudged Irving Messing. He went off to war soon after the dinner and served in WWII Europe, writing a letter to my sister each day, without fail, for six years. (My mother, it's sad to report, took peeks at them.) When he returned home in 1946, Dollie became frightened and ran off to be with a girlfriend in the Adirondacks. He pursued her. They married and have been together for sixty-five years. I'm not sure I know of a better love story.

I had no idea that we were poor. My mother kept reminding me of how fortunate I was. ("There are boys who would give their eye-teeth to be in your shoes.") Which boys? Did they all live in Somalia? Still, on the whole, I did feel blessed. We lived within walking distance of not one, but two ballparks, the Yankee Stadium and the Polo Grounds. I had the finest t-shirt collection of any boy in the neighborhood. We had a maid, who was paid a salary of seven dollars, which my mother borrowed back at the end of the week. (Queenie also served as a therapist, patiently standing at the sink for hours while my mother smoked her Chesterfields and told the poor black daughter of slaves of the many ways that life (and her in-laws) had conspired against her.) We had a step-down living room, which seemed grand to me. I was free to have adventures in the street. And I was a theatergoer. An aunt Esther ("Essie") worked for the Schuberts in the box office of the Broadhurst Theater. From age five on, whenever a show flopped and was about to close – I was tapped on the shoulder and whisked down-town to fill one of the empty seats. Unknowingly, I became an expert on bad plays. More than one had to do with Joan of Arc who was always being burned offstage. A woodsman would stare off into the wings and say:

"My God, I believe they're about to torch the poor thing."

It occurred to me, at a tender age, that it might be more effec-tive to have key scenes enacted *onstage* and not off in the wings somewhere. Other plays that did not fare well featured a central character who had dropped dead before the curtain went up. *The Starcross Story* was one such production. Poor Starcross had expired long before the proceedings began. The actors were reduced to chatting for several hours about what a remarkable fel-low he must have been. A theatergoer beside me muttered:

"For God's sakes, if he's so interesting, why don't they get bloody Starcross out here?"

I'd like to say that these early experiences were useful when I tried my hand at playwriting. They weren't particularly. A play is a slippery animal. Though I've had some successes, I'm not sure I ever got the hang of playwriting. But I did manage to hold an audi-ence's atttention, even if it meant hitting each theatergoer over the head with a a program. Still, I lit up a few offstage Joan of Arcs of my own.

Despite our pinched circumstances, I was sent off to camp each year at the first whisper of a summer breeze. I learned even-tually that C.J.I. (Central Jewish Institute) was a charity camp. Had I known that – even as a child – I would have been indig-nant. At the age of five, I was packed into a grim and antiquated train to Peekskill, New York, there to live in a tent with heavy-legged Israeli pioneers. To be fair about it, the air was fresh. The Israelis were good-natured and spent most of their time tramping

through the woods in search of blueberries. I was issued a pair of
yarmulkes (skull-caps): one for daily use, another, a lovely white
satin one for the Sabbath, that brought me to the edge of becoming a serious Jew. Still, I did not do well. Turnips, the featured
course at most meals, caused me to become deathly ill. My
mother came up to whisk me out of the infirmary, nurse me back
to health in the Bronx and then return me to the camp for more
turnip-eating. But there was a single bright feature to the experience. On Friday nights, I would gather round a campfire with
other 5-year-olds and listen to Dr. Schoolman, the camp director,
tell a story about the Wise Men of Chelm. They weren't wise, of
course. In the style of Sarah Palin, they built bridges to nowhere.
But I found the stories (written by Sholom Aleichem) spellbind-
ing. Did they ignite a need in me to take a try at (slightly bent)
stories of my own? It's not inconceivable, though the forces that
turn an individual into a teller of tales – instead of a salesman –
are varied and mysterious. It might be genetic. It certainly can't
be a hunger for riches.

We were not, as an example, an especially bookish family. My
father would occasionally take on a serious demeanor and page
through a biography of one of his heroes, generally a white-haired
patrician type such as Edward R. Stettinius, a secretary of state in
the Roosevelt administration (considered by some to be one of the
worst to hold the office). Still, my father would stop after a few
pages, shake his head in wonder and say, "He was some guy."

My mother was a passionate theatergoer, her favorite actors
being Gertrude Lawrence and Tallulah Bankhead (irritatingly
referred to as 'Taloo.') Ethel Merman was "that bitch," spoken with
admiration. It was the performers who were key. My mother paid
little attention to the playwrights. When my play, *Scuba Duba*,
became a surprise hit in 1967, I called her, expecting to be showered with adulation.

"I could not take my eyes off that boy," she said.

"But mom, he wasn't reading the phonebook. What about the
play?"

Her response?

"Thank your lucky stars you had that boy."

On reflection, she may have been on to something. "The boy" was Jerry Orbach, later to star for years in the television series *Law and Order*. He was brilliant.

For all her love of the stage, my mother, too, would occasionally say:

"I know what's wrong with me. I've got to get into a good book."

And off she would go to the corner candy store which housed a Lending Library. Books could be borrowed – for a few pennies a day.

Enormously popular in the forties was Kathleen Windsor's scandalous novel, *Forever Amber*. The great clarinetist Artie Shaw berated his wife, the actress Ava Gardner, for reading such "trash." Then he promptly divorced her and made Windsor his sixth wife. Following the publication of my short story collection, *Far From the City of Class* in 1963, Shaw called and asked to have lunch. And then, there I was, at the Carnegie Delicatessen, eating a tongue sandwich and sitting opposite the man whose renditions of "Begin the Beguine" and "Stardust" had provided the soundtrack for a million summer romances, mine included. I felt I owed him royalties. And I wanted to hear about his marriages, to Windsor, of course, but also to Ava Gardner, Lana Turner and a favorite of mine, the maddeningly sexy and under-rated Evelyn Keyes. He waved all of this aside. He wanted to talk only of short story construction.

My sister wasn't especially bookish, but she devoured movie magazines. She clipped out pictures of her favorite stars and pasted them to the walls of the cabinet in which she slept. In 1970, I saw the very same sepia-toned pictures of the identical stars (John Payne, Loretta Young, Robert Taylor) affixed to the wall of Anne Frank's bedroom hideout in Amsterdam. It was the only time the Holocaust got through to me with full force. *Anne Frank. My sister*!

The same age? Fans of the same movie magazines? Never mind the "good Germans." The ones who were "kept in the dark." At the time, I was capable of tearing out the throat of anyone who spoke with a German accent.

Of course, Hitler, too, liked Betty Grable movies – which was maddening.

And why this lifelong need of mine – still unfulfilled – to set aside some time and learn German?

There were five volumes actually on display in our apartment, each with the faux leather binding of a classic. My father won them in a contest sponsored by the Hearst-owned *Journal American*. One was *Westward Ho*, which I still haven't read. Another was *The Autobiography of Benvenuto Cellini*. I pored over the latter half-a-dozen times, thinking it was the confessional of a foreigner, an Italian at that. Surely it would include some naughty passages. No such luck. Nor did I fare much better at the sanitized local library. Virtually all of the books seemed to be written by (Janet) Taylor Caldwell, the Joyce Carol Oates of her time. I took home a sack full of Caldwells every few days, along with a thick diversionary volume dealing with Manchuria. But never once was I rewarded with so much as a heaving bosom, a verbal glimpse of thigh. This was understandable in the case of *Grandmother and the Priests*. But to come up empty after a thorough search of *Melissa* and *Your Sins and Mine* was inexcusable. Actually, there were several passages about Manchurian washerwomen that were moderately arousing.

"Innocence" did not begin to describe the period. In the mid-fifties, and on into the mid-sixties – I worked as an editor of a group of men's adventure magazines. When sales dipped a bit, the publisher agreed to have the phrase "dark triangle" put into play. ("She stood before Hemmings, a dark triangle visible through her flimsy negligee.") Before getting a dark-triangle go-ahead, we had to wait until the publisher had removed his name from the mast-head so that his Long Island neighbors would not connect him with rakish behavior. The word "risqué" on a book jacket gave off a promise of bedroom shenanigans. Raphael Philipson ("Phipsy") an English teacher at DeWitt Clinton High School, reading aloud from a novel, would wink, and alert us to a passage that was "a bit hotcha." A biology teacher had an internal debate before explaining, in a sweat, that a male frog mates with a female by using – and here he paused – "the pressure of his limbs." He then surveyed the room carefully as if to check for any erotic damage.

It is often said that the forties and fifties were a better time, when much was left to the imagination, and giant cascades of pornography did not come showering down upon us from every direction. I wonder.

A book that appealed to me at an early age was *The Wonderful Adventures of Nils.* An illustrated volume, it was, for some reason, kept under glass in a special reference room and had to be read while two librarians, like prison guards, folded their arms and looked on warily. Nils is a young boy who falls in love with a flock of geese and hops on the back of one of them to fly off in search of adventure. (Were the librarians concerned that I might fly off with their book?) The appeal of the classic story to a boy who, all theater-going to the contrary, slept in a kitchen and lived in a world of concrete, was obvious. 'Adventure' remained my favorite word in the language. At one time, throughout the eighties and nineties, it meant traveling, as a journalist, to darkest Haiti under Duvalier ("Papa Doc") to witness voodoo ceremonies and adversaries hung by the neck and left to swing on poles in a village square. Or flying off to investigate the fleshpots of Hamburg. Now it's more likely to mean a visit to a new restaurant. But adventure it remains. In the self-serving department (which will no doubt grow as this hallucinatory memoir moves along) William Emerson, editor of the *Saturday Evening Post* (I was a contributor) wrote of me:

"Friedman is a modern-day Huck Finn, sailing down the Mississippi on a riverboat, stopping off here and there to see what he can see."

This from a child of the Deep South, writing with affection about a Jewish boy from the Bronx. Does anyone doubt that this is a great country?

Other favorites in the Taylor Caldwell-dominated library were the *Blue Book of Fairy Tales, The Red Book,* etc. which continued to appear until the publisher ran out of colors. There was to be no Chartreuse edition. Like many short story collections, they were front-loaded with the most delicious tales – Ali Baba and the Forty Thieves, Sinbad the Sailor, Aladdin and his Magic Lamp – and then tailed off a bit. I don't know if it was a direct route, but I was soon caught up in the irresistible Hardy Boys series, which held me in high excitement until the tenth volume or so. Here again, in terms of quality, the narratives seemed to go off a cliff. Had my interest flagged? It was more likely that new – and ineffectual – writers had been brought in, an unthinkable measure at the time in a series of beloved books. There was no such tail-off in the mystery novels of Agatha Christie. I tend not to read anything twice, but it was entirely natural to wolf down *And Then There Were None* and *Ten Little Indians* a dozen times, marveling each time at the author's ingenuity.

When the first copy of *Superman* appeared, the earth shook for me. Though Superman himself never became a particular favorite of mine – too super, much like the invincible and corporate-like New York Yankees, who played their games just down the street. *The Submariner* and *Human Torch* were more like it, especially when the Torch took on the boy Toro to help him along. Freud claimed that sexual stirrings begin in the cradle. Such longings came over me when I held a fresh new copy of *Captain Marvel,* for example. The very feel and smell of it. The trick was how to get my hands on it. A dark note was sounded in my life when my father, in the late thirties, awakened me in the middle of the night, handed me a coin and whispered: "That's the last dime I'll ever be able to give you." (I keep stressing that mine is not a sad story. On reflection, perhaps there were a few less than blissful moments along the way.) I felt awful, of course, not for me, but for my poor father. No doubt he'd been asked to take a cut in his anemic salary. I would get along very nicely; all I had to do is resume the seduction of Albert Beitler.

He was the rich boy in our building. Both his parents were teachers which, in the Bronx, positioned him in the wealthy category. He could always be counted on to be holding a fresh copy of the latest comic book, which he would breeze through in a few moments and be about to dispose of when I cornered him in the building courtyard. There I would argue, with less than Churchillian eloquence, why it was only fitting that he hand it over to me.

"C'mon, Beitler, you know what *Batman* means to me. You've already read the damned thing."

After holding the comic out of reach, as if protecting his virginity, he would inevitably "yield," and fork it over. He wasn't mean. A thin, bespectacled boy, he wasn't terribly popular. I think he enjoyed the attention, the almost daily courtship.

Years later, in Hollywood, when I was attempting the seduction of a fringe Hollywood actress, she lowered her eyes in B-movie style and said: "You always get what you want, don't you, Friedman . . ."

I did, when it came to Albert Beitler.

A word here about the Big Little Books. A shrine should be built in honor of the creator of those fat little beauties. The adventures of Dick Tracy or Flash Gordon or Little Orphan Annie, for that matter, seemed to take on new layers of meaning when read in this strange and tasty new format. As thick as it was wide, the Big Little Book was a comic all right, yet it was also a (cardboard-covered) book as well. Tarzan, Prince Valiant, Popeye, and the beloved hamburger-eating Wimpy – could all be savoured one delicious panel at a time. The road to acquisition of these robust little treasures led through Murray Cohen, a much tougher nut to crack than Albert Beitler. Nor, to my knowledge, was he ever cracked. Dark, round-shouldered, and furtive-looking, he was the first boy in the neighborhood who needed to shave. A Big Little Book tease, he would invite me to his parent's dark apartment for a look at his collection. After unlocking a rolltop desk, he stood by as I hungrily stared at the stacks of them, each in mint condition, probably unread.

"All right if I borrow a few?" I would ask.

Shaking his head in the negative, he indicated that they were only for display and led me back to the street. Though I was disappointed, a more grave concern was that he would go forth in life, perpetuating age-old slanders about the covetous ways of the Jews. (He became an accountant.) Yet I forgave him. His father, a cab-driver, had a degenerative back condition and walked at a 45-degree angle, his nose almost touching the ground. Finally, he broke, like a pretzel, and that was the end of poor Mr. Cohen.

Radio was a great friend, especially when I was ill. It was almost a joyous occasion to wake up with a fever. There were the medieval mustard plasters and enemas, a favorite of my mother's, often inserted, forgetfully, without lubrication. (Is it a wonder I didn't wind up as an afternoon regular at S&M parlors?) But once these horrors were out of the way, the treats began. Fortified with slices of toasted Wonder Bread, and propped up in my parents' bed – an actual bed – I got to listen to afternoon radio shows – Lum and Abner, and Fibber McGee and Molly for a taste of the heartlands. Later in the day, there was the wildly non-P.C. *Amos and Andy*, *The Shadow*, *The Green Hornet*, *The Lone Ranger* and my favorite of all, *I Love a Mystery*. Jack, Doc and Reggie were the three heroes. How I wished I could have tagged along on their adventures, as a fourth. Years later, I was to feel the same about Gus McCrae, Pee Eye Parker, Joshua Deets and Jake Spoon, characters in Larry McMurtry's magnificent novel, *Lonesome Dove*. When I came to the end, I was ready for another thousand pages. And how I longed to have tagged along on one of their cattle drives. I'm not sure I would have been welcome, but I felt confident I could have proven my worth, the Bronx background nothwithstanding.

I'm not the first to observe that those invisible *I Love a Mystery* characters, cooked up in a radio studio, and embellished by a boy's imagination – were more real than those on the screen, or on the street, for that matter.

Saturdays were set aside for the Fleetwood Theater and a visual banquet of two full-length movies, a newsreel, several cartoons (Bugs Bunny, Looney Tunes), and a serial adventure, each chapter ending with a "cliffhanger," which made a return trip mandatory. A favorite featured twenty or so Lone Rangers. One of the masked law enforcers was killed each week. Only after the twentieth episode would the real Lone Ranger be revealed. None of these afternoons came together without a beloved box of chocolate-covered Goobers. Years later, the writer Sally Kempton told me, astonishingly, that she was able to nurse a box of Raisinets through two movies. My Goobers were usually gone by the end of the opening credits. Small wonder that the patient Kempton became a swami in far-off India.

Queenie was my silent partner at the movies. At the end of the program, and on special occasions, a birthday, for example, she would buy a five cent toy soldier for me at Kress Department Store. I was heartbroken when I played with it. Where had she gotten the five cents? Clearly, she would have to do without something, now that she was even more impoverished. Neil Simon's title for a 1972 movie based on my short story, "A Change of Plan," was *The Heartbreak Kid*. I'd never met him, but apparently he knew something about me.

I loved the movies when I was a boy and didn't much care for them while I was actually working on them in Hollywood. Sunshine, room service, pretty girls – it could hardly be called work. I was actually offended when someone suggested I leave the tennis court and write a scene or two. But whatever interest I had in writing scripts tapered off with the arrival of a group I think of as The Arc People. Fresh from MBA courses, they became studio executives and weren't quite sure what an arc was. When asked to describe one, an executive might shape one in the air. But arcs were known to be terribly important and there was an insistence that several be sprinkled into each film.

With the dreaded arcs behind me, I'm back to loving movies again. With a rare exception (*Donnie Brasco*, for example) it's unusual for me to want to see a film a second time. Yet, as a boy, I thought nothing of watching *She* a dozen times or returning week after week to watch the climactic scene of *The Last Days of Pompeii* in which Preston Foster holds up the collapsing Coliseum on his shoulders, so that his fellow Romans can escape being crushed in the destruction. Even *Sh! The Octopus* demanded several viewings.

A dreary aspect of youthful movie-going was having to walk out into the streets and be confronted with everyday life in the Bronx, which seemed stale by comparison. No cocktail parties, no South of France. No David Niven for instructions on sophistication. Not so much as a cattle drive in the West. To this day, I have a glum sensation as I leave a movie theater. Unless it's one of the many films about family dysfunction, in which case the outoors comes as a relief. Still, that may be one of the advantages of watching DVDs. You can be glum in the privacy of your home.

For all of my being enraptured by movies I had no interest in the process of making them. I wanted to *be* Humphrey Bogart and Gary Cooper – Cary Grant was a bit of a reach – but that was the extent of it. As a boy, I had no idea there were people who actually wrote whatever was spoken on the screen. When that finally sunk in, screenwriting, for literary aspirants in the fifties and sixties, had come to be thought of as a déclassé activity. The Gods were Hemingway, Fitzgerald and Faulkner. Scribners – and not Warner Brothers – was the temple. The editor Maxwell Perkins the High Priest. Writers "sold out" when they went off to Hollywood. There were women in Greenwich Village who refused to sleep with a writer who had anything to do with the screen.

"You mean you'd actually *sell* your book to the movies? Or *write* for those people? *Prostitute* yourself?"

All of this spoken in horror, and generally by those who had never received a film offer.

Writing seemed such a romantic profession when I was a boy. The same could not be said of orthodontia, for example, and certainly not of theatrical press agentry, my mother's appointed career for me. Although in truth, the first job offer I received came from Bill Doll in the early fifties. He was a legend in the profession who had long locks of gray hair and swirled around theatrically in a black cape. My theater-connected Aunt Essie had introduced me to the iconic press agent. After asking me a few questions in Schubert Alley, he reached beneath his cape, whipped out thirty dollars and told me to commence writing press releases for a play starring Boris Karloff. Sadly enough, it closed after a weekend try-out in Boston, bringing down the curtain on my career in theatrical press agentry as well.

It was the novelists who fascinated me. The idea that someone knew enough to "fill up" an entire book was beyond comprehension. It seemed the most noble of professions. When a writer visited Public School 35, I had little interest in what he had to say. It was the way he dressed that interested me, his stance at the podium, the way he smoked. Irving Caesar was not quite a novelist (he composed the lyrics for "Tea for Two"), but he was a writer of some sort and I made do with him. When he came to address our class, I secured a seat in the front row. Half-way along in his talk, he stopped and said to me:

"Why are you staring at my socks, young man?"

Hollywood fed into the portrayal of the novelist (or foreign correspondent) as romantic figure. Writers wore trenchcoats, stood at the railing of ocean liners, jaws clenched, a pipe between their teeth. They stared off at the horizon, bemoaning failed love affairs.

"Why can't we continue?" a puzzled lover would ask.

"Because it just wouldn't work out" was the usual answer, though exactly *why* it wouldn't work out was never explained.

Still, how I longed to be standing on the deck of one of those ocean liners, with a pipe between my teeth, bemoaning a hopeless love affair. Off I went as a young man, egged on by the movies, in search of a doomed romance; I had little difficulty in arranging for several of them. It took decades for me to realize that a successful romance was better than an awful one, although in truth, it was the latter that made for better fiction.

Still, there must have been more to writing than striking poses.

It occurred to me that women would notice me, even find me attractive, if I became a writer. After all, clenched jaw muscles, poverty, insecurity – what woman in her right mind could resist such a package? I adored women, lusted after them, of course, but I had a tendency to become strangulated and to clutch at my throat when I was actually in the presence of one. The women in my family were not supportive. Whenever I received a rare phone call from a girl in my public school class, my mother and sister would howl with derision and then gather round the one phone to hear my end of the conversation. This forced me to burrow deep into the clothing closet and to speak hoarsely with overcoats piled on top of my head. In preparation for the few dates I had, I would scribble down half-a-dozen jokes on my cuffs, taking sly peeks at them and hoping they would launch me into an actual conversation. The jokes were borrowed (stolen?) from the routines of Borscht Belt comedians – who stole from one another. A representative greeting to a puzzled young woman might be: "I don't have to do this. I can make a living selling bagels to midgets for toilet seats."

I became convinced that if I wrote a little something, affixed my name to it, girls would see that I was more than a boy who became strangulated when he approached them. This was an odd thought, since there didn't seem to be any girls in the Bronx. The few that existed were kept indoors and could be seen on the second floor of apartment buildings, peering through the drapes. Nonetheless, I pressed on with my plan and, through great good fortune, came under the care of the aforementioned Raphael

"Phipsy" Philipson, a teacher who headed up a program for a group who were called "newsers" at DeWitt Clinton High School. I was assigned a weekly column for the *Clinton News*, which I cleverly (or so it seemed at the time) called "Anybuddy's Business." (My nickname was "Buddy.") It was filled with breezy items about one thing or another on Broadway, about which I knew little. This didn't matter. The main thing was to be breezy and to see my name in print, which was addictive. There was no turning back. After years of being referred to by my mother as a pronoun ("*It* has a voice?") I had an identity, albeit a breezy one. Women did not, as I had expected, fall at my feet. For one thing, DeWitt Clinton was an all-boys' school. And for that matter, I never met a single individual of either sex who read the column. Never mind. I was on my way. Sort of.

A next step, after graduating from high school in 1947 was to begin angling for a college – and some semblance of a profession. There was something amorphous and fanciful about a writing career. One didn't just jump in and begin whipping out novels. To Jewish mothers in the Bronx, medicine was the only profession of any consequence. Why someone would choose to become a writer – and not a dermatologist – mystified them. As a result, hordes of boys in the forties dutifully trooped off to become surgeons and gastroenterologists. Allen Sandler, at ten, strutted regally along Sheridan Avenue with a serious demeanor as if he was weighing a diagnosis. (He became a heart specialist of renown.) Allan "Muff-diver" Procter, trailed along behind him. He had earned his nickname by claiming to have committed (performed?) cunnilingus on a superintendent's daughter. "The Muff," as he was called, also famously celebrated his first ejaculation by throwing open his bedroom window and shouting to the neighborhood: "I just shot." For all of his lubricious activities, off to medical school he went. A boy in the Bronx could not show his face unless he'd been consigned a nickname. Doodles, Ref (for 'refugee'), Pickles, "Half-Ass" Schneider, the great three-sewer stickball legend, all stormed the gates of medical schools. Here and there, parents reluctantly indulged a stray daughter and permitted her to enter law school. In search of a livelier career path, a few of the rowdier boys chose Murder, Incorporated and spent only a brief time on the planet. Young Tommy McKenna, a regular at bar mitzvahs, had a tryout at shortstop with the Yankees and was swallowed up in the minor leagues. Woe to watery-eyed Cantrow who became a shoe salesman.

Setting aside my frail literary aspirations, I joined the herd and took a try at becoming a doctor. Years later, I suggested to my second wife Pat that had I not become a writer, I might have done well as a therapist.

"But you don't listen," she said.

"Oh, that," I said. "I'd forgotten."

An important hurdle on the path to a career in medicine was the obligatory interview with the aforementioned Dr. Pasachoff, reigning physician of the Grand Concourse, who had saved my arm when I was fifteen. It was felt that with a wave of his distingished hand, he could deliver a qualified boy into the finest of premed programs. (Beset by private demons, he was later to meet his end by hurling himself through the window of his seventh-storey apartment.) The Doctor agreed to see me and listened gravely as I told him of my authentic love for Bunsen burners. I went on at length about the paramecium, which had always intrigued me.

"It's a restless little organism, isn't it? Always wandering off in search of adventure."

The doctor was baffled. He was also unimpressed and led me to the door in silence. All in all, this was a good thing. Who knows how many suffering souls would have gone to an early grave had it not been for Dr. Pasachoff's intervention.

Nonetheless, I stubbornly pressed on and sent out a single application for premed school at Columbia University, not thinking for a moment that anyone would have the gall to reject me. One college application was plenty. I've always had trouble with applications, and generally become bored after filling in the blank for my mother's maiden name. The Dean of Admissions, Dr. Arbolino – and why do I remember his name? – called me down to his office and explained that all the premed openings were taken up by returning World War II veterans. The year was 1947. But he'd seen a flicker of writing ability in an essay I'd sent along on the pride I took in my t-shirt collection. He suggested that I forget premed for the moment and reapply for Arts and Science.

"Once you're in the school, you can change your mind. If you're still interested, it's an easy matter to change your major to premed in your second year."

"I'm afraid I can't do that, sir. It would be misrepresenting."

"Let me explain again," he said patiently. "Just put down Arts and Science for the moment. *It will get you into the university.* After that, you can do what you like."

"Out of the question, sir. It's premed, or it's no go."

He shrugged. *I've done all I can. Why am I bothering with this individual?* Off I went to be a waiter at summer camp. Unsurprisingly (to a normal person) a letter awaited me from Columbia saying that my application was impressive but that there were no openings in the premed program.

"Regrettably, we are forced to turn you down."

This was distressing. Fall was approaching. It seemed that everyone I knew was going off to some leafy college in the Mid-West. And I would remain behind in the Bronx, taking lonely walks along deserted railroad yards. I was particularly upset about not being admitted to Harvard. It's true that I hadn't bothered to send the school an application. But somehow I assumed that Harvard would find out about me and send a delegation to my apartment in the Bronx, pleading with me to return with them to Cambridge, there to begin eating popovers and poring over Platonic dialogues.

Once again, fate happily intervened on my behalf, this time in the form of a young woman the novelist Terry Southern would have called "a blonde nifty." Her name was Doris Donn. We met on a volleyball court. She was going off to Missouri University, which

had a fine journalism school. There was no need to concern myself
with applications. Anyone could get in. You simply walked onto
the campus and began studying. That's all I needed to hear. I
immediately headed to the MidWest. Harvard might offer
Suetonius. At Missouri there would be farming journalism, Serbo-
Croatian cabals and, of greater importance, three women's col-
leges, attended by the most beautiful creatures I'd ever seen –
every bit as lovely as those who were to show up, years later, at my
local Whole Foods each day at five-thirty in the afternoon.

4

"You wrote the vagina story?"
> The author, to a woman in Hiram Haydn's cele-
> brated writing course in Greenwich Village.

After four years at the University of Missouri, I was issued a B.J. (Bachelor of Journalism) degree, which sounds a bit like something that one sends off for in the mail – like a Russian bride. Two years in the Air Force followed; I returned then to the Bronx, in 1953, as a fat and unemployed fellow. (Those delicious Air Force veal cutlets.) I quickly learned that there was little demand for individuals who had been schooled in farming journalism and Serbo-Croatian cabals. Still, it was important to a find a job of *some* kind, or so it seemed. How long could I lounge around in my mother's apartment in the Bronx and, in the evening, make unsuccessful attempts to seduce lesbians in Greenwich Village? (In truth, my mother would have preferred keeping me there until I was seventy.)

I had the two short story publications, but brandishing them about at parties did not get me very far. And the pressure was on. My girlfriend in St. Louis had become an instructor with Arthur Murray Dance Studios. I wasn't much of a dancer and could proceed in only one direction. When I came to a wall or a partition I would have to stop, walk my partner back to our starting point and begin dancing again. This did not sit well with Ginger Howard. I had a fear that a colleague of hers, who could dance in several directions, would waltz her out of the Arthur Murray studio and I would never see her again. And no woman, much less an attractive one, would ever again have anything to do with me. It wasn't so much that I wanted Ginger that badly. But I couldn't bear the thought of losing her to a terrific dancer.

So much of life at the time had to do with dancing. And hair loss. The fifties to me were about hair loss and dancing.

There was the possibility of cringing back to Gottfried Underwear, my father's "place of business" to see if there was a job available in the stockroom, but somehow that was unthinkable. (Not that I was sure I could cut it in the stockroom. There were veteran stockroom fellows who knew what to *do* in there. No doubt there were stockroom cliques – and I would be viewed as an outsider.) So off I went, to midtown Manhattan in search of employment, much like the innocent Dick Whittington, a fairy tale favorite, who came to town, carrying only bread and cheese.

Magazine publishing seemed a logical target. It wouldn't thrust me into the limelight as a novelist, but there was the matter of my not *having* a novel at the moment. A position in the magazine world might at least nudge me in the right direction.

At *Life*, I was offered a job at FYI, a house organ that would enable me to travel from floor to floor and to rub shoulders with people who were actually employed by the company. I said I preferred to have a job of my own, rather than be among people who *had* one and be constantly reminded that I didn't. The personnel director seemed puzzled by my position. Thinking somehow that it might shore up my credentials, I had brought along a picture I'd taken of Ginger Howard, leaning against a refrigerator in St. Louis. The personnel director took what I thought was an inordinate interest in the photograph and kept staring at it soulfully, bringing it close to his face and taking a few sniffs of it. When I asked to have it back, he seemed irritated and turned me over to a young man with a thick British accent who was recruiting people for a new magazine called *Sports Illustrated*. He smiled at me thinly, took me for a walk through several corridors, the last of which led me out to the street. Despite the snub – and as a demonstration of my character – I remained a staunch Anglophile.

At *Newsweek*, I was told there might be something for me in the storage room, which I declined, thinking it sounded suspiciously like the stock room at Gottfried Underwear. *Colliers* came next. An editor there granted me an interview, but warned me in advance that he was terribly busy. As if in demonstration, he shuffled papers as I sat there, went through files, typed a few lines, then told his secretary that he was up to his ears and couldn't take any calls. Finally, it all became too much for him. He groaned, put his head on the desk, waved me off and said it was a mistake, he was much too busy to see me.

"Perhaps some other time, when things quiet down a bit."

On my way down the hall, I peered in at some other rooms and saw editors who bustled about and seemed every bit as busy as the fellow who was too busy to see me. The magazine folded soon after. For all of their labors, the staff apparently wasn't busy enough to keep it afloat.

And that was it for my job search, at least for the moment. Some chilling news had arrived. George B. Leonard, my former commanding officer, had published his first novel, *Shoulder To the Sky* at a new company called Atheneum. I didn't *hate* Leonard for this treachery. But much as I admired him, I was foaming over with envy and some panic. A novel at the time was everything (and it still might be). To quote Philip Roth, "nothing can compare to the novel – nothing, nothing, nothing. "

I felt that one "nothing" would have been sufficient, but I got his point.

Here I was, popping along in my twenties. I didn't have an idea for a novel. Nor did I know how to get one going. But it was important to jump in as soon as possible and take a try at it. Thirty was the cut-off point. If you didn't have one at that age, you might as well hire a skiff and set out to sea, never to be heard from again.

George B. Leonard, now a published novelist, suggested I hold off for a bit and begin my efforts by taking a famed course in the novel that was taught in Greenwich Village by a man named Hiram Haydn. Seats in the class were much coveted and difficult to come by. Leonard assured Haydn, a fellow Southerner, that I had promise and was able to secure one of them for me. An appeal of the course was that Haydn was the publisher of a company called Bobbs-Merrill. It was tacitly understood that a gifted student might very well end up having his novel published by Bobbs-Merrill. William Styron had taken the course. His first novel, *Lie Down in Darkness* had been brought out by Bobbs-Merrill in 1951. It was unimagineable at the time that Styron and I would later become friends.

The class was made up, for the most part, of returning World War II veterans, many of them still wearing combat fatigues. They might have been the same bunch that had kept me out of premed at Columbia, the program in which I had little interest, though I stubbornly insisted that I did. There was a woman or two in the group. At the first session, Haydn, a towering figure who had written Dust Bowl novels, introduced a graduate of the class who was about to have his first novel published. He was a relaxed and preppy-ish fellow whose book, we were told, was in the Salingeresque mode. I was terribly envious of him, of course. As he addressed us, characteristically I studied him closely, trying to worm out the secret of his success. He kept falling back on the phrase "sort of."

"I sort of had an idea for the novel, and I sort of wrote it and sort of sent it off to an agent. He sort of liked it."

That night, at the kitchen table, I threw this new verbal style into play.

"I'm sort of hungry and I'd sort of like another piece of chicken."

"Is that why I paid for your college?" my mother said. "So you could come home and talk like a moron?"

The style of the course was to have Haydn read one of the anonymous submissions and to go round the room and have the class comment on it. He would then weigh in with remarks of his own. Haydn particularly enjoyed performing the female dialogue, going over to a high-pitched falsetto that I felt, quite frankly, was uncomfortable to listen to. The first selection appeared to have been written by one of the few women in the class. It focused on a scene in which a prepubescent girl is circling a kitchen wearing imaginary ice skates. She peers down at the linoleum floor at one point and sees clearly a reflection of what could only be "the sly curve of her vagina."

Haydn paused here. There was a hush in the room. This was, after all, the repressed fifties – there were no known vaginas at the time. Finally, the combat veterans could restrain themselves no longer and cried out their approval.

"*Terrific.*" "*Keep going.*" "*Let's have some more of that.*" "*Don't let anyone try to stop you.*"

Haydn generally concurred with the group's opinion and went on to read the next piece. When I realized it was mine, I slumped down a bit in my seat. Never in my life had I felt so exposed. The narrative centered on a young boy who is awakened each night at midnight by his mother and brought out to the living room in pyjamas to sing the ballad "I Understand" to an assemblage of visiting neighbors. He is accompanied on the piano by his father. The piece wasn't entirely autobiographical. My mother didn't haul me out of bed *every* night.

What I'd written was four or five pages long. I had no idea of where it was going, and, of course, this was a class in the novel.

Haydn read my submission and even crooned a few snatches of the song.

"*I understand. And darling you are not to blame. . . .*"

The first comment came from a pale and slender young Village resident who wore a beret. He had clearly been tormented by the reading.

"What we have here is a sick piece of work," he said. "Sick in its conception, sick in its execution. Clearly it's the work of a sick individual. And frankly, I think we're all sick for sitting around and listening to it. Sick, sick sick is the way I see it."

Exasperated, he threw up his hands, swiveled his chair around and turned his back to the class.

"Sick" I should mention, was a term that was in vogue at the time and was thrown around casually in social circles. Psychoanalysis was in full flower. "Penis envy" and "toilet training" were phrases that had some popularity as well. One or both would inevitably pop up in conversations. ("Obviously. Feingold hasn't been properly toilet-trained.")

"As you know," Haydn told the class, "we all work anonymously here. But before we go any further, I'd like, on this *one* occasion, to ask the author of this piece to remove the mask and tell us what on God's earth he's getting at and where's he's headed with this 'thing' of his."

"Gladly," I said, getting to my feet and breaking into a voice that was an ocatave higher than usual and sounded suspiciously like Haydn doing one of his female characters.

"To begin with, I don't think my work is all that sick. It might be a *little* sick, but nowhere near as sick as the gentleman suggests. Now where is the work headed, you ask. An excellent question."

And here I thought I'd pick up a few points by using the terminology of Haydn's star graduate.

"What I thought is that I'd sort of press on and sort of let the work tell me where it wants to go. Rather than me sort of dictating to the story, if you get my drift."

And then I fainted. It's a family trait. The Friedmans were always known to faint in a crisis. When I came to, my head was in the lap of one of the women in the class. Somehow I'd been transported to a nearby parking lot. I was still groggy. She had on kneesocks. She wore a plaid skirt. I could smell the freshly laundered wool. She was painfully beautiful.

"You poor thing," she said, stroking my head. "I thought your piece had great promise. And I know just how you feel. I was in last year's class. When Professor Haydn read the first draft of my vagina story, I was attacked viciously."

"*You* wrote the vagina story?" I said, suddenly alert.

"I've polished it quite a bit, of course."

It was all too much for me. The kneesocks, the skirt. The whole vagina business. To hear a vagina spoken of, written about, freely discussed by a woman who no doubt had an excellent one – was overpowering. And before I knew it, we were having an actual conversation, my first with a woman. It had some literary content. Stendhal came into it, though I hadn't had much luck with him. I wanted to run off with her. Clearly, there was a connection between us. Otherwise, what was I doing with my head in her lap. She was married, had two children. That might be an obstacle. I'd had a brief flirtation on the Jersey Shore with a married woman whose child threw a pile of mashed potatoes in my face. Hers might do the same. Then, too, there was the girlfriend, now a dancing instructor, who was waiting for my call in St. Louis. We'd had something along the lines of sex a few times in my car. Marriage was the only feasible option. After all, hadn't I "ruined" her? "Spoiled her" for other men. At twenty-one? Or at least that was the thinking in the fifties. So I felt I had no choice but to say good-bye to my vagina friend. There hasn't been a day that followed that I haven't thought about her. (Well, perhaps a day.) The plaid skirt. The kneesocks. The young mother fragrance. The openness – oops! – the casual mention of her vagina.

What would my life have been like with her, even with the mashed potato flinger?

I resigned from the course after a single session, feeling it was unfair of me to take up one of the highly coveted seats. Haydn said, in a letter, that he felt I'd made the right decision.

"It takes courage for a young man to acknowledge that he has chosen the wrong profession. Whatever the future holds, I salute you, Friedman."

5

"I really wanted Isaac Bashevis Singer."

> University of Southern California Professor Max
> F. Schulz, after writing a book about the author
> for the Twayne series on American novelists.

I often think of my mother as being flighty, flirtatious, spending
much of her time at corsetières and dressmakers, concerned
about hemlines and her "shape." Making a very big deal out of
having our small apartment painted and fighting with butchers
over the price of lamb chops. Such was the life of many an intelligent woman of the time who hadn't had much schooling. A few
may have led union rallies, but that was not my mother's style.
And yet, at every critical juncture of my young life, she was there
for me. As a first-grader, I was dyslexic, before there was a name
for the disability. I recall her standing before me, fully dressed for
an evening on the town, yet patiently holding up "flashcards" for
long hours into the night. She kept this up for days until I got the
hang of reading properly; quickly I shot up to being the second
best speller in my grade at public school. This, perhaps unfortunately, set a pattern in which I was to be a perpetual runner-up.
Voted Second Funniest Fellow in Junior High School. (The

winner, truth be told, campaigned.) Runner-up at the Academy Awards for *Splash*. When Professor Max F. Shulz of Southern California University, had completed his biography on me for the Twayne series on American authors, we met for the first time in 1970. He confessed (after a few drinks) that he'd really wanted Isaac Bashevis Singer.

As I walked the streets of Madison Avenue there seemed to be a Great Wall separating me from a job in publishing. I found temporary work in a warehouse, unpacking umbrella stands that had come in from Finland, inspecting them, and shipping the defective ones back to the Finns. I developed some skill at this. To this day, it takes little time for me to spot a defective umbrella stand – but I didn't see much of a career coming out of it. And once again, my mother flew to the rescue. Holding court at the bar of the House of Chan restaurant on Broadway, she struck up a conversation with a woman whose nephew, Ray Robinson, worked for an unusual group called the Magazine Management Company. It didn't "manage" magazines, so much as publish them by the dozens, the hundreds, actually, in every imagineable area – adventure, comics, movies, confession, paperback books, sex, or some simulation of it. The woman arranged a meeting with Robinson, a short feisty fellow who was later to have a career writing books about famous (and feisty) athletes. Quite graciously (since it may have cost him his own job) Robinson introduced me to his publisher, Martin Goodman, a silver-haired man in his mid-fifties who smoked thin cigars and spoke very little. Yet his very silences were chilling and had caused more than one of his employees to seek psychiatric care. (His own brothers, who worked for the company, addressed him as "Mr. Goodman.")

The publisher looked me over, took a puff of his thin cigar and said: "We'll give'm a try."

Then he walked off in some grim direction.

I became an assistant to James A. ("Big Jim") Bryans, III, a towering New Englander with a crew cut and a bull neck that he scratched at continually. He lived in fear of his father, who had struck him regularly throughout his childhood. When approached unexpectedly, Bryans would cringe back and throw up his hands protectively.

"Jeez, fella," he would say, "I thought you were going to crack me over the head."

Recovering, and as if he were a human magazine, he'd ask "What's new and unusual?"

He brought little cucumber sandwiches for lunch each day, prepared by his wife, "Mrs. Jim," as he referred to her. The sandwiches were sorrowful-looking and hardly seemed sustaining. I felt awful for him having to eat them, although I did taste one and it wasn't bad, with a little dill spread over it. He explained them away by saying:

"Big Jim is in a negative cash flow situation."

Bryans was editor of a robust and newsy little tabloid magazine called *Focus,* which was pocket-sized and sold in the millions. He had a predilection for photographs of women who were fire-eaters in what were then called "scanty" costumes. It fell to me to write blurbs – or "selling" lines – that would make the photographs more inviting to readers. As a *rite de passage*, Bryans kept me running back and forth to his office with revised versions of the blurbs, all the while reminding me that I had taken the job away from a man who had been fired by *The New York Star.*

"And he had kids, BJF, *kids.* Let's not forget that."

Eventually I got the hang of writing blurbs. Concision was the trick. "What's Worse Than Sex?" was a favorite title of Bryans' (of mine, as well). The answer, of course – violence – was disappointing. But the title resonates. When I was given my own magazine, in 1970, I hired Mario Puzo, whom I'd never met before, and (sadistically?) put him through the same drill. He almost cracked under the pressure and claimed to have had nightmares about the difficulty of composing a workable blurb. He may have written *The Godfather* as a means of never having to write one again.

*

Bryans had accumulated mounds of fire-eater photos, which had been sold to him by Viennese émigrés who treated him to expensive lunches and praised his editorial skills.

"You take a subject (fire-eating, for example) which seems like *nussing*. Then, Big Jim, you *tvist* it and it becomes *vunderful*."

The photographs were to be Bryans' undoing. When sales fell apart in a sudden recession, each member of the *Focus* team was required to carry a pile of them into Mr. Goodman's office. He smacked each one with the back of his hand, while Bryans stood by, cringing at each blow as if his father was at it again. (There were, I was to learn, "good" smacks, a kind of light tap when Goodman tossed a magazine on your desk and said "It's moving" – from the newsstand, that is.) The smacks that day were not good ones. Big Jim had accumulated thousands of dollars worth of fire-eater inventory. Pictures of bullfighting and log-rolling also went into the mix along with images of IRA activities. The shady Viennese salesmen had flattered Big Jim into purchasing packets of them by the dozens. All were of subjects Goodman felt were death at the newsstand. ("You can't give them away.") Years later, he felt the same about Vietnam stories, which sold poorly compared to those related to World War II.

Soon after that dark day, Bryans was released – along with his inventory. He had a secretary named Helen Heitkamp he had nicknamed "Helen Hideaway." She had giggled at his every pronouncement and wept profusely as he was about to leave. And then she followed him out the door. Bryans held a few odd jobs in publishing and ended up in a nursing home. One of our contributors had been Walter Wager, later to become author of the popular John Tiger suspense novels. Wager had a prosthetic hand. On visits to Bryans' office, and as a means of announcing his presence, he would unscrew it and toss it into Big Jim's lap. With time running out for the aging editor, Wager went to see him at the nursing home. As a result of excessive drinking, Bryans had lost a foot. For old times' sake, Wager tossed him the hand. Big Jim tossed his artificial foot back at Wager. They made a little game of it.

Despite his questionable inventory, (and it remained inventory – it never appeared in the magazine) Big Jim taught me to focus, editorially, on what he called Big Emotions – Love, Hate, Greed, Hunger, etc. I thought of this years later when a fellow who'd begun a new magazine asked me to do five thousand words on the annoyance he felt when people coughed in the theater. (I felt I could squeeze a comment or two out of it, but not much more. Where were the Big Emotions?) His magazine folded quickly. The man who was too busy to see me at *Collier's* had been laboring over a favorite presentation of his titled "Airports at Night." A parade of photographs of jetliners slumbering peacefully in their hangars. Somehow he felt they would seize the imagination of the reading public. Unless a wily Viennese outdid himself in salesmanship, they would not have passed muster with Big Jim.

When I first began at the company in 1955, under Bryans' tutelage, my office was a small one that may very well have been a stockroom. If so, it was a *publishing* stockroom which gave it some distinction. My desk was of an ancient rolltop variety, awarding the little space a Dickensian flavor. No sooner had I settled in than the company moved itself off to grand offices on Madison Avenue which were less pleasing to me. Here, I was placed in a cubicle that was contiguous to one occupied by Stan Lee, the celebrated founder of Marvel Comics. Before I arrived, and almost overnight, sales of comics had plunged; Lee's staff of two hundred was pared down until all that remained was Lee himself and a comely secretary who twitched. (When my marriage collapsed, I had a brief romantic entanglement with her, doing my all to ignore the twitch. When that failed, I twitched with her.) Martin Goodman, who was Lee's cousin, had set out, virtually, to force him out the door. Lee, in an act of great bravery, cheerfully stayed at his tiny desk until suddenly *The Fantastic 4*, *The Hulk* and *Spider-Man* brought Marvel Comics back to life; Lee's staff of two hundred was hired back.

After a month or so, I was given a surprise raise, my salary going from ninety to one hundred and twenty-five dollars a week.

Feeling affluent, I decided to have a suit made. Round the corner from our offices on East Sixtieth Street was a small brownstone with a sign outside that said: *Otto Perl, Fine Tailoring for Gentlemen.* A bit self-consciously – I'd never had a suit made – I entered the shop and was greeted by Perl himself, a small and slender man with a tailor's tape around his neck. He began making shapes in the air, ones that indicated that he approved of my measurements. Before we looked at fabrics, he said he'd like me to meet another of his clients and led me into a fitting room. There, astonishingly, standing before a mirror, was Joe DiMaggio. The Yankee Clipper wore a suit jacket, flowered boxer shorts and shoes and socks. His legs were hairy and unimpressive, but the effect on me was stunning. That Joe DiMaggio and I were to share the same tailor was almost more than I could bear. Who would be today's equivalent of the Clipper? Obama? Derek Jeter? In terms of fame, there *is* no contemporary equivalent. This was the Second Coming.

"Hi'ya doin', kid," he said, then went back to examining his reflection in the mirror.

The only writer I was to meet who had been an Otto Perl client was Gay Talese. A fashion plate, second only to Tom Wolfe, or perhaps his equal, Talese had Perl suits made by the dozen. I had the one, a Navy Blue Pinstripe. But we do have the tailor, Otto Perl, as a bond.

Magazine Management people seemed not so much to have been hired as to have washed ashore at the company like driftwood. We were all slightly "broken" people. A few had gifts, but we were "rejects" all, having clearly been unable to cut the mustard at the Luce and Hearst empires. There was an astronomically high divorce rate. Every now and then, an editor who found life intolerable would run head first into a water cooler and have to be carried off to a rest home, never to be seen again. I fit in nicely, walking about, slightly bent over, and with a palm pressed to my forehead in an effort to conceal hair loss, and, of course, drawing attention to the very site I wanted to go unnoticed. One of the confession book editors, a disheveled blonde woman in her forties, stayed late each day and had a sideline. For a fee, not that modest, actually – she would "pop" the hair of employees who had the same fear of encroaching baldness as I did. That is to say, she would gather up a clump of thinning hair and lift it from the scalp, presumably allowing blood to flow freely into the deprived sections. Sometimes, frighteningly, the clumps would come out in her hand. Reassuringly, she would say they weren't of much use. ("It was time for them to go.") Their absence would allow the remaining strands to flourish. Employees who stayed late would have their work interrupted by strange popping sounds coming from the cubicles of clients, of whom I was one. Visits to her home were encouraged. The services offered there were said to have gone beyond the pops.

There was a great deal of backbiting going on. Each day, an editor with a mole-like face would sneer in on my cubicle and say:

"So we're going to write the Great American Novel, are we?"

Yet another fellow who was the editor of *Eye* magazine went around with wet lips, announcing that his wife had "a great tushy," miming the kisses he'd rained down upon her rear quarters and implying that others had no such treats awaiting them at home. He went off to Hollywood where I guessed he would find his equivalents and fit in nicely.

There was one fellow whose very appearance and attitude offended me. He had a large head and seemed to do nothing but strike poses and stare out of a window languorously, as if he belonged on Corfu, writing cantos. Yet the fates had consigned him to be trapped in a magazine purgatorio, and a down-market one as well. Astonishingly, with the publication of *Wittgenstein's Mistress*, David Markson, the individual who had so irritated me, became not only a close friend but one of my favorite authors. His novels had even less plot than those of his hero, Samuel Beckett. Yet the very absence of narrative mysteriously made them all the more compelling. (It's a difficult feat to pull off. I wouldn't advise this method to aspiring young novelists.)

Markson, or so I felt, was the master and perhaps creator of the one-word poem. *Lidice*, as an example. The name itself has resonance. But the placement of it is everything. When surrounded by seemingly unrelated (scholarly) references and coming out of nowhere to stand alone, the effect is that of a thunderclap.

The underappreciated Markson (adored, of course, by the French) lived for decades in proud (though rent-controlled) poverty in the Village. When last I saw him, it was at Gristedes. We watched a legless Vietnam veteran in a cart snatch a jelly doughnut from a pastry bin and then, not stopping to pay for it, go motorizing off down the street. Infuriated, Markson chased after him with a raised fist, screaming at the man.

"For God's sakes, Markson," I said, running along with him, "Give the poor bastard a break."

"Never mind," said my beloved but slightly crazed friend. "He had no right doing that. I can't, why should he."

I was stunned when I learned of Markson's death in 2010. He'd had one illness after another. But it was my feeling (it's in his books) that he died of bone-deep loneliness. The year before, he had finally been "recognized" with a glowing review in the *N.Y. Times* of his last novel (*The Last Novel*). He spoke before a large group of admirers at the the Y.M.H.A. It was heartening that he had that time in the sun.

Slightly less irritating to me than the young Markson was a small and pockmarked Harvard-educated man who seemed to spend all day with his arm draped over the office partition of the fellow who ran Lion Books. This was Donald Fine, who was to become a powerful figure in book publishing, bringing out the novels of James Jones, Elmore Leonard, Ken Follett and several of mine. A perpetually grumpy man, he was, in literary circles, either loved or despised. I fell into the former category. Before my agent Candida Donadio sent me to see him, she told me that he was both brilliant and cheap. ("Tight as a clam's ass.") That may have been so, but he was also loyal to certain of his authors, almost blindly so in some cases. He continued to publish book after book by Irwin

Shaw when the novelist's star had faded. By rough count, he must have brought out twenty novels by the author Jerome Charyn. It's doubtful he earned a dime from any of them. But once he cared about an author, there was no more to be said. He was my favorite of the five publishers I've had over what has turned out to be a long career. I'm told that in today's climate, that is not a great number. And yet, once again, my snobbery intruded, I could never grant Fine full credibility. After all, hadn't he also begun as a grunt at the same noble and gloriously "schlock" company that I had? How good could he be?

He died, in his mid-seventies, of colon cancer. His last words to me were: "They could have caught it."

From time to time, I ran into my benefactor, Ray Robinson, who did a masterful imitation of Sen. Joe McCarthy of the House Un-American Affairs Committee. ("Don't be cute," the red-baiter would snap at uncooperative witnesses.) Each morning, Robinson discussed bowel rhythms with Thérèse Paul, a faded beauty who had been the lover of Sartre, Camus and many of the distinguished philosophers of France. Now an assistant editor of *Stag*, she continued to have a world-weary charm. Her teeth were nicotine-stained. Yet such was her forlorn appeal, that I imagined myself, with a little encouragement from the aging temptress, chain-smoking my way into her romantic orbit. This was not to be.

Martin Goodman's every move was studied. An enormously wealthy man, he had never paid much attention to the stock market. Suddenly, it became his obsession. Word filtered down to the minions that he had invested in a company called American Machine and Foundry. Thinking I was privy to privileged information (after all, his brokers must have been of the finest) I raced out and bought ten shares of AMF for several hundred hard-to-come-by dollars. Neglecting my responsibilities, I stole off each day and spent hours watching the tickertape at a brokerage firm on the floor below, feeling great bursts of elation when the stock rose a point, falling into a depression when it fell off a bit. The experience wasn't entirely a loss. Some years later I published a story called "The Investor" in which a man develops a mysterious disease, his temperature fluctuating between 97 and 103. A doctor, who has an interest in the market, realizes that the man's fever is tied to the price of a munitions stock. An effort is made to control the price of the security. It fails. The stock splits. The man dies. It pains me to quote the words of a Hollywood studio head, but even such individuals are human beneath the skin:

"Nothing should be wasted."

Soon after he'd lost interest in the market, Goodman discovered psychiatry and hired a tiny bearded Freudian who came to his office each day to analyze him. (House calls? From a psychiatrist?) One day, the usually taciturn publisher came racing out of his office. In shock and confusion, he cried out:

"The man just asked me if I wanted to suck his cock."

The therapy loosened him up a bit. In sexual matters he was constricted, if not confused, which, in the fifties, was not to separate him out from the rest of us. He was terribly concerned that his Long Island neighbors would tie him into some of the naughtiness in his magazines. "Naughty" is the word, too. Certainly, by today's standards, the magazines were almost churchlike in their innocence. Still, he kept taking his name on and off the mast-heads. He ran a huge corporation. Yet hours each day were thrown over to airbrushing out aureoles on the breasts of "cheesecake" models who appeared in the magazines. There had been a man named "Manny" assigned to this function in the art department, but the publisher did not trust him entirely and felt his own fine hand was needed to do a follow-up. On one occasion, a picture of the actress Barbara Logan in a swimsuit with a strand of public hair showing almost made it into *Wink* magazine. This created mayhem. At least one head rolled. (Not that it was an issue, but Logan was married to the director Elia Kazan at the time.)

When sales fell off, Goodman, for all of his prudishness, pushed the envelope a bit. The word "Nympho" was a Goodman favorite and was thought to be a circulation-booster. Hence the title, in 2000, of my non-fiction collection: "Even The Rhinos Were Nymphos." There was a battle within the ranks of Chicago University Press as to whether the title was suitable for what Terry Southern called a "quality lit" quarterly. Against all odds, the nympho supporters won out.

Some years later, the quiet and meek-mannered Charles "Chip" Goodman, one of the publisher's heirs, was to brush aside all of his father's sexual reticence and establish a towering empire of porn, piling up a fortune not only in magazines, but in vibrators, penis-extenders and hand-cuffs as well. I'd been asked at one point to "train" him, to pretend I didn't work for his father, and to show him no favoritism. This was impossible, of course, though I did play at it.

When the "tushy man" left for Hollywood, and James A. Bryans III was dismissed, I was asked by Goodman, at the tail end of the fifties, to write captions for *Eye* magazine, which was essentially a picture gallery of models in bikinis (make that swimsuits) winking at the reader. All were "amply endowed," as the phrase went. The previous captions were of the "How'd ya like to?" variety as in: "Tess Jones is a native of Toledo, Ohio. How'd ya like to get your hands on some of that?" I gave the captions an upmarket touch by ascribing to the models a familiarity with distinguished authors.

"Each night, before I go to bed, I make sure I've dipped into a little Emerson."

Goodman was impressed. He appeared in my cubicle one morning, took a puff of his thin cigar and said:

"I am throwing you a magazine."

6

You Are Your Own Hors D'Oeuvres
> Title of the author's first (and never published)
> attempt at a novel.

I awakened one morning, soon afterward, (the tail end of the fifties) to discover that I had three sons, a house on Long Island and a wife with whom I'd barely exchanged a few words. (Admittedly, we'd had a brief but spirited exchange about Barbra Streisand. And yet another, of course, about Sinatra. Both performers had our admiration.) I had only the vaguest notion of how all of this had come about. Once I had the job at Magazine Management Company, Ginger Howard had traveled East in 1954 with a large family, each of whom had tagged along, presumably to watch Broadway musicals. In a flash, arrangements were made for Ginger and me to get married at the Grand Concourse Hotel in the Bronx. And there I stood, with a wedding about to take place, sensing that something had gone terribly wrong. There hadn't been a single person in my life I could talk to about my confusion. (Admittedly, my mother had suggested that I go off to live in Paris for a few years. I'd said, no, no, I'm fine.) I couldn't bring myself to admit that I was nauseous and vomiting about the coming nuptials. Nor was I willing to hurt Ginger Howard's feelings. What would become of her? A ruined woman at twenty-one.

Before the ceremony, I recall charging down the halls of the hotel in a rented tuxedo, in a last minute search for some wise individual to advise me. I was finally reduced to asking the salad man if he felt I was making a mistake.

The wedding took place as scheduled, followed by a brisk honeymoon in Miami. Three boys came along in quick succession, along with a house (and a mortgage) in Glen Cove, Long Island. I was about to turn thirty, my cherished dream of publishing a novel hadn't materialized and a magazine I cared little about had been thrown at me.

The marriage, to put it gently, was a shaky one, although I thought we did nicely on our occasional vacations. If we'd been able to continue doing limbo dances in the Caribbean the union might have survived. It was only when life intruded that we ran into difficulty. And after a time, ran out of Caribbean islands.

My sons were to insist, years later, that I was a good father. My only recollection of parenting (the very word makes me wince) is one of Sundays – packing the three of them into a car, and driving all over the tri-state area, in search of new roller coasters, ones that had to be thrilling – and more perilous than the previous ones. Years were spent hunting for the ultimate roller-coaster.

I suppose I needed the job at Magazine Management, although I wasn't obsessional about keeping it. I was unthreatened by the Goodman silences that had so unhinged others. After all, I was a novelist. The normal rules didn't appiy to those in such an exalted profession. That I hadn't actually *written* a novel (I'd made a start at one) was beside the point. All of that would come – or I would kill myself.

In some odd way, the house we lived in, or at least its remote location, helped to push me along a literary path. It had a Hansel and Gretel look to it and might have been made of gingerbread. I'd fallen in love with it. Anyone who had slept in a kitchen chair in the Bronx for seventeen years would have been equally smitten.

That it was outrageously far from the city – a two and a half hour commute on the average – didn't especially trouble me. (It took some time for it to become maddening.) In the meanwhile, there were solitary hours to be spent on the Long Island railroad, writing short stories and beginning to sell them at a decent clip – To *Mademoiselle*, *Harper's*, *Esquire* and the "quality lit" quarterlies, such as *The Antioch Review* and Northwestern's *TriQuarterly*. Despite these modest successes, the writing of what Norman Mailer called "the bitch novel," standing alone on its icy peak, remained daunting. And then one day, after I'd changed trains at Jamaica, I jumped in and began to write *You Are Your Own Hors D'Oeuvres*. It centered on an early Martha Stewart type named Grace Dowdy who toured Air Force bases, buoying up the spirits of service wives who felt they had failed at being hostesses.

"Don't concern yourself with dips and canapés," she advised them. *"You are your own hors D'Oeuvres."*

Hence, the title. Why I thought this theme would capture the attention of anyone, much less a publisher, is beyond me. In any case, this first effort wasn't born to be a novel, or anything else, for that matter. Nonetheless, I plodded on, clinging to the hope that it would turn itself into a fictional entity that had some shape to it. There is probably a level of hell, unknown to Dante, for those who've consigned themselves to such a task. The four years I spent on this work in my twenties whilst (my first 'whilst') holding on to a job, was much like climbing a steep hill with an old Buick on my back. Age thirty, the cut-off point for aspiring novelists, or so it was felt at the time, loomed up ahead. As did a nervous breakdown. (We were to learn later on that the nerves do not break down, although something else that's awful does happen.) It was The Time of the Ulcer, a condition that was thought, incorrectly, to be brought about by tension or – as James A. Bryans III would have put it, in magazine lingo, "inner-fears."

A major concern was my sons, Josh, Drew and Kipp, all named after actors in late-night movies. They each had ferocious appetitites and prided themselves on being "four-bagel" people.

They were excellent sons; turning my back on them – packing myself off to a rest home – was not an option.

Frank Sinatra had said famously that he needed a bottle of Jack Daniels "to get him through the night." That seemed an excellent idea. I followed the crooner's advice until I woke up at midnight, on the divider of the Long Island Expressway, cars whizzing by in both directions and having no idea of how I'd gotten there. The closest I came to total collapse was an unannounced visit to Martin Goodman's office. I simply paraded into my employer's office and broke into tears. Martin Goodman was reassuring; he said he'd take on the mortgage if that was a bother – and that he would help in any way he could. So much for his fearsome reputation.

Still, with that fateful thirtieth birthday coming up, and feeling close to the edge, spiritually, novelistically, every which way, I swerved off in a new direction and dashed off four fantasy and sci-fi stories. I'd never "dashed off" anything before. But this one time, in a state of frenzy, I *did* dash them off. All four sold to *Playboy* in a single weekend. I spent the $6000 fee on a a baby blue MG, stacked my three sons up in the front seat and off we went in search of that ultimate roller coaster. Of greater importance was that I had negotiated that critical birthday and hardly noticed it.

As for my poor novel, or fictional entity, it did have one and a half advocates. The half was a prominent editor who admired it greatly, but felt he needed a second opinion before recommending it for publication. As reported to me by Candida Donadio, he handed the manuscript to a colleague, then left the man's office, and knelt outside the closed door, listening through the keyhole for the fellow's reaction. At first he heard horselaughs and guffaws and a clumping sound as if the reader had fallen out of his chair in hysterics. There followed a howl or two and then a series of chuckles that gradually petered out. What seemed to be an endless silence effectively sealed the fate of *You Are Your Own Hors D'Oeuvres*.

Donadio remained a passionate supporter of the book and insisted, literally, to her dying day that she would see it in print. I have a letter from her, in the kind of "dead man's scrawl" seen in movie Westerns, in which she swears allegiance to the manuscript.

Something decent did come of the experience. In slogging through a dreadful novel (with some nice touches) I did learn how to write a decent one. I would hesitate to advise a young writer to invest four years in writing something awful in order to create something good. But that's the way it worked for me.

Once I got past the four years of nausea, I rarely had a writer's block. For one thing, I couldn't afford one. And then one day, it happened. At some point in the seventies, I ran into my very own writer's block. Not a single thought in my head. Flailing around, I consulted an ancient Viennese psychiatrist who might have studied at Freud's knee. After five minutes of listening to my lament, he stopped me and said:

"You forget, Mr. Friedman. What you do is very hard."

"Oh," I said, "I'd forgotten that."

I made out a check for $150, considering it money well spent. Then I returned home and finished a story.

For all of that, I was thirty and hadn't even risen to the level of failed novelist, since I hadn't actually produced one. And I'd been "thrown" a magazine.

7

I wanted to be Henry Kane, holed up in a basement apartment with a Chinese valet, and on the run from a third blonde wife.

The author's fantasy, after meeting one of his favorite writers of mystery and suspense.

Mr. Goodman asked me to lunch one day, presumably to discuss the magazine he'd "thrown" me. I suppose I should have been thrilled, but the expired body of my first try at a novel, *You are Your Own Hors D'Oeuvres*, bless its shapeless and unruly heart, was still warm, and I hadn't summoned the courage to start another.

To be alone with Mr. Goodman was unnerving. (To this day, he's still *Mr.* Goodman.) It's not that he frightened me, but I'd always been uncomfortable in the presence of prominent individuals. When I was a boy, my mother would often point one out to me at a restaurant – a landlord, or a banker.

"He's there," she would say, "and you've got to get there."

I found this irritating, if not maddening. Why did I have to get there, wherever it was? What if I wanted to get somewhere else? Or remain where I was? Still, my mother had spoken. Perhaps I did have to get there, whether I wanted to or not.

On the way to the restaurant, Mr. Goodman offered me a cigar.

I declined.

"Maybe later," I said.

"But what if I don't offer you one later?" he said.

"I hadn't thought of that," I said, sheepishly, and accepted the cigar. I was doing a great many sheepish things at the time.

We stopped at a store on Madison Avenue, one that offered a full complement of magazines – and cigars.

"Now that's the kind of place I always dreamed of owning," said the publisher of a zillion dollar company. "No hassle, all cash, a clean little operation."

I sympathized with him, although I had no interest in owning a store of any kind, even one that was a clean little operation. But here again, perhaps I was wrong and ought to have been yearning for the ownership of one.

At lunch, Goodman was a bit more voluble than usual. Still, he had trouble describing exactly the kind of magazine he'd "thrown" me.

"I'd like it to be classy," he said, "but not too classy."

He grabbed my arm as he said this, as if I was about to run out and start throwing together a magazine that was too classy.

I assured him that I would try to come up with a magazine that was just classy enough. *Esquire* was mentioned as a model. That seemed to satisfy him. We were joined by two advertising men, each of them named Sid, who had gotten wind of the project. It was their feeling that such a magazine should kick off with several pages of truss ads for men with hernia difficulties.

Mr. Goodman took this in neutrally and asked for my opinion. I'd never been asked for one before and found myself speaking in an odd and elevated Cromwellian tone.

"Sirs, I understand full well the need for revenue to offset the cost of this unusual project. But it's my feeling that hernia ads would run counter to the classy audience we're trying to reach."

"Oh, so they're too classy to use trusses," said one of the Sids.

Sensing an argument was about to break out, Mr. Goodman quieted us down. We smoked cigars and returned to the office, where the publisher set about to select paper stock for the proposed new magazine. In this area, he had no peer. He put together a strange blending of slick (classy?) paper for the early pages, followed with some medium-grade stock for the body of the publication and then tapering off to a third section of essentially pulp-grade paper. Having read along that far, the reader would, presumably, forgive the fall-off in paper quality – and perhaps not notice it at all.

The two Sids from advertising won out. The hernia companies signed on and were only too happy to do so. With a slender budget, I did what I could to hold up my end, buying stories from the trunk, the very bottom of the trunk, of celebrated authors that I could feature on the cover of the new publication, which was to be called *Swank*. Graham Greene was one. William Saroyan was another. He was a towering figure in American letters, whose reputation had fallen off a bit in his late years. This was not unusual in the case of literary greats. (The major playwrights seem to have an especially difficult time. That Arthur Miller and Tennessee Williams, as they became older, were unable to have their plays produced is surprising, but no longer astonishes me.) Toward the end of his career, after a long silence, Saroyan had turned up with a play that had been produced and warmly received. I'm a great fan of comeback stories, and I recall how thrilling it was to read Richard Watts' review in the *N.Y. Post* with the heading: "Welcome Back, Bill." I longed to be welcomed back some day, after a long absence.

With no fanfare, Saroyan strolled into my office one morning. I expected such people – literary giants – to be twelve feet tall and to reek of greatness. He was a man of average height with a gentle style, and there was no reeking. It seemed that the higher an author rose in the pantheon, the more modest he or she became, at least in demeanor. I was to meet others. The Nobelist Isaac Bashevis Singer comes to mind, as does Nelson Algren. Add Irwin Shaw to the list, and surprisingly, Norman Mailer, when he wasn't drinking. Saroyan thanked me for buying his story, as well he should have since it was resoundingly unpublishable. Then he attacked the hernia ads.

"What's the *point* of them?" he wanted to know.

I told him they weren't my idea, but I'm not sure he was convinced of this. He may have thought I was the kind of fellow who insisted on having hernia ads in a magazine before I would have anything to do with it. We chatted a bit; I may have hinted that I was struggling with a novel and that I preferred not to be thought of as just another hernia magazine person. He went off to Paris soon afterward to write a short, brilliant book called *Not Dying* which went largely unread. I must have been down in the mouth when we met. My domestic life was a shambles. He sent me a letter, avuncular in style, saying that anything is better than "the other." I knew what he meant by "the other." When he died, I toasted him by checking into The Great Northern Hotel for an assignation. It was a musty and shambling old place on West Fifty-Seventh Street that he favored during the declining years. It closed – or collapsed – soon after my stay there.

Years later, Saroyan's daughter Lucy approached me at a restaurant with an interesting proposal.

"If you're ever in the mood for an affair, call me."

I did not take her up on it. (She lived on the West Coast, for one thing.) But I had never had it put to me that way, and I can assure you that it remains branded in my memory.

A robust and barrel-chested man came rollicking into my office one day, on the heels of Saroyan's visit. He was instantly likeable and full of good cheer. I could have sworn my unannounced visitor was Ernest Hemingway. Saroyan had turned up, why not the king himself. As it turned out, the new arrival was Leicester Hemingway, the great man's brother, who could have easily passed for his sibling. In many ways, he seemed more authentic.

"Don't look puzzled," he said. "You're not the first to confuse me with Ernesto."

He had just come off a fishing boat and tossed a bait-stained manuscript onto my desk, then went rollicking back to the East River. I read the piece immediately, anxious to love it. How could I not? It was the work of 'Ernesto's' brother.

"Hi, ho, me hearties," it began, disappointingly, and continued along in a nautical spirit that seemed to be directed at adventure-loving boys of twelve and under. I believe it was called "Avast." It wasn't a question of it not being classy enough. But it struck me as being the wrong kind of classy for our readers, not that I had any idea of who they were. Here I was in the awful position of having to turn down a story by Ernest Hemingway's brother. I suppose a kinder soul would have bought the piece, and stashed it in the inventory. But I did not want to go down that same fire-eating path of James A. Bryans III and be shown the door. And so, borrowing a phrase from *The New Yorker* rejection book, I wrote and said: "It's awfully good, and it pains me to say this, but I just don't see it here."

While I never got to meet 'Ernesto' himself, I kept circling round the Hemingways. A.E. "Hotch" Hotchner, became a friend. His book, *Papa Hemingway* is as good a portrait of the iconic novelist as any I've read and seems to keep improving as the years roll along.

"Did Hemingway actually refer to groups of women as "womanies?" I asked "Hotch."

He replied: "I'm afraid he did."

"And did his third wife, Martha Gelhorn, unforgiveably refer to some friends as being "whipped-cream fun?"

In sadness, "Hotch" verified this.

At a party, I met Mary, the fourth wife of the Master, and told her what a fine fellow Leicester was.

"That swine," she said. "You dare to mention his name in my presence."

She wheeled off in another direction, but then came back to apologize. Apparently, she'd been locked in a nasty financial dispute with Leicester. All the involved parties hated one another. I have a history of women I've just met saying awful things to me and then wheeling around to apologize. I probably should look into that.

Leicester. The charm of the man. Yet there is something about brothers. In the early nineties, I auditioned Jim Hanks for a televison comedy. An attractive and much heftier version of his famous brother Tom, his acting style was decent enough but much too restrained for the character he was being asked to play. I had to turn him down, too. I met Tom Hanks, just once, incidentally, on the set of *You've Got Mail,* in which I had a cameo role.

"Was it difficult for Jim as an actor," I asked him, "having you for a brother?"

"The time it really bothered Jim," he said, "was when I appeared in *Splash.* I was really hot then."

He went on, of course, to star in *Philadelphia, Saving Private Ryan,* and the multi*billion*-dollar-grossing *Forrest Gump,* among others, feeling all the while that he had cooled off.

Actors.

Of the authors who passed through the *Swank* offices (actually, it was one little room) my favorite was Henry Kane, a writer of mysteries, who was always thought of, unfairly I felt, as being a notch or two below Raymond Chandler and Dashiel Hammett in ability. In some ways I preferred Kane. He was on his heels and agreed to write a 30,000 word Book Bonus for our fee of six hundred dollars. (James A. Bryans III, a Francophile, called the form a Book *Beaunous.*) Kane wrote it quickly. I went over to collect it at a basement apartment on Central Park West where he had "holed up" for the time being. The setting was noirish. He was a slender and

roguishly attractive man who would have fit in nicely as the lead
in a B-movie. When I arrived, he summoned a Chinese valet, gave
him some cash and sent him out for a bottle of Scotch. He was edgy
and kept glancing out of the one window. Apparently, he was
behind on alimony payments to a gorgeous blonde wife, his third,
whose attorneys and their thick-necked "representatives" were
pursuing him. Such was my domestic state at the time that I
wanted to *be* Henry Kane, holed up in a basement apartment with
a Chinese valet, and on the run from a third blonde wife. The story
he gave me was awfully good, too. Just classy enough.

Soon after it went on sale, Goodman tossed the maiden issue
of *Swank* on my desk, tapped it lightly with the back of his hand
and said "It's not moving." Then he went off, ominously, with a
puff of his thin cigar. To energize the magazine I began a feature
called "Swank Dines Out" which had me sharing a meal with a
succession of pretty young actresses, taking a few notes and
returning home to write a spiced up version of whatever we'd
chatted about. On reflection, I can see that the column was a cheap
ploy designed to put me in the company of women who would
now be called "hotties." Though my marriage was virtually
non-existent, I wasn't quite nervy enough to have affairs. This was
my way of testing (dipping my toe) in the extramarital waters. The
first to come by was Tina Louise, later to become famous as a star
of the television show *Gilligan's Island*. She was nineteen, had just
come back from the Caribbean sun, and was so paralyzingly beautiful that I found myself unable to move my jaw muscles. I muttered something about having just had a rough session at the
dentist, and managed to get out a few limp questions. It was not a
case of being smitten. It was more like stupefaction. Several
decades later, I saw her at a party in Hollywood, standing on the
sidelines, something of a wallflower, looking out at a sea of young
starlets. I thought of introducing myself, but in truth the spell was
broken. She was a perfectly normal person, no longer an unattain-
able goddess. What would be the point of pursuing her? And – in
the interest of scorching honesty – it has to be reported that I found

her feet to be disproportionately large. Somehow I hadn't noticed this at our first meeting. Perhaps it was the lighting.

It was the age of the Marilyn Monroe look-alike. Cleo Moore was a cheerful, appropriately buxom version who became serious when referring to her craft. (There's another word that sets my teeth on edge, when it relates to acting. Isn't it carpenters who have a craft? Glass-blowers? Did Cary Grant ever go on about his craft?)

Lowering her voice an octave, Moore, the star of *Congo Bill* and *Women's Prison* said to me:

"My ambition is to work opposite (Marlon) *Brahndo*."

Jayne Mansfield, "the other Marilyn Monroe" was also a candidate. She received me in her hotel suite. Two words come to mind when I think of her. Too much. Too much bosom, too much make-up, perfume, the peignoir, all of it a serious setback for sex. Before I'd cleared my throat, an Alitalia pilot dashed in, flung off his cap, knelt beside her and literally began kissing her from head to toe.

"Let's go on," she said, as he licked at her ankles. "And don't mind Marcello. He doesn't understand our industry."

Quite the opposite in style was the understated, and unassuming, Gloria Mosolino, who was Marily Monroe's body double in the film *Monkey Business*. She wasn't a bit actress-y. I had lunch with her at Reuben's Restaurant and found her terribly appealing. She was soon to marry the novelist James Jones and go off to Paris to live with him. When I met her, several years later, she had taken on airs, having become the doyenne of the expatriate literary circle.

"What do you do?" she asked, at Elaine's restaurant in New York.

"I'm a writer," I said.

(Actually, my book *A Mother's Kisses* had been on the *Times'* list for several months.)

"Oh, good," she said with a lack of interest and looked away.

Her husband, James Jones, who had written the powerful *From Here to Eternity*, was warm and friendly. But as he left the restaurant, Jones called back at me, "You still haven't written The Big One."

I had the perfect answer.

"What about *Candide*, Jim? A Little One, only ninety pages long, but the only Voltaire that's still being read. His 'Big Ones' are moldering in the Louvre."

Unfortunately, I thought of the response hours later, long after Jones had gone off in a cab.

I became friendly with Gloria when I moved to Water Mill, Long Island, in the early eighties. The usual reasons. She liked my short stories. And she had dropped the airs. I may have taken on some. She was crusty, charming, fierce in her honesty. Jones, who died in his fifties, was her great love. She never married again. Sinatra, with affection, called her "one of the the great broads."

The magazine quietly fizzled out after a few issues. The mix of hernia ads, starlet interviews and unpublishable stories by great authors never quite came together. Even Martin Goodman's alchemist's touch with varieties of paper stock couldn't save the poor thing. What had been needed, evidently, was the hand of Martin Goodman's son "Chip," who was later to flag *Swank* on to pornographic glory. The opinions of his Long Island neighbors mattered little to him. Many no doubt were secret fans.

Before I could clear off my desk, Goodman appeared in my office and said: "I am throwing you another magazine."

In short order, he threw me three more. I became the editor of *Male*, *Men*, *Man's World* and the beloved runt of the litter, *True Action*. *Stag*, a friendly competitor, was being published down the hall. I steeled myself, fearing that it might be thrown at me, but happily this never came about. Clearly, having buried one magazine, I was Failing Upward, a phenomenon I was to encounter years later on the West Coast. It puzzled me that a Hollywood producer I knew who was responsible for a series of box office disasters had little difficulty finding financial support for his next project. He explained testily:

"I got them *made*, didn't I?"

At the company, the titles assigned to me were referred to as "adventure" magazines. In other quarters, particularly the lofty offices of *True* and *Argosy,* leaders in this field, they were sniffed at as "armpit" publications. We did some sniffing of our own at magazines we felt were shoddier than ours. There was a great deal of sniffing going on. The magazines featured stories of World War II GIs storming the beaches of islands such as Iwo and Corregidor. I had to buy roughly seventy stories a month. When we ran out of beaches to storm we made up others, with rarely a protest from readers. (Occasionally, someone might question the designation of a tank tread, but never an entirely fictitious battle.) Also popular were "Sintown" or "Scratch the surface" exposés. "Ellensville appeared to be a sleepy and innocent little village, but *scratch the surface* and what you discovered was a cauldron of gambling, prostitution and total depravity." This is virtually the same formula used by the popular cable show, *Investigation Discovery.*

Readers, unfathomably, could not get enough of first-person accounts of people who had had animals chew at them ("A grysbok ate my bones") and mechanics who'd been trapped on electrical wires. ("I'm frying. Get me off this thing.") There were the reliable nympho-yarns. ("GI King of Nympho Island"); accounts of escape from captivity were a large draw. ("No Prison Cell Can Hold Me.") Each issue had a "set" of pin-up pictures, with nipple aureoles responsibly airbrushed away by Mr. Goodman himself. It wasn't quite a formula, but all in all it was a robust little mix that worked. The magazines had few subscriptions. Relying on newsstand sales, each title having a bare bones budget, the "books" as they were called, were alarmingly profitable. A strong issue could actually scrape the edge of a million copies sold, much of it resulting in cash for the Goodman coffers.

Along the way, I'd put together a hardy little band of associate editors. One of the first to come aboard in 1960 was John Bowers, a tall and handsome Tennesseean who had been having a promising career at the State Department. Why he chose to throw over the life of a diplomat to join the staff of *True Action* remains a mystery to me. But join us he did with great enthusiasm. George Fox, "the mad Englishman," was another hire. A pudgy nondescript fellow with a mysterious appeal to women, he was later able to support himself in Hollywood for decades with repeated sales of a single story – one that featured a ten-foot tall Japanese soldier who hid out on the Pacific Islands after World War II, creating chaos and never to be captured. Fox had also written a mystery novel and took pride in the *Times* review:

"This book is above the routine ruck."

The brilliant Jules Siegel joined the team. He had been a classmate of Thomas Pynchon at Cornell and made a formidable case that he was far the superior novelist. That he never quite wrote a novel was beside the point. To this day, I remain convinced of his claim. Thomas Chastain, later to become the author of bestselling mysteries, signed on with us. The poor fellow was riddled with arthritis and had trouble getting around. Callously, I modeled the character Teener in my 1970 novel *The Dick* after him – a homicide detective who had stopped more bullets than anyone in the Bureau. In a film version, I changed his name to Lead. To light their cigarettes, detectives struck matches on his head.

My next choice, in a way, was an historical one. There were two excellent candidates for a single opening. One was Arthur Kretchmer, later to become, for many decades, the editor of *Playboy*. The other was the jolly and rotund and cigar-smoking Mario Puzo. Oddly enough, considering the towering future that lay ahead for Puzo, this was not a simple choice. The lugubrious Kretchmer clearly had a crisp intelligence. I had read one of Puzo's two novels, *The Dark Arena* and found it sullen and without narrative forward motion. Additionally, Donadio had told me the gifted Simon & Schuster editor Robert Gottlieb had rejected him as an author ("Italians with hooded eyes? I wouldn't be right for him.") In the end, with all those pages to fill, I needed a writer and not an executive. I hired Puzo for the princely sum of $150 a week. Taking the call at his home in Hicksville, he reacted in disbelief and asked me again and again if I was serious. He'd never held what he described as a "straight" job before. Previously, his "employment" had been arranging deferments for young men who were about to be drafted. Though Kretchmer was, graciously, to publish a great many of my stories at *Playboy*, I'm not entirely sure he ever forgave me.

Rounding out the team was a pretty young secretary named Jo Eno, one of the first hippies to make her way east from California. She delighted the group by doing headstands on her desk, first thing in the morning, yellow hair streaming, flowered panties on full display. Goodman, perhaps wishing he could be one of us, came by each morning for an envious peek.

8

A group of editors complimented the author on his jacket. "Thank you," he tells them. "My mother bought it for me at Saks."
They were referring to his book jacket.

Having buried the body of a first novel in the early sixties, I thought I might as well get started on a second. It was my great good fortune that *Time* and *Newsweek* had shown no interest in me as a journalist. I can't imagine it would have been possible to file dispatches from Lebanon and to write novels on the side. (The French can do that.) But somehow, being the editor of four monthly magazines (I was in my seventh year at the company) was only a minor inconvenience. Though I gave out assignments and thought up cover lines, I did not actually have to *write* anything, which, for an aspiring novelist, would have been a nuisance.

Stern was written in five months – most of it on subways and trains. My sons, on their way to school, report seeing me slumped over the kitchen table, having worked through much of the night. Not to dramatize (perhaps a little), but I recall writing the book in a heat, as if I was being chased down an alley. This was a new experience for me. I was writing about feelings I preferred to keep secret.

Was it a cry for help? Whatever it was, I shipped it off to the agent, fearing the worst and receiving it.

"You have written an ugly book," said Candida Donadio, a comment she later denied making.

This was awful. I'd sensed there was something wrong with the book and now I knew what it was: It was ugly. It was as if she'd called *me* ugly and I didn't feel I was that bad-looking. What followed may not have been the worst week in my life, but it was awfully close. Then she phoned and said she'd thought of the one person in all of publishing who might respond to such a book (an ugly one?). The individual she had in mind was Robert Gottlieb, a rising editorial star at Simon & Schuster, later to continue rising at Knopf. (We were all rising stars.) Gottlieb, a young, owlish-looking fellow (make that thoughtful) met me in a gloomy setting at the Algonquin Hotel. He spoke in hushed tones. We might have been planning a murder. He liked the book, but the ending had to be revised. It dealt with a child in jeopardy. Gottlieb, personally, felt that, as written, the novel would have been unbearable to read, which was the whole idea. Would I agree to "feel my way back into it" and make a change? Would I agree to saw my arm off? Ridiculous question. Of course I would. I was about to have a first novel published. There was very little in the richest imagination that I wouldn't do. So I set about to make the change, which was no easy matter, even technically. I had never "felt my way" back into anything. What if I got lost along the way? But I gave *Stern* what passed for a "happy" ending. Or one that was less bleak. Those that liked the book, and there were many, failed to notice what I thought was a momentous shift in tone. So much for author sensitivity.

The weeks that followed were excruciating. The book had been accepted, but not "officially." It was very much like the World War II Sitzkrieg, a period during which Germany, France and England for a time *seemed* to be at war but did nothing, essentially, but glare at one another. And what if the "acceptance" fell apart. Who else would take a chance on the book, which was still a little ugly, despite the glimmer of hope I'd thrown in at the end.

Finally, it became official. I was a novelist now, no longer the same person. A door had opened, I was admitted to a charmed circle. There would be no turning back. Or so I felt. And little did I realize how difficult it would be to avoid being shoved back into the corridor.

I was invited to meet the editorial staff at Simon & Schuster. My mother insisted on selecting an outfit for me. When I arrived, a group of editors complimented me on my jacket.

"Thank you," I said. "My mother picked it out for me at Saks."

They were referring, of course, to my *book* jacket, which was later to win an award for cover design. (And how I miss the young man who had gotten it all wrong, though my wife Pat insists that nothing has changed.)

Mr. Schuster came doddering down from an office above to congratulate me.

"The man who writes those wonderful Dust Bowl novels. I've always wanted to meet you."

I said: "Forgive me, sir, but I'm afraid you've confused me with another author."

"No, no," he said, "I'm never wrong about these things. For God's sake, don't you know your own work, young man?"

He doddered off. Robert Gottlieb had asked me to lunch. I joined him in his office, thinking we would be off to Pavillon or some other such elegant establishment. There was a huge plate of carrots, celery and radishes on his desk. That was lunch, Gottlieb being ahead of his time on crudités. What he did, essentially, as we nibbled on raw vegetables, was to mime typing gestures in the air, encouraging me to get on with the next book, before this one showed up in the stores. I followed his advice – at least in this instance.

I met Joseph Heller in the hallway. *Catch-22* had been published the year before. After a shaky start, it was on its way to becoming a global phenomenon. Gottlieb was his editor and had worked shoulder to shoulder with Heller, pulling the novel together out of hundreds of little notecards that the author had written. Apart from suggesting a new ending, the only work Gottlieb had done on *Stern* was to point to a single line and say: "You didn't write that." Without looking at the line, I knew the one he was referring to. I still shudder when I think of it.

Stern reeled as he had never reeled before.

The Magazine Management influence.

Heller had a trademark toothpick in his mouth and wore a bad suit. What I took to be a white Arrow shirt was open at the collar. He reminded me of a Fuller Brush salesman I would often see in the Bronx, hawking his wares, door to door, then setting his valises aside to join a stickball game. In a high, hectoring voice, Heller advised me on how to get ahead as a novelist.

"What you have to do is make friends with wholesalers."

This was the first of many wisdoms he was to pass along. It wasn't quite what I had in mind when I set out to have a literary career – but who knows, perhaps he was right.

We began a prickly friendship. It seems a miracle that in his late years I came to love him as I did few other men.

Stern sold "only" six thousand copies, but, according to Gottlieb, they were "the right copies." (I later wondered: Would it have been so awful to sell a few hundred thousand of the "wrong" copies?)

The reviews were quite good. I don't recall a clinker in the lot. The one that continues to resonate – and how could it not? – was written by Stanley Edgar Hyman in *The New Leader*.

"Friedman," he said in summation, is "greatly gifted, fiercely honest and very welcome news indeed." (The "indeed" put it over the top.) Hyman said I had written the first totally Freudian novel, and indeed (that word again) the book was popular in psychiatric circles.

Dr. Norman Kaye, a Great Neck, Long Island, psychiatrist, made what amounted to a pilgrimage to my house in Glen Cove. His eyes watering over with admiration, he congratulated me on my comprehensive knowledge and mastery of Freudian psychology.

"Your innovative thinking on the male pregnancy fantasy literally took my breath away."

Actually, apart from a quick riffle through Krafft-Ebing, in search of naughty passages, I hadn't read a word of the literature. Still, I couldn't bring myself to point this out. I nodded humbly, and with a wan psychiatric smile, I signed the copy of my book he'd brought along and sent him on his way.

Dr. Harold Greenwald, who had written *The Call Girl: A Social and Psychoanalytical Study* told me that one of his patients (not a call girl) had walked into his office one day in a mixed state of high excitement and anxiety. Dismissing the three years of treatment he'd undergone, he slammed *Stern* down on Greenwald's desk and said: "*This* is the way I feel."

Yet another Greenwald patient, a bearded, towering ex-Klansman from South Carolina said he longed to be "a big strong fearless Jew – like Stern." (Stern is described in the novel as an innocuous-looking man with "pale, spreading hips.")

The novelist Daniel Stern, who was to become one of the best editors I'd ever had, thought he recognized himself in the book. He threatened to retaliate by writing a novel called *Friedman*. There were several unauthorized screenplays written. Each was presented to me with fanfare and the expectation that I would be thrilled to have them and immediately turn over the rights so that the filming could proceed. The scripts looked nice and were typed beautifully, but I hated them. I'd writtten a *book* and not a movie and didn't understand – and probably still don't –the great adjustments that have to be made from the book to the screen. The basic requirement in such a transfer is loving fidelity to the spirit – and not necessarily the text of the novel.

Later, in the seventies, I met Warren Beatty in Hollywood. He was convinced that he could play the part of Stern in a film version. The actor was – and still is – one of the handsomest men who has ever appeared on the screen. (*Graced* the screen is the way it's usually phrased. I had a few cameo roles in films. In not one of them did I grace the screen.) I told Beatty his idea was absurd. No one would believe him as the meek and frightened Stern.

"I can do it," he insisted. "You've got to trust me on this."

(The lesson: Never tell a good actor there is a role he can't perform. Or a good writer, for that matter, that there is something he can't write.)

One of the weaker offers that were made to me came from a woman whose brother, a novelist, was also named Stern.

"My brother is scheduled to speak at the Harmonie Club," she said. "He'd like you to act as his foil."

A much more appealing proposal came from *Mademoiselle* magazine, which had a literary bent at the time. The editors had the inspired idea of pairing up first novelists and playwrights with Swedish models for a photo shoot. We were arranged in teams. Mine, the fifth and last to be photographed, included the playwright Jack Richardson and George Plimpton, a man I knew nothing about. There was a great deal of drinking going on. There was always a lot of drinking going on. This was the early sixties before drugs took over. Based on his two plays, *The Prodigal* and *Gallows Humor,* Richardson was considered to be the great new hope of the American theater. I'd seen the latter play. It was stunning in its impact. A tall, trim, handsome man, he wore a cape and – is there another way to put this? – he cut a dashing figure. After we'd been photographed, he gathered up two Swedish models beneath the cape and swept them off to rehearsals of his new play. How I envied him. I was wearing a tweed suit and about to go home to a loveless marriage in Great Neck. Why had I become a novelist? Had I picked the wrong profession? As a playwright, I could be gathering up Swedish models beneath a cape and sweeping them off to rehearsals. As it turned out, Richardson had never behaved quite that way before. When his wife learned about the cape and the models, she demanded a divorce.

When I got to know Richardson, it turned out – as it so often does – that he had envied *me* – author of a new and well-received novel, house in the country, happily married to a lovely wife, children. Getting it all wrong, of course. What he thought he saw was a façade.

Plimpton offered me a ride to Penn Station. There was something about his car. It wasn't a new model, but the interior had a kind of shabby genteel feel to it. It was a foreign make, probably an Alpha Romeo. I would have bet, correctly, that it had been to Paris. (I was a Chevrolet man at the time.) Plimpton was another tall, attractive and highly agreeable person. I couldn't quite place his accent. No one ever could. It wasn't Etonian, nor was it New England. Or Upper East Side Manhattan. With my eyes closed, he sounded like Audrey Hepburn. (In his oral history, I was quoted, incorrectly, as saying he sounded like *Katharine* Hepburn, which was absurd.) Years later, he appeared on a panel with the essayist Roger Rosenblatt, who could take being puzzled no longer and erupted in frustration.

"What on God's earth is that accent of yours, George?"

In a splendid moment, Plimpton replied: "Affectation, my dear boy, affectation."

The author Leslie Kopit was later to define the accent definitively as "mid-Atlantic."

Plimpton invited me to "a little get-together" the following Friday night. I said I'd be happy to show up. Despite the attention the book had gotten, I was lonely and in need of a new friend. George seemed the perfect candidate. Little did I know what he had meant by "a little get-together." Nor did I have any idea of the astonishing evening that lay in store for me.

9

"You're married to Friedman? Isn't he the guy who writes like Philly Roth?"

> An agent to Ginger Friedman, who was auditioning for a part in a play.

My new friend lived in a quiet and understated brownstone on East Seventy-Second street. I didn't know of anyone my age who had a brownstone alongside the river all to himself. It seemed the most comfortable way to live. There were no doubt advantages to being in a small house with children and dogs and a broken marriage, but at the moment I wasn't aware of them. Years later, Bernard Farbar, who knew everyone, said that George was envious of *me* of all people, when I bought a house he admired in Water Mill.

The door was open. The place was empty. Apparently I'd arrived early. Showing off my excellent Bronx manners, I called upstairs and asked if I could wash some glasses before his guests arrived.

"No, no, dear, boy," he called down. "Make yourself at home, Take a walk. Whatever you like. The others should be along shortly."

I did take a walk. When I returned, the "little get-together" had gotten underway. I recall a scene in Fellini's *The White Sheik* in which there is a slow parade across the screen of comic book characters who have come to life. I watched a somewhat similar parade – or slow march – of what seemed to be every major literary figure in America, with Jacqueline Onassis and a few Vanderbilts thrown in for good measure. Philip Roth, Jules Feiffer, Norman Mailer, William Styron, Truman Capote. I felt I was in a theater, watching a glorious play that starred all of my literary heroes. I'd read their books, and, of course, expected each one to be twelve feet tall. A door had been opened; I'd been admitted to a charmed circle. My new friend George hadn't let on that he knew the neighborhood grocer much less this group of luminaries.

Then too there were what came to be known as the *The Paris Review* women, pretty, vivacious, each one a walking heartbreak with, unforgiveably, a literary sheen. The evening might have been a casting call for Sally Bowles or Holly Golightly. I didn't know where to look first. I was in love with all of them. (And didn't they each sound a bit like George Plimpton, now that I think of it.) Though I'd had some modest success with the women at Stevens College, ("The Vassar of the MidWest") this was new territory. I did not know how to approach such people – and I didn't. Each one gave the impression of having just returned from the Dordogne – or from a skiing trip at Klosters. After that, it would be off to follow the bulls at Pamplona. I was in no position to follow along with them. George gave the impression that he was – though I never had the feeling that his attraction to these heavenly creatures was a sexual one. There is a story told to me by a girlfriend – of mine, actually. It's naughty, but that's never stopped me before. She and George had arranged for an assignation. At the appointed time, he arrived at her apartment. Expecting to be caught up in his arms, she watched him take off his trousers and arrange them neatly on a hanger, making sure to keep the crease.

"Oh, George," she said. "Why don't I just go and cook some dinner."

I chatted briefly with Philip Roth – Philip *Roth*, for God's sakes. I'd read his stories in *The New Yorker* and knew of his stunning ability. But who could foresee the thirty novels that were to follow – all held to the highest standard. He praised my story "The Punch" that had appeared in *Esquire*. (*The New Yorker* had rejected it for being "unpleasant," thereby, in a sense, rejecting in advance all of my writing in the coming years.) Roth took an inordinate interest in my arms. Did I work out? Or did the shape of my arms come about naturally? Actually, as if to compensate for a lost marriage, (broken, shattered, lost – all of the terms accurate) I'd been spending some time in a gym, no doubt in preparation for the next romantic adventure . . . or calamity. Further along, I would run into Roth from time to time. I'm not the first to note that Manhattan, in its way, is just another small town. I noticed a pattern in our brief encounters. For the first minute or two he was affable. Then, as if assured he was safe from attack, he would slowly elevate his jaw and his tone would become aggressive. ("You're wasting your time on those ridiculous movies.")

I've always been envious of Roth's career – what novelist wouldn't be? It's not that I *wanted* his career – to a degree I was satisfied with mine. But I was in awe of it. Sticking to his last the way he did. A friend, long after the Plimpton party, consoled me when I made my feelings known.

"How can you be envious of Roth? You have a (second) wife who adores you, four childen who do as well, grandchildren." (By this time I'd been married to Pat O'Donohue – we adored each other – and my daughter Molly had joined the team (been born).)

All of what the friend said was true . . . And yet. . . .

I fired a literary agent because of a related remark he made at a small dinner party.

"There is Philip Roth and there is everyone else."

There was some truth to this, but I thought it was rude of him to announce this to a group, with a client sitting beside him.

On the subject of envy, Martin Amis, who had known Anthony Powell, another literary hero of mine, said that the author of the *Dance to the Music of Time* series, admitted to being envious of everyone and everything, including a horse that had won the Derby.

As for the Roth experience, my wife at the time aspired to become an actress. She auditioned for an agent who learned she was my wife.

"You're married to Friedman?" he said. "Isn't he the guy who writes like Philly Roth?"

I became friendly with Jules Feiffer that night at Plimpton's and was to see him often at Fire Island in the summer. In a brief moment of affluence – the mid-sixties – Ginger and I had hired a housekeeper. At five in the afternoon, Mrs. Sullivan would place a bowl of potato salad and a platter of coleslaw on the dining room table. And each day, promptly at five, Feiffer would cycle up to the house, sit down at the table and wolf down Mrs. Sullivan's freshly prepared treats. And for a time, I thought he'd been showing up for the pleasure of my company.

For all of the bookish stars that had been assembled at the Plimpton party, one outshone them all. I'm not sure that all eyes were on him, but I know that mine were. He was The Next One. He was the Annointed (and was to continue annointing himself). Hemingway, Fitzgerald, Faulkner, James Jones (with an asterisk) and now Norman Mailer, whose *The Naked and the Dead* had electrified the literary world. (It was accurate, in this case, to say there was Mailer – and there was everyone else.) It was something to lay eyes on him for the first time. He was small and stocky and did not cut the dashing figure of my new friend Jack Richardson. But he had a look of the literary lion that he was. A youthfully craggy face, a knowing twinkle in his eyes. Magnificent hair, almost provably the best of any novelist.

In his late years, when he was even craggier, I said to him: "You're our Spencer Tracy."

He kept a whiskey glass in front of his face, almost defensively, as if to protect himself from a sudden blow. He was often photographed that way. It might as well have been a trademark. I had the feeling he kept glancing over at me now and then, and the look was not friendly. My ego hadn't run amok. The ubiquitous Bernard Farbar told me some years later that I reminded Mailer of a classmate at Harvard who would beat him mercilessly and regularly at tennis.

I made a mistake then, telling myself all the while: "You are about to make a mistake." I approached Mailer and told him I had written a novel (*Stern*) and would he care to read it. He looked me over, taking my measure – if that's what he was doing – then said there was no reason to send him the book.

"Tear off the front dust jacket flap," he said, with an elaborate tearing gesture. "Send it to me and if the subject interests me, I'll take a look at the book."

In retrospect, it seems a reasonable response. The last thing a novelist needs is for a stranger to approach him at a dinner party and say here's my book, would you please stop everything and read it. Especially when the novelist is at the center of the universe.

"Care to shoot a few hoops, Mr. Jordan?"

What I thought unneccesary was the flamboyant tearing gesture he made, as if he was tearing up my novel. I met Mailer a second time perhaps a year later. He said he'd read and enjoyed the novel. I began to apologize for it. Too short, never got my teeth into it. Expect to do much better on the next one.

This amused him. He said: "You make the same mistakes that I do."

The party began to peter out. As I was leaving, Philip Roth called out to me: "Remember, Saul Bellow am de daddy of us all."

Though I admired Bellow's novels of the time, *The Victim* in particular, I did not feel he was my daddy. But this was Philip Roth. I let the comment go unanswered.

And why, incidentally, did people keep calling out to me as I was leaving restaurants and parties?

10

"I've been writing a novel. What do you think of 'The Godfather' as a title?" "Not much," I said. "Sounds domestic. I'd give it another try."

> An exchange between the author and Mario Puzo at the Magazine Management Company.

Not that long ago, the publisher of a small imprint told me he was anxious to bring out a book of my essays.

"Unfortunately," he said, "we don't have pots and pots of money."

Though *Stern* had gotten considerable attention, there were no "pots and pots of money" coming my way. Though I now walked an inch or two above the ground, the job at Magazine Management continued to be important to me. I had used Martin Goodman as the model for Stern's employer in the novel. Though I'd taken every precaution to disguise him, short of turning the publisher into a Dutch housewife, I was convinced he would recognize himself and fire me.

The dreaded summons to his office came soon after publication. He surprised me with a congratulatory handshake and a raise. Later in the day, a woman who worked on the floor below followed me into the elevator and began to shriek at me.

"How could you do something like that? Expose my secrets. Who gave you that right, you lowlife."

And then she disappeared. I'd never met the woman before, but she was convinced I had based a minor character in the novel on her life. That set a pattern. It was rare that someone I had actually written about or 'used' in a book or story was aware of it. More often, it was a perfect stranger who was outraged.

One friend felt he had spotted himself as a character in my second novel, *A Mother's Kisses.* He was annoyed. Yet when the character didn't work out in a stage production and had to be eliminated, he called and was outraged.

"You dropped me? How could you drop me? The play is nothing without me."

I assured him that we'd made every effort to keep him in the play but (and here I was lying) we couldn't find an actor who was able to get across his character's unique charm.

Puzo took to the job at the Magazine Management Company with great enthusiasm and cheerfully pumped out stories by the dozen. Though salaries at the company were minimal, there was an opportunity to move up to a living wage by doing freelance articles. We called it "fweelance," mimicking, cruelly, the pronunciation of our art director. Puzo, who had six children to support, fattened himself up on "fweelance." The fee for a 30,000 word Book Bonus had stood resolutely for years at five hundred dollars. I became Puzo's hero when I insisted that Martin Goodman raise his figure to seven-fifty. He did two a week. His only grievance, a minor one, was that I refused to let him pick out cartoons for the four magazines. It was one of the perks of the job. In my ego, I thought I was better at it. A sly and witty man in his way, Puzo was concerned that he wasn't funny enough. Years later, at the height of his fame, we had lunch and I recall him looking off wistfully into the distance and saying: "They never call me for comedy." ("They," being the Hollywood people.)

That same insecurity, I've noted, is not uncommon among writers, no matter how substantial their reputation. Gore Vidal often said that Norman Mailer, with whom he had skirmished, verbally and physically, had no sense of humor. In the late sixties, my first play *Scuba Duba*, had become a surprise hit (no one was more surprised than I was). Mailer's stage version of his novel *The Deer Park* was floundering. A mutual friend, Bernard Farbar, took him to see my play and reported that after the final curtain, Mailer pounded on the armrest and said: "I know what it is. Friedman's a wit." This, as if the play succeeded because I'd pulled a sneaky and underhanded trick. Though he was no Oscar Wilde, Mailer himself had a rough wit, but it was never one of his strengths.

There is a theory – who knows, maybe it's mine – that no writer can make a claim to greatness unless there is a streak of comedy in his work. I'm hard-pressed to think of any merriment in Thomas Mann's novels. But in *The Death of Ivan Ilyich* Tolstoy himself includes a funny scene in which Illyitch's wife waves away her husband's agonizing death-throes by telling a doctor that he always goes on like that, don't pay any attention to him. (Perhaps you have to read the book.) Stavrogin, in Dostoevsky's *The Possessed*, is also a funny character. Oh, those Russian cut-ups.

While not neglecting the treasured magazines, our merry little band became increasingly literary. John Bowers weighed in with *The Colony*, an affecting memoir about the year he'd spent at the Handy Writer's Group – along with James Jones. I set about to begin a second novel, to be called *A Mother's Kisses*. I worked (or 'labored', after all, it was a comedy) late at night, often all through the night, with my heart in my throat. My marriage, which I'd described in a play as being "A Gibraltar of a union," had crumbled like an old Graham cracker. (An image that Gottlieb would never have permitted.) Still, I've never needed tranquility in order to tell a story. Often, a little chaos was useful. But my situation at that moment was ridiculous. Quite apart from the four magazines, the five-hour commute and the doomed marriage, there was yet another distraction – the new neighbor who had moved into a house across the road. A Polish concert pianist, he practiced each night by pounding out variations of Aram Khachaturian's "Sabre Dance," perhaps the most grating of all musical compositions. Summoning up the courage, I walked across the road to have a word with him. Confrontations have never been easy for me. (Are there people who love them?) A character in a movie I wrote, *Stir Crazy*, tells a prison warden: "I only have one speed, sir."

I myself had two, or at least I did during that troubled time: embittered silence or extreme violence.

I knocked on the pianist's door at midnight and explained that I was writing a second novel.

"It's terribly important that I have some quiet. Would it be possible for you to practice during the daylight hours?"

He said that was out of the question. He was preparing for a concert.

"Midnight is when I'm at my best."

"Now look," I said. "I'm not just any old novelist. I can assure you, I'm taken very seriously."

To prove my case, I returned to my house and gathered up the reviews for *Stern*. He was waiting for me on his lawn with glowing reviews he'd gotten for his concerts in Gdansk. We stood there comparing reviews in the moonlight.

He refused to give an inch. I thought about it, but decided it would be an overreaction to throw him through a window. With clenched teeth, I returned to my house and pretended to be writing. Soon afterward, and once again, my mother rode to the rescue with a little machine that gave off a pleasant sound (White Noise) and was designed to counteract an offensive one. The machine, or gadget, commonplace now, was a rarity in the sixties. How she knew about it is beyond me.

Mothers.

Puzo approached me one morning in 1963 – it was his turn to be sheepish – and said he was moonlighting a novel and wanted my opinion of the title. We were all moon-lighting. None of us short-changed the magazines. So it wasn't as if we were cheating. But where he found the time to write a novel was beyond me. Where any of us found the time was a mystery. We were young. But Puzo wasn't all that young. He was moving along in his forties and was later to say that his huge success came too late. Smoking giant-sized Dunhill cigars in the Elizabeth Taylor suite of the Beverly Hills Hotel, he said, somewhat contradictorily, "There had been too much illness, too much hardship. . . ."

At the moment, and with regard to the title, he said to me: "What I have in mind is 'The Godfather.' What do you think?"

"Frankly," I said, without hesitation, "it doesn't do much for me. Sounds too domestic. What if we used a title like that on *True Action*? It would drive readers away. I'd take another try at it."

A look of stone came over his face. You would not want to see that look. It would come over him at odd times, when some-one, for example, challenged his expertise on the proper ingredi-ents for a great spaghetti sauce. For years, he maintained that *The Godfather* was all make-believe, that he had no connection what-ever with organized crime. Whenever I saw that look, I had my doubts.

Oddly enough, I felt I was right about the title. It would not have worked on any book other than *The Godfather*.

This strange mixture we had of writers who produced adventures and exposés by day and turned out often acclaimed literary works at night did not escape the attention of the outside world. Gloria Steinem was doing investigative reporting at the time. For back-ground material on Hugh Hefner's empire she had gotten herself hired as a *Playboy* bunny. She dropped round to see what we were up to. And the novelist Richard Yates turned up one day. He sat down behind an empty desk as if he worked on the magazines and hung around for weeks. It was difficult to know what to do with him. He was a disheveled-looking man with a handsomely ruined face and the hangdog demeanor of a sheepdog who had wandered in off the street. I knew of his quality. I had read *Revolutionary Road* and the word-perfect *Eleven Kinds of Loneliness*. But there was no job available at the time; nor did he ask for one. He just wanted to sit there, as if we were operating a shelter of some kind. He rarely spoke. Though I do recall him mumbling bitterly that *Revolutionary Road* would have been a runaway bestseller if *Catch-22* hadn't been published simultaneously. Writers, gifted ones, often have the strangest notions. The books were totally different in style and execution. But he was convinced of his theory.

After work each day, when our "books" were put to bed, a group of us repaired to a bar called Tobo's on East Sixtieth Street. I was in no rush to get home. I didn't have much of a marriage and there was an Israeli waitress who'd caught my attention. There were the unshaven legs, de rigeur at her old kibbutz, but she was awfully attractive. We had a new secretary, a young Barnard graduate with green eyes and a lovely name – Craigh Brohel. I may have hired her because of her name. And the green eyes. Yates joined us, as if he'd put in a hard day's work. It was no secret that he had a drinking problem. No doubt we all did, but his – much like his literary gift – was monumental. Quietly, he knocked back three or four martinis and fell forward, cracking his head on the table. Brohel, who had previously taken no apparent interest in him, rushed forward, cradled his head against her (capacious) bosom, got him to his feet and walked him out to the street. They set up housekeeping. That was the last we saw of either of them.

I would get a call from Yates now and then when he was teaching in the MidWest. Did I know of a job for him? Some way for him to make some money? He saw me as a producer of some kind, never once acknowledging that I was a writer. This may, unfortunately, have been the impression I gave off. I had the same problem, if that's what it was, with Terry Southern, during his lean years. (All of his years seemed to be lean.) He felt that with a snap of my fingers I could get him hired on major motion pictures. Blake Bailey, in a biography, noted that as an academic, in the MidWest, Yates taught only three books. One was *Stern*.

Yates died in bitterness and squalor, a familiar story for many a gifted writer. *Revolutionary Road* was made into a major film, decades too late to do him any good. Would it have made a difference if the film had been bought and produced in his lifetime? Seems unlikely. He came across as having a demon or two more than the rest of us.

There was a memorable day at the company that began much like any other. I had breakfast at The Boyd Chemists, a drugstore on the ground floor of the building. The counterman, Eddie, was convinced I could get him a toehold in the film industry (another one). As he did each day, he ticked off all the reasons he would do well in the industry as I tried to get down a tuna on rye. Though I didn't know a soul in Hollywood, apparently I was stuck with the look of someone who could get people jobs in the film industry. He would have had more luck with my mother. A freelancer named Martin Fass showed up with a Confederate Prison camp story I'd assigned. Hands clutched to his mouth and writhing in agony, he needed one hundred dollars immediately to pay a dental bill. I took the request in to Martin Goodman, who approved it. Then he said that sales were off a bit. He took a puff of his thin cigar and said: "Throw 'em a few hot words." I passed this advisory along to John Bowers, who was our man on the writing of sex scenes, mild ones that would not offend Mr. Goodman's Long Island neighbors. Dutifully, he tossed a few "dark triangles" into a story he was doing called "The Rock-Around Dolls of New Orleans."

I exchanged glances with one of the secretaries, a silent agreement that we would stay late and make love (have sex, really) in my office after hours. My wife had embarked on her own romantic pursuits. I felt "covered." It was maddeningly erotic. The building had emptied out. The door was locked. Amyl nitrate had come into use. The air conditioner gave off a high mentholated whine. Yellow hair streaming in my lap. Smokey blue eyes beaming with delight. Martin Goodman's son, "Chip," sniffing suspiciously at the door. After he'd left, and to raise the erotic stakes, we had sex now and then in the temple itself, Martin Goodman's office. There was once a stain on a couch that I would rather not think about.

And then it happened. Our managing editor, Bernard Garfinckle, kept changing his name to Garr and then back to Garfinckle. I believe he was Garfinckle when he came charging into the office, flushed and excited.

"I've just just read the first eighty pages of Mario's novel. It's a battering ram."

The Godfather almost instantly became a publishing phenomenon. I felt entitled to share in Puzo's success. After all, hadn't I "discovered" him. He was a born storyteller. Yet he claimed, and there may have been a grain of truth to it, that he learned how to write a compelling narrative at the Magazine Management Company. I never got the knack of it myself, though I had some expertise in telling others how to do it. Puzo considered me "a great coach," not exactly the role I had in mind for myself.

Mr. Goodman, understandably proud of *The Godfather*'s success, said to me: "Maybe you'll do something, too, some day."

Soon after the novel's publication, I recall hearing Puzo on the phone to his publisher. Though he'd been given a healthy advance, he felt he needed more money.

"Two hundred grand," he explained. "does not last forever."

There was a film sale, of course. His flimsy percentage of the profits brought in millions.

"The money came out of the ground like oil," he said. "The studio didn't have time to hide it. But they made up for it. I didn't see a dime on *Godfather II*."

He was not greedy. Far from it. He was the most generous of men. As his fortune grew, he took care of more and more friends and relatives. At lunch, a year before he died, in 1999, he said: "If only I had dropped dead a year ago, I would have been in much better financial shape." But throughout the Hollywood years, he remained fascinated by film profits, the *definition* of profits, his dream being to get a percentage of the *gross*, much like the major film stars. That is to say, he would be paid a penny or two – or more – from the first dollar taken in at the box office. One day, long after he'd left the company, he signed on to write a film and called me in triumph:

"I got it. A piece of the rolling gross."

I said I didn't know much about grosses.

"But what I think you're after is a *stationary* gross. If it's rolling, the chances are it will be rolling away from you."

Though I've never made a decent financial decision, it turned out, in this instance, I was right.

After that first *Godfather* publication, his habits didn't change much, but he began to live on a larger scale. After being mugged several times in Hicksville, he moved his family to a larger and more reclusive home in Bay Shore.

"There was nothing wrong with the other place," he explained. "But I had something to lose now, and the people who attacked me didn't."

His legend as a famous eater (gourmand?) began to grow. When one of us arrived a few minutes late for a dinner date at a Chinese restaurant, he would make use of the delay to slip around the corner for a quick pizza. After the *Godfather* enriched him, he hired a special mozzarella man, who would race down the street and deliver the cheese while it was still dripping with freshness.

"After fifteen minutes," he explained, "it starts to lose its flavor."

As a host, at dinner for his friends, he would order every pasta on the restaurant menu, so that his guests would be able to sample each one.

Weight had always been a concern. When it got out of hand, he checked into what he called a "fat farm" in the Swiss Alps. After a week of dieting, he could take it no longer. In his pyjamas, he left the facility and somehow found a cab in the mountains. He instructed the driver to take him to Paris, three hundred kilometers away, where he found a restaurant that was open and ordered a beloved pizza.

We continued our friendship until he passed away – I can't bring myself to say he died – at the age of seventy-six. His belief had always been:

"After seventy-five, you are playing on the casino's money."

11

The great screen legend raised her skirt and literally kicked me out of the apartment and into the hallway.

Marlene Dietrich, a fan of *A Mother's Kisses*, when the author failed to recognize her at a cocktail party.

Any temptation I might have felt to be envious of Puzo was greatly reduced with the publication of my second novel, *A Mother's Kisses*, in 1964. The book caused a commotion of its own.

The reviews were extravagant, the one exception coming, almost predictably – it was, after all, a second novel – from Stanley Edgar Hyman, who had been so fulsome in his praise of *Stern*. I actually enjoyed his summarizing comment.'

"Friedman's book might as well have been called 'A Mother's Titties.'"

No matter. The book went sweeping up the charts and remained there for months. The attendant stage and film offers came in, the most aggressive from the fellow who had made the film of *Portnoy's Complaint*, which I didn't much care for. Nor did Philip Roth, I was told. I turned him down.

Marlene Dietrich, of all people, had come through from London with a ringing endorsement for the bookjacket. I was to meet her once at a party given by Mike Nichols at his Central Park triplex. The place was jammed. The director introduced me to a slip of a woman, perhaps in her seventies. I shook hands with her and looked around to see what was going on. Inadvertently – I have no record of being rude – I had snubbed Marlene Dietrich. The great screen legend raised her skirt and literally kicked me out of the apartment and into the hallway. I did not return. I sensed that it would not have been a good idea.

David Merrick, the reigning king and "the abominable showman" of Broadway wanted to do the book as a musical comedy. His office was red, plush, heavily brocaded. I don't know if he was shooting for an upscale bordello effect – but he'd achieved it. He stood at the window, parted the drapes and pointed to Forty-Fifth Street. Three of the major hits were Merrick productions.

"Do this show and you can have any one of those broads down there," he said.

His reference was to Carol Channing (*Hello Dolly*), Ethel Merman (*Gypsy*) – and other assorted "broads" who were appearing in Merrick productions. Despite the ferocity of his reputation, he had a hurt little boy quality about him. *If you don't do this show, I may have to cry.* (This was the seduction phase. The ferocity would come when you were actually working with him.) Nonetheless, I decided to pass. For one thing, I had no idea of how to do a libretto – and still don't. Merrick was later to produce my play *Turtlenecks*. The Yiddish phrase for the result is "*Aliva shulem*" – may it rest in peace.

Much more tempting was an offer from a producer I remembered from summer camp named Gabe Katzka. He never left his tent and was presumably making deals at age fifteen. The lure was Richard Adler, the composer/lyricist of *Damn Yankees* and *The Pajama Game*. And there was a vague promise that Neil Simon would write the libretto. Simon was later to do film adaptations of my short story "A Change of Plan" and my book *The Lonely Guy*. When Simon was asked, at lectures, why he didn't adapt the classics, he said: "I only adapt Friedman."

Katzka's option expired, but *A Mother's Kisses* as a musical was to come back into my life a year or so later. In the meanwhile, it was fun seeing the books pile up in the stores and disappear. (I never did befriend Joseph Heller's wholesalers.) I was where I suppose I wanted to be, yet for all the attention and clangor I felt somehow let down. It was as if I missed the struggle and had found it more satisfying than the book's success. (And how I wish there was a better word for "success.'" Hedge fund managers are "successful." Writers, or at least good ones, never feel they are. Or shouldn't.)

Then, too, there was a glum feeling that came along with those early victories. Though there was considerable evidence to the contrary, I felt that I had personally failed as a husband and – more important to me – that I had let down my sons. The feeling nagged at me and prevented me from enjoying myself at what should have been a trimphant time of my life. What good was it all if I had a broken personal life. My mother's advice had been: "Never, no matter what, break up your family." Though I'd had plenty of help, this is what I'd done. And those early victories came at a price.

An intelligent next move would have been to press on and do a sequel to my second novel, picking up Joseph and his outrageous mother (the central characters in *A Mother's Kisses*), where I'd dropped them off. There was plenty of life to cover. Yet I had no appetite to do this. Promiscuous fellow that I am, the fun was always to strike out and explore some uncharted area. To fail, if necessary, with a new work rather than succeed with the tried and true. Hardly a recipe for the building of great fortunes. (And does a novel ever "fail" because no one reads it? Only in the eyes of the publisher – or Joseph Heller's wholesalers.)

I still had to contend with my job at the Magazine Management Company, the four magazines and the occasional "special issues" and the mountain of stories I had to buy each month. For all of the press and the foreign editions and an advance on the next novel, there weren't any great cascades of money pouring in.

Yet, in what seemed like a split second, I could no longer face another "GI King of Nympho Island" story. Martin Goodman asked me to stay on and said, essentially, that I could write my own check. As an added inducement, he gave me a key to his private men's room and unlimited access to his humidor. (He'd graduated from his trademark thin little cigars to fat and expensive Por Larrañagas, brought in illegally from Cuba.) When I hinted that I might be ready to say goodbye he said, ominously: "You're a year away."

I was to hear a version of this advisory in Hollywood, years later, delivered by a producer, to the most sought-after young actress of her time.

"You're a picture away, babe."

She did a film with the producer. It failed. She was never heard from again.

Motion picture actors, the most frail of creatures, always feel they are "a picture away."

Did Trollope, too, after fifty efforts, feel he was a novel away?

My father signed on with Gottfried Underwear at the age of fifteen and stayed with the company until he died at age seventy-five. That was the model. That was the way it was done. You took the subway to work in the morning and came home at night (holding the *Journal American*.) But I was thirty-five – in 1965 – an old man, or so I felt. This was my last chance to break free. I could have continued to edit the magazines with my left hand, but I had no wish to take someone's money when I couldn't in turn make a strong effort to earn it. Add to this – I was sending Puzo and Bowers to places (Vegas, San Juan) I wanted to visit. In a brief (split-second) moment of either clarity or madness – I decided to quit my job. It took a good part of a year for me to work up the courage to resign (to dive into the abyss?) – and roughly twenty minutes to get used to my new freedom. (*I can swim, I can really swim.*)

There were last-minute temptations, which, for all of their promise and very real riches, weren't all that tempting. I was, for example, offered the job of editor-in-chief at *Playboy*. It had been held by A.C. Spectorksy who had written a few freelance pieces for our magazines. This is wince-inducing, but at the time there was a much written-about tabloid phenomenon of girl-pinching in Rome, the local rakehells tweaking at the behinds of visiting American women. I assigned a freelance essay on the subject to Spectorsky, who delivered a piece called "Girl-*Bumping*." I explained that this wasn't quite what I had in mind. His next effort was titled "Girl-*Tickling*." Still not what I'd ordered. We went on this way until I paid him his fee and forgot about it. When he called, several years later, he said:

"Hef and I are offering you this job because of your stubborn and quite proper refusal to accept anything other than *Girl-Pinching*."

The job was considered – by Hugh Hefner and perhaps by the magazine world – to be a step up. I didn't see it quite that way. I had no interest in continuing on with magazines. Dreaming on, had I been offered the editorship of *The New Yorker*, I would have felt dismally the same. In the case of *Playboy*, I had the feeling that you would never know – as an editor – how good you were. Was it an article on the Scottish wetlands that caused an issue to sell, or, more than likely, a picture of a nude and busty blonde carhop in Seattle? Arthur Kretchmer, who had almost made the cut at *True Action*, got the job and continued to hold it for decades. I had no compunction about *writing* for *Playboy*. The payments were generous, the staff convivial, and the assignments took me all over the world. One morning, I received a memo from the magazine, wondering if the editors could induce me to write a story on "The Natural Blondes of Iceland." A handsome fee, all expenses paid, of course. John Metcalf, an iconic figure in Canadian letters, smacks his lips in envy when he hears this story. (And once again, I didn't feel that Iceland's finest could hold a candle to the home-wreckers who assemble at my local Whole Foods at five in the afternoon – after finishing up work at *Condé Nast*.)

As for my journalistic efforts at *Playboy*, there were distinguished jurists, political figures, and financiers who would stop me in the years to come and thank me for being their "cover" (beard?) when they were caught with a copy of *Playboy*.

"I had to buy it, dad. There's a new Friedman in this issue."

The Magazine Management Company was acquired, just as I left the company in 1965, by a pair of businessmen whose background was in electronics and who knew nothing about publishing. They invited me to lunch and offered me the job of running the company, Martin Goodman to be kept on as a consultant. This meant, unthinkably, that the formidable and much-feared publisher would have to report to me. Would I now be compelled to give one of his efforts a little tap, tell him "It's not moving," then walk off with a puff of a thin cigar? Unimaginable. Great classical (Oedipal?) themes were at work here. I had little doubt that I could oversee the editorial side – perhaps I'd need some help on the confession magazines, although the formula – *sin, confess, repent* – was a simple one. Once again, I was asked to name my own figure. And once again, I backed away. There was no sum of money that could tempt me. Nothing heroic about this position. I'd simply had enough. And so off I went, into the abyss, with a mortgage, little in the way of savings, a thin façade of a marriage and three sons with increasingly voracious appetites. But never again would I have to sit in an office. Admittedly, there were times when I did miss the water cooler, the camaraderie, a steady income and the after-hour dalliances. (Did I say 'dalliances?' You can lead a boy out of the pulps, but you can't, etc.)

Martin Goodman, after graciously accepting my decision to leave the company, put together a farewell banquet in my honor. There was a prominent and much admired couple at the time who seemed to have the perfect marriage. Suddenly, to the surprise of their friends, they filed for divorce. The wife explained:

"We said and did unforgiveable things to each other."

I'm sure my ex-wife has her examples of my unacceptable behavior. Close to the top of my list was the hour or so she spent applying make-up on the day of the banquet – while I sat fuming in the car. (I have no history of fuming. I may never have fumed before. But fume I did that day.) Finally I drove off and arrived – alone and humiliated – as dessert was being served at a banquet in my honor. I was asked to speak. I choked out the words "Thank you" and sat down. Mario Puzo jumped to his feet and rescued the moment with a jolly twenty minutes of comments about Martin Goodman, the most generous of supposedly ungenerous men. *Martin* – and I'd finally worked up the courage to address him as such – took me aside and surprised me with a five thousand dollar farewell "gift." I thought this was one more magnanimous gesture on his part. On reflection, this was a time when we had no union, no benefits, no protection of any kind. Our health and well-being was tied to the largesse of our employer. In today's world, a severance payment – for more than a decade of pounding out dozens of money-making magazines – would have been ten times the amount I was given. The bone I was thrown. Still, I was grateful. He might have seen me off with a handshake – and no banquet at all.

On reflection, there was a fellow at the company named Arnold Hano, the editor of Lion Books, who put his family at risk by attempting to organize a union. He was found out and dismissed and had to go off to California to find work. At the time, some looked upon him with contempt. Was I one of them? Did he have to upset the applecart? I remember seeing Goodman speak quietly to him, explaining why he had no choice but to let him go. He may have secretly admired Hano. He was a brave man.

12

Writing screenplays is not enough. To succeed in the film world, you have to be able to "pen" them.
                    The author reflects on his time in Hollywood.

So there I was, with all that freedom. No need to wear a suit. (These were the "Mad Men" days. We wore suits to the office.) And no particular fears, although anyone of sound mind would have had some. I'd broken the nine to five (nine to midnight, actually) pattern, which was like spitting on my poor father's grave.

Before I had time to flounder and feel rudderless, an offer came through from Hollywood. I was asked to adapt a book for the films about an Eskimo (now Inuit) photographer who becomes an Andy Warhol-like cult figure in Manhattan. I had never tried a screenplay before. Despite warnings from Philip Roth to avoid them at all costs, I decided to move ahead with this one. With the exception of bungee-jumping, I'm generally inclined to try whatever it is that I haven't done before. Mr. Smugness would rather fail with the new than succeed with the tried and true.

Alan Pakula was the producer. He later became a director of note. (Warren Beatty, a Hollywood kingmaker of sorts, had walked across a studio commissary one day, stopped at Pakula's table, scrutinized him with chin in hand, then pointed a finger at him and said: "You should direct.")

Pakula was wearing a bathrobe and pyjamas when he greeted me at his Manhattan offices, which were still under construction. Excusing himself, he stood on his head for the next few minutes, wanting me, I would imagine, to know that he was fascinating. (Hollywood notables had nicknames at the time. Burt Lancaster, for example, was Burt Lungbuster. Pakula? Alan Peculiar.) Back on his feet, he showed me to a room that was the size of a small hotel lobby. Assuming it was to be my office, I thanked him.

"Has my name on it. I'm sure I'll be quite comfortable."

"No, no," he said, "It's for my brother-in-law." (Pakula was married to the actress Hope Lange.)

The producer then led me to a room that was no bigger than a broom closet. There were actually a few brooms in it and some cleaning supplies.

"I think we can fit a desk in there for you," he said. "What do you think?"

I said, diplomatically, that it was fine but there was a chance that I might feel a little "hemmed in" and I'd prefer to work at home.

He was disappointed. What he had in mind was for me to sit there, all hunched over, surrounded by cleaning supplies, and to slip him pages (under the door?) as soon as I'd finished them. In one stroke, he had defined the writer's position in the Hollywood hierarchy.

After some time on the West Coast, Mario Puzo would say that writers were only hired out of bitter necessity.

"There's never been a producer who didn't feel he could write a screenplay – if only he had the time. "

I tried one hundred pages in this new form – all of them set in an Eskimo village. The scenes were of dogsled competitions, the cooking of whale blubber and naughty behavior in igloos. I thought I'd better try them on the producer before I went any further. (A screenplay is generally 120 pages.) Pakula pointed to a single line of dialogue on page one hundred:

The Lead Eskimo: "My destiny is in New York."

"Here's where we begin," said Pakula.

This was upsetting, but once I'd calmed down, I saw that he was absolutely right. I'd been clearing my throat, showing off my writing skill, which was beside the point. Carol Baron, an excellent producer who had enjoyed my books, warned me later on that a singular voice would actually work *against* me in Hollywood. This was, after all, the motion *picture* business. Much preferred was a generic voice. The writer who can find it in himself to write the line: "We have to talk," spoken by one of two characters who for an hour have been doing nothing but – will go far in Hollywood. The critic Pauline Kael said that Alan Pakula, author of screenplays now, had not written so much as "penned" the screenplay for *Sophie's Choice*. That's another essential. Writing is not enough. To succeed in the film world, one has to be able to "pen."

My first effort never made it to the Big Screen. (Apropos of which, years later, after I'd written a novel, short stories, journalism and a play, a man in a steambath said to me:

"I notice I've never seen your name on the Big Screen."

Wisdom attained? There will always be a man in a steambath.

I ended up – if indeed I've come to the end – with half-a-dozen screen credits. It seemed a paltry number. It embarrassed me. Until Hollis Alpert, who had become a film critic and biographer – assured me that novelists who come West rarely earn more than a credit or two, if that. F. Scott Fitzgerald, who actually loved the movies, had only a third of a credit on a single film (*Three Comrades*). Anthony Powell, whose *Dance to the Music of Time* series is provenly a masterpiece, did not even get a third. In the six months he spent in Hollywood not a soul in the film business acknowledged his presence, much less offered him an assignment. The high point of his trip came when he spotted F. Scott Fitzgerald in a gathering at a cocktail party.

On reflection, my Eskimo village scenes might have made a movie unto itself. If only I had kept those pages.

*

Some years later, on the set of *Stir Crazy*. I made the mistake of sounding off to Richard Pryor on the poor treatment I'd received from a studio on a previous movie. He listened patiently, then asked quietly: "Did you get paid?" I did indeed get paid for my Eskimo saga, not handsomely, but enough to take my family off on a trip to Europe. We rented a palatial villa in Cap D'Antibes. Twenty-five hundred dollars covered the rental for an entire summer. Maid service, a pool, magnificent gardens were all part of the package. (The year was 1965.) Still clinging to the shards of a marriage, I brought along my wife, three sons, a Mrs. Sullivan who had joined the team as a housekeeper, and a cat.

"That's fine with me," my mother said. "I'm sitting here in the Bronx and the cat is going to Europe."

When we got off the plane in Nice, a gathering of the press was there to greet us. Reporters, flashbulbs popping off, all of which seemed unusual. At this point I'd published two novels, a collection of stories (*Far from the City of Class*) and some magazine journalism. The books were published in France, but still . . . You would have thought I'd won the Nobel.

Not a word about our arrival appeared in the local French press. I learned that a college friend, who had gone into public relations, had arranged the faux press reception as an affectionate prank.

We arrived late at night. The boys were starving. A Vietnamese restaurant was the only one we could find that was open. My youngest son ordered a pizza. After biting into a slice, he cried out:

"This isn't pizza. There's no cheese in it."

Kipp was a quiet boy. Until that moment, we'd barely heard a peep out of him. But apparently the culinary setback had driven him over the edge. We explained that the Vietnamese had a different take on pizza; they felt that cheese was unnecessary. This was puzzling, but it did calm him, if only slightly. The trip had begun poorly. Matters did not improve when we arrived at the villa. It was splendid-looking as advertised, but still, I felt cut off, isolated. I'd never been out of the country before. And then, suddenly, I heard the song "If I Were A Rich Man," from *Fiddler on the Roof*, come booming out of a seaside home across the Mediterranean. That's all it took. I felt connected. I've told this story on several occasions to Sheldon Harnick, the lyricist of the musical, to little effect. Clearly, he'd heard quite enough about the show.

My sons learned to swim at the glorious Hotel du Cap. For the crawl, the instructor taught them to turn their heads and say *New York* for the left stroke, *Cap D'Antibes* for the right. They learned little French. The phrase "Donnez la note à mon père" ("Give the check to my father") got them by very nicely. My wife and I went off to visit the lovely red-headed novelist Edna O'Brien at her home in London on Deodar Lane, adjacent to the Thames. (*The Thames . . . Deodar Lane . . . the very sound of it – for an Anglophile – on a first visit to London.*) O'Brien had created a stir with her first novel, *The Country Girls*. She was later to write other celebrated novels, and also one of the finest biographies in the language on James Joyce. I'd read five hundred pages on major figures such as Balzac and Tolstoy . . . and felt I knew even less about them after I'd finished their biographies. Difficult task, bringing to life, *inhabiting* a great subject. Not so for Edna O'Brien in her one hundred pages on Joyce . . . and then doing the same for Byron.

She greeted us by telling of a date she'd had with the novelist Bernard Malamud, who disappointed her by showing up, unforgiveably, with fingerless kid gloves. O'Brien's male characters were lusty. This was not the lustiest of get-ups. After setting out the largest cooked salmon I'd ever seen (the Moby Dick of salmons) for her assembled guests, she tiptoed upstairs, put on some symphonic music and continued along with her second novel. I was baffled by this approach to writing, but it seemed to work out nicely for her. Seated beside me at dinner was one of the most beautiful women I'd ever encountered. Never mind The English Rose. She was an entire country garden. She said to me:

"*Hours and hours of lovely lovely love.* Don't you find it the most wonderful of activities?"

I agreed, of course, though I had little experience at it. As Joseph Heller would have put it, "Maybe a quick bang or two . . ."

I took her words as an invitation. Decades later, the words still haunt me. There was a gentle and chubby man beside her. I believe he was part of the package. I could have slipped away with her, and even worked in the chubby man. I probably wouldn't have been missed. My wife and I no longer shared a bed. But it would have been rude. Throw a little cowardice into the mix. (*"We could do it. But it would be wrong."* Richard Nixon.) And yet, there it is, branded in my memory forever . . . *Hours and hours of lovely lovely love.* Hours that got away.

My wife and I took a (self-) consciously literary sidetrip to Paris and stayed at Oscar Wilde's favorite hotel on the Rue de Bac. (Was there a caged jaguar in the lobby? There was.) We were much too late for Hemingway, and even the *Paris Review* group. But still . . . it was Paris. My mother had emptied out her poor bank account and encouraged me to take this trip *before* (in lieu of?) getting married. A chance to starve romantically in an attic, sit in the cafes and to be filled with tremulous dreams of the grand novels I would write some day. Instead, I was forced to actually *write* the bloody novels without the support of cold attics and tremulous dreams. Had I traveled abroad, at that earlier time, I would no doubt have ended up with virtually the same wife – Ginger, with a French accent. Pat, my second, wife, even gave her a name: *Genevieve.*

Rome next, a tacky hotel, but, as if in compensation, the matchless light. Then on to Venice, sad and narrow little streets leading to the astounding Piazza San Marco, almost blinding in its space and magnificence. To just come upon it that way, without preparation. Home of the sixteenth-century Doges – my favorite, Enrico Dandolo, ninety and blind, but insisting nonetheless on limping off to sack Constantinople. Exquisite trip. Wrong marriage. Decades later, I sought to duplicate it with Pat, the love of my life. Same scenario, London, Paris, Venice, even the Hotel du Cap. Yet everything was a beat off. (Did I miss the torment?) Perhaps we needed a trip of our own. And we were to take many.

13

*"Exuse me, sir, but I've come to see a play and not to hear you bab-
bling on that way."*

> The author, unknowingly shushing down Edmund
> Wilson, the most formidable literary critic of the
> century.

My wife took the boys off on their own field trip. I stayed behind in
a cold castle, wearing a bathrobe no less, pacing up and down, for
no good reason, and carrying a scythe. Stone walls, isolation again,
little French. I was good, fittingly, at the cry for help. *Au secours . . .*
My wife was off somewhere. It all felt like a play. Hadn't I been
told that there were dramatic "unities"? (I had gotten that much
from my farming college, along with the history of silos.)

*A single space, some conflict (the absent – and straying – wife), one
night.*

I had my unities. Though I'd never tried one, I'd been caught
up, turned upside down really, by several plays I'd seen before
we left for Europe. Edward Albee's *The Zoo Story*; Jack Richardson's *Gallows Humor*; Arthur Kopit's *Oh Dad, Poor Dad,* . . . . Add
to the mix *Machinal* and Jack Gelber's *The Connection*, which had
been ridiculed by critics until Kenneth Tynan arrived from

London and explained to us that it was a classic. I was so caught up in the Gelber play that I recall shushing down an elderly gentleman who kept chatting with his companion after the performance had begun.

"Excuse me, sir, but I've come to see a play and not to hear you babbling on that way."

The manager took me aside during intermisson and said I'd silenced Edmund Wilson, at the time the most formidable literary critic in the country.

"Excitement" is a word that's thrown around like loose change in Hollywood. The whole town is in a constant state of excitement, everyone is excited about a film, an actor, an idea (generally for a remake). All meetings end with someone (the producers) saying "We certainly are excited." ("Amazing" is the new "excited.")

But in the early sixties, when the word was fresh, I was truly excited by the theater and its possibilities. More than one patient had given *Stern* to a psychiatrist and said: "*This* is how I feel." When I saw the theater of Albee and Richardson and Kopit – and Beckett and Ionesco – my feeling was:

"This is how I *think*."

"Absurdist" is a catch-all word for the spirit of this new (form) style of theater. I suppose it's as good as any. The plays I had seen previously – the flops I'd been rushed down to see by my aunt who worked for the Schuberts – were all formal, manicured, tidy. Drawing room comedies. Terence Rattigan. Noel Coward (and bless him for it). But this was theater turned on its head. And as an infant, hadn't I been dropped on my head on more than one occasion by my sainted mother? (How difficult is it to hold on to an infant, even a squirming one? My mother couldn't quite manage it.) In any case, slightly brain-damaged as I was, the Theater of the Absurd made perfect sense to me.

And so, filled with presumption and crawling with embarrassment (I hadn't even seen *Hedda Gabler*) I set out in a rented chateau in Juan-les-Pins to write a play. I finished *Scuba Duba* in five days. Which is to say I finished *something*, some pages, that vaguely resembled a play. There were nauseating revisions to come over a period of two years – before it reached the stage. For one thing, I hadn't realized the importance in a play of assigning dialogue to more than one character. What I'd come up with was a single disgruntled actor in a bathrobe shouting grievances at the moon, while several (salaried) cast members looked on in silence. Elia Kazan said that the great plays he directed (*A Streetcar Named Desire, Death of a Salesman*) each came to him whole. The ones that needed patching and mending never worked out quite as well. Mine – and skip the greatness – came in dribbles. But it did come eventually, and I've yet to have a (literary) experience more thrilling than sitting in a theater and having a live audience react favorably to a piece that I'd written. Of course there is the disappointing other. In the mid-seventies, during the 1972 try-out of my play *Turtlenecks* in Detroit, audience members began to file out of the theater in mid-perfomance.

I'd had nightmares about droves of people leaving the theater.

"Are they droves?" I recall asking the director, Jacques Levy.

"I'm afraid so," he said.

I shipped *Scuba Duba* off to a theater agent, the ageless Robert Lantz. When asked how old he was, he would say, even then, "I am in the public domain." When someone asked *me* about his age, I would ask in turn:

"How many people do you know who've had lunch with Pirandello?"

Which he did at the Hotel Adlon in pre-Hitler Berlin.

"H.G. Wells," he would say, "came by, stopped at my table and took a bite of my dessert. He could not resist."

"Robby" as he was known with affection in The Industry, along with his friend, the producer Sam Spiegel (*On the Waterfront*) were alleged to be the last two Jews to escape from Nazi Germany before the borders were closed.

"Hitler," said Robby, "would never have *dreamed* of closing the borders until he was certain Spiegel was gone."

Lantz was later to shove me into a suite for a night of madness at
the Beverly Hills Hotel with the actress Jean Seberg. My kind of
agent.

In his last interview, John Updike recalled a time (the fifties, sixties,
perhaps the seventies) when it was possible to patch together a
reasonably comfortable existence by writing short fiction and
assorted journalistic pieces. I was able to do so – barely – for the
several years that followed my exit from the Magazine Management Company. Updike had his "home" at *The New Yorker*; I had
mine at *Esquire*, *The Saturday Evening Post*, and, to a lesser extent,
at *Harper's*, *Playboy* and any of the publications willing to ship me
off somewhere and write a check for the result. (Screenwriting,
apart from the Eskimo venture, was yet to come.) The journalistic
pieces were useful in that they had a cross-pollinating effect on the
fiction. The (venerable) *Saturday Evening Post* had asked me to tail
along with a pair of homicide detectives for several weeks in
Chicago. The piece was published: (*"Arrested by Detectives Sullivan
and Valisares. Charge: Homicide."*) and that should have been the
end of it. But there was a residual atmosphere of violence that
stayed with me and formed the background of my next novel, *The
Dick*, published in 1970.

Parenthetically, and perhaps because of my homicide reporting, I recall being early to pick up on the public fascination with
crime, which now so dominates television and the screen. I suggested a Colombo-style series to a TV producer named "Stu"
(Everyone in television at the time seemed to be named "Stu.")

Stu gave me one of the worst pieces of advice I'd ever
received. "Forget crime. The networks won't touch it."

And for decades to follow, of course, they touched little else.

I didn't consciously use the magazine assignments as research
for fiction (I needed the money), but it often worked out that way.
In Jerusalem, an Arab-Israeli room service attendant pleaded with
me to smuggle him out of the country so that he could attend his
brother's wedding in Queens.

"Please, Mr. Friedman. Take me to Lefrak city."

I could not find a place for the episode in my magazine story, didn't think much about it, but suddenly the experience formed the basis of a novella (not yet published) called *The Peace Process*.

Harold Hayes, the brilliantly quirky editor of *Esquire*, carved out a (brilliantly quirky?) sub-genre of story in which a writer of literary note would attempt and fail to land an interview with some luminary. The approach caught fire for a brief period. Jack Richardson did not quite get to interview the singer Eddie Fisher. He did spend time with Fisher's press agent which was good enough for Harold Hayes. In Bimini, I came within a hair of spending time with Adam Clayton Powell, but was turned away at the last minute, although we did have a quick exchange of cigars. (The Congressman had been treated poorly by a *Time Inc.* reporter and held me accountable.) Shame. Fascinating man, or so I felt. I gave up, went fishing, enjoyed the finest gumbo I'd ever eaten. The *Post* editor called, said don't despair, just go ahead and describe my frustration at *not* getting the story. He was convinced it would be compelling. I followed his instructions, and who, knows, maybe it was.

I actually did get to meet and to train (six miles a day) with the unknown (at the time) Joe ('Smokin' Joe) Frazier, in preparation for his fight with the Canadian George Chuvalo. Frazier was a smallish man, for a heavyweight. You wouldn't be concerned if you sat next to him at a bar. His great strength came up through his powerful trunk. And, as we learned, he was a 180-pound pit bull. At a press event, he was asked to armwrestle with the powerful Chuvalo, who might as well have been carved out of granite. The Canadian, with little effort, pinned Frazier three times, a man against a boy. I feared for my new friend. I'd been assigned to cover Frazier. My money, so to speak, was on him.

"Don't worry, Bruce," he assured me. "We ain't gonna arm-wrestle."

In his sixty-eight fights, Chuvalo had never been knocked out. To put it in sportswriter terms, Frazier "accomplished the task" in four rounds. Instructive. It's not a matter of how well a fighter is built. The story I did for the *Post* led to a friendship and ringside seats with my father at the first of the three legendary Ali-Frazier fights. Each time I meet the director James Toback, he tells me that everyone he knows claims to have been at that legendary fight. *"But we were actually there, Bruce."* Frazier took the first fight. I had mixed feelings about the result. For all of my affection for the almost unbearably decent Frazier, my heart was with Ali. His stance on Vietnam, (a refusal to fight the war) and the four prime years that were torn out of his life as a result of it. (*"Ain't no Viet Cong ever called me 'nigger.'"*) When I was five, my uncles took me to see the fights at an outdoor arena in the Bronx. It was a gentlemanly ritual. Cigars, a suit and tie, an occasional ironic catcall ("Stop that bloody battle") when the fighters were sleeping on their feet, just going through the motions. I've been following the sport ever since and I've never seen a fighter – or an athlete, for that matter – who could compare with Ali. It was my feeling that he could have beaten – or figured out a way to beat – anyone who preceded him or any fighter who came later – including the massive Klitchsko brothers. At Chasen's Restaurant in Los Angeles, years after his career had ended, I found myself standing next to the legend at a urinal. I completely lost it.

"*Ali, Ali'*" I began to chant. "You are the greatest. We will never see your like again. *Ali, Ali.*"

I poured out my divided feelings about the first fight with Frazier "that decent decent" man – (and why did I keep calling him "decent"?) and how, despite my feelings for his opponent, a fine man, a *decent* man, my heart was secretly with Ali.

"It was awful for me."

He listened patiently to this outburst, then asked quietly:

"Who are you, brother?"

I told him it wasn't important who I was – although I did throw in a few credits – it was *him* . . . Ali . . . The Greatest . . . And then I flew out of the men's room and told the whole story to my wife Pat. In a fine moment, she asked: "Did you let the poor man take a leak?"

But on the night of Frazier's victory, and in my father's last days, he got to shake hands with the new heavyweight champion in the fighter's dressing room.

"Your dad's got quite a grip," said Frazier.

I'd always felt shabby about not doing a good enough job in looking after my father before his death. But I did have a moment or two.

This mix of short fiction and journalistic assignments was enriching in some ways, but not monetarily. I'd moved out. There were two households to take care of, a one-room flat for me, a house in Great Neck for the family. It's said that freelance journalists burn out after a few years. I recall being envious of a writer named Charles Einstein in the fifties, whose byline appeared in virtually every publication I picked up. And then it was gone. His byline. Him. As if he had fallen off a cliff. I hadn't quite reached that point. Indeed, some years later, I became infuriated when some CAA agent asked me if I was "burned out." I'd turned down a film assignment. But *burned out*? I was breathing, wasn't I? But at the time, in the late sixties, the cupboard was virtually bare. Each of my short stories at the time began with the main character "backed against a wall, the IRS drawing closer..." or some variation thereof. I told an interviewer that I did my best work when I, too, was "backed against a wall," but that's something one tells interviewers for dramatic effect. I'm sure I could have performed effectively if I'd had a bank account.

I had dreams of returning (slinking back) to my old company in defeat and finding a strange individual at my desk. I thought I'd been essential, and here were my old magazines being pumped out as if I'd never worked there. And then the play, or play-like entity, I'd written in France came to the rescue.

14

"You, me, Truman Capote. People like us should put our skulls together."

> A three A.M. call from the singer Bobby Darin, following the opening night of the author's hit play, *Scuba Duba.*

Scuba Duba eventually ran for several years, "without an empty seat" as I'm always quick to add. The play had been turned down by virtually every theater management in Manhattan, a development that I've found is not necessarily a bad sign. Both *Stir Crazy* and *Splash* were received coolly by all of the major studios. Columbia finally came around and went ahead with *Stir Crazy* in 1980. Disney began a new division and took a chance on *Splash* in 1985. Both became huge commercial successes.

The producer Alex Cohen took some momentary interest in *Scuba Duba* and arranged for me to meet Elaine May, whose idea it was that she would act as the director and play all the female characters. There were five in all. One was a 21-year-old woman in a bikini, another an elderly French housekeeper. I didn't see how this was possible, but such was her charm that I decided it was a splendid idea. I drove back to Long Island, slightly in love with her. When I reached Exit Forty my infatuation began to fade. As I pulled into the driveway, I hated her. Play *all* the female characters? And direct as well? What was she thinking? What was *I* thinking? As evidence of my constancy, I fell right back in love with her when I saw *The Heartbreak Kid* in 1972. (The first version.) It was my favorite experience in the movies. Neil Simon wrote the screenplay. The film was based on a short story, "A Change of Plan" which I'd published in *Esquire*. Elaine May directed it. No re-writes. No dreaded "notes" from teenage executives. All I had to do is buy some popcorn, go to the movie and love it – which I did.

I asked Neil Simon how he had gotten the tone of the movie to be so faithful to the story.

"I pretended I was you," he said.

"But you'd never met me. You don't know me."

"I don't?"

The Producer Ivor David Balding took an interest in *Scuba Duba* though he announced to virtually everyone he met: "We don't know if Friedman can write a second act." (We still don't. Sadly enough, it's the one trick the internet can't quite pull off – at least not well.) But somehow, I did get a second act written.

Balding, the son of a legendary British polo player, ran The New Theater, a lovely space in midtown that had thrown off nothing but hit plays. The theater was adjacent to a popular disco called *Arthur's*. Rock music could be heard thundering through the walls during performances; somehow this did not interfere with – and perhaps added to – the flow of triumphs. Mike Nichols had directed George Segal in *The Knack*; *Sgt. Musgrave's Dance* with Roy Scheider was staged at The New Theater. And there was *The Mad Show*, put together by the brilliant young Englishman, Steve Vinaver, who agreed to direct my play. He told me that when *The Mad Show* was in terrible trouble, he decided to disappear for a long weekend.

"Then I called myself in and fixed it."

The show then ran forever.

Vinaver had a crush on the actress Lainie Kazan, and wanted to cast her as the ingénue. This may have been what attracted him to the play. I've noted that directors will often attempt to shoehorn a wife or mistress into their projects. When Gene Saks signed on to direct a musical version of my novel, *A Mother's Kisses*, his wife, the brilliant (and miscast) Bea Arthur had to be folded in as the star.

"This time, baby," I recall him telling the mannish Arthur, "*you're* the one coming out in a white gown."

I tried, some years later, to have a single line ("Hi, there") written into a television show for an actress I knew (all right, a girlfriend) who was in dire financial need. I was told by the producers that it was out of the question. The casting couch was only to be used by producers and directors. No writers need apply.

With high excitement, we were about to begin casting *Scuba Duba* when Vinaver calmly abandoned the production and took himself off to London to direct *Darling of the Day*, a musical produced by Harold Prince and starring Vincent Price. Clearly this was a much bigger deal than my poor play, and welcome to the theater. I tend to be calm in a crisis, and to fall apart when it's been resolved. In this case I fell apart immediately. Such infamy. Not since Pearl Harbor had I lived through the like of it. And that was only the start of a *war. This was my first* play, *for God's sake*.

Schadenfreude Department: *Darling of the Day* closed after a few performances in Manhattan.

With British aplomb – he was *sort of* British – Balding called upon Jacques Levy, who had directed and written a segment of the hit play *America Hurrah*. There were puppets with giant heads in it. They scrawled dirty words on walls, in some kind of sixties anti-establishment statement. It didn't matter. There were puppets in the play. That's all it took to intrigue me. And, indeed, we ended up with puppet-like figures in my play. (Harold Pinter did not care much for Levy's directing. He did not feel his plays needed to have puppets parading around in them. Very strange.)

Levy had begun his career in psychology and had been "a rising star" at the Menninger Clinic when he spun around on a dime and decided he wanted to direct in the theater. (In the years that followed, he would look off in the distance now and then and say:

"You know, I was a rising star at the Menninger Clinic.")

I accepted this. Then I began to wonder. Was he *really* a rising star at the clinic? Or was everyone there a rising star? Perhaps it was the Menninger's way of buttering up interns, whether or not they were rising.

Levy announced his decision to change careers to his parents, who had invested so heavily in his education. His mother accepted the news calmly, then handed the phone to her husband who sang "Hello, Dolly" into the receiver.

My first impression of Levy was not a good one. Enormously pleased with himself, and convinced he had the perfect icebreaker, he told me a joke – a Jewish joke – that I'd heard at least a dozen times that week. It was virtually impossible to step out the door and not have someone tell you the joke, which wasn't all that wonderful. It was one of those "two Jewish guys" jokes. I told myself: *This is not going to work out.* But on the other hand, there were those puppets. And as so often happens, the best of friendships often begin on a flat note. Such was the case here.

There was little else to do at this point – order the puppets and begin casting. Levy did have one idea. There is a party girl, or "light hooker" who has a brief moment in the play. Levy was something of an *enfant terrible* in the theater. (He stayed mysteriously connected to Abbie Hoffman when the leader of the (infamous?) Chicago Seven was on the run.) Levy's suggestion was that the louche (my first *louche*) actress wander across the stage bare-breasted, which sounds like weak tea now but was unheard of at the time. The idea was to "shock" the audience, and in this it succeeded. So as to indicate that he (now "we") didn't intend the scene to be titillating (but only to shock), great care was taken to avoid casting a nubile with perfect breasts. The performer chosen, a very good one, was a middle-aged woman whose breasts were on the matronly side. (Margaret Thatcher?) Nonetheless, you could hear the intake of breath in the audience and sense the stomachs tighten when the actress strolled across the stage. This, after all, was the hallowed and sanctified *theater*.

It's unusual now, of course, to see a play in which at least one nude body doesn't prance around at some point. But this was a famous first. Do I take pride in the 'breakthrough'? Not especially. It was Levy's idea, not mine, although I didn't put up much of an objection. (The "just following orders" defense.)

For the role of the lead ingénue, Levy suggested an actress named Brenda Smiley, who unsurprisingly turned out to be the director's ex-girlfriend. No matter. She was fine. Then began the search for the lead actor, the "charming young man" with some skill at comedy who is virtually impossible to find. No sooner does such an actor shine on stage than he is immediately whisked off to Hollywood to do a film or television series. We looked at dozens. The relatively unknown Jerry Orbach did a twenty-second scene. All agreed there was no other actor who could play the part. Before his audition Orbach had told friends and family he had no chance of being hired.

"They're flying in Big Guys from the Coast," he said.

The producer had indeed flown in a few Big Guys, none of whom had worked out.

Soon after Orbach had been hired, a young actor named Dustin Hoffman stopped me on the street and insisted that he was born to play the role. I had seen Hoffman in an off-Broadway play, *Journey of the Fifth Horse*, and knew how good he was. Still, I had to explain to him with patience that we had already signed Orbach.

"I don't care, Mr. Friedman," he said, virtually – and nasally – following me to my doorstep. "You're making a big mistake. And you've got to give me a shot."

Next stop for Hoffman, the lead in *The Graduate*. But I never felt we'd made a mistake.

Rehearsals and then previews went smoothly. Romantic affairs were had by virtually all, which I learned was fairly traditional. The loneliness. The boredom. And everyone was so attractive. At one point in the play Orbach's character is called upon to mention the Fifth Avenue boutique Henri Bendel. I'd always thought it was pronounced Henri *Bendle*. Orbach thought otherwise. In his view, the accent was on the second syllable. Henri Ben*dell*. I actually called in Geri Stutz, the owner of the store, to confirm that my pronunciation was the correct one. The actor was undeterred. From first performance to last, Orbach, clinging to his independence, cried out "Henri BenDELL" so that it could be heard clearly in the last row.

The final preview was a disaster. The actors walked about in a fog, mumbling their lines. The atmosphere was that of a funeral parlor. *Well, that's it, I thought. Two years down the drain.* Surely this would be registered as the unfunniest comedy in memory. The conventional wisdom was sound: novelists have always washed up and broken their backs against the unforgiving shoals of the theater. Think (presumptuously) Scott Fitzgerald, Henry James. To add to the general despair, Steven Vinaver, who had deserted the show, turned up and watched a preview. Shaking his head sadly, he threw up his arms as if to say: "What can I tell you?" then disappeared with a show of sympathy.

The play opened the next night, in October of 1967. I was untrained in how to encourage actors before an opening performance.

"Just relax," I told Orbach, in his dressing room. "It's no big deal."

"You're right," he said. 'It's just a couple of lousy careers."

Still, from the first, the lighting and the very mood seemed brighter. The cast might have been injected with some miracle potion. After the first laugh, which seemed to take forever – and was unplanned – the play seemed to race happily and exhilaratingly along to the final curtain.The audience raced happily alongside the play. As for the final preview, I hadn't realized that it was all preparation, that actors saved their best for the opening night. And why should they not. A grade school student could have figured that out. But I hadn't.

The play opened to unanimous praise. Clive Barnes of *The Times* led the press in its approval, calling the play the finest comedy since Arthur Kopit's *Oh Dad*, which was high praise indeed. He also pronounced it an unqualified hit, which apparently ran counter to the newspaper's policy. A play couldn't be *declared* a hit. It had to *become* a hit. Not too long afterward, Barnes was working for the *N.Y. Post*, and may never have forgiven *me* for causing him what appeared to be a career setback.

Joe Levine, the reigning film mogul of the time, insisted on seeing me immediately.

"From this day forward," he assured me, "you will never have to worry about money."

I felt wonderful. To think that I would never again have to worry about money. This from the producer of *The Graduate*. Actually, not a day has passed since that I *haven't* been worried about money. I brought this up to him a year later in Beverly Hills.

"Oh well," he said, "you have so much of it."

This was disappointing. I'd expected something catchier in response.

Attention came from every direction. The singer Bobby Darin awakened me with a call at three in the morning.

"You, me, Truman Capote. People like us should get our skulls together."

Laughable, but in retrospect, it might have been a fascinating combination.

A telegram arrived from Paris, asking (begging?) me not to assign the French stage rights.

"Will arrive tomorrow night. Staying at the Ritz Carlton." Signed: "Irwin Shaw."

Irwin Shaw. Tip on A Dead Jockey. Sailor Off The Bremen . . . "The Girls In Their Summer Dresses." Talk about a *frisson*. This was *beyond* a frisson. A telegram from J.D. ("Jerry") Salinger himself would not have meant more. Shaw's estranged wife, a producer who lived in Paris, wanted to do the play at the Comédie Française. (*Molière*, for God's sake.) The great Romain Gary, whose *The Roots of Heaven* had won the Prix Goncourt, was enamored of the play and was anxious to take on the translation. (*He sent me a telegram.*)

"I've enjoyed your novels, but *this*."

I instructed Robert Lantz (who was not accustomed to being instructed) to do nothing about the foreign rights until I'd met with Shaw.

There is something about a play. It's rare that a writer catches someone reading his novel. But to have people sitting in a theater each night and enjoying (laughing) at your work. It's as if you've thrown a party each night, for a diverse and fascinating group of guests. Though the play had a comic veneer, there were powerful emotions boiling up beneath the surface. Or so I thought. (I'd called the play "a tense comedy.") One night, there was a long-simmering eruption. A man in the audience advanced on Orbach with his fists clenched and had to be wrestled to the ground by ushers. At intermission, a fistfight broke out in the lobby, one so vicious that an ambulance had to be called. Every punch seemed to land. José Torres, the light heavyweight boxing champion, witnessed the brawl.

"I never saw that much blood in the ring."

Happily, (fortuitously) the screenwriter Bill Goldman was on hand that night to record the events faithfully in *The Season*, his book about one year in the New York theater world.

Tickets were hard to come by. Congressman Adam Clayton Powell, who had refused to speak to me on Bimini, showed up with an entourage and was told there were no seats available for the indefinite future. Despite the rejection in the Caribbean, Powell remained a defiantly heroic figure to me. It gave me great pleasure to leave a message at the box office:

"Give this man anything he wants, whenever he wants it."

Geri Stutz, the Bendel's owner, girlishly pounded me on the chest ("You big strong man.") and said:

"Why, oh why, can't my friends get tickets to your show?"

The producer David Merrick came along with a solution. He offered to transfer the show to a huge theater on 45th Street and to replace Orbach with a major film star. My mother, in her last days, had given me two bits of advice: 1) Don't follow buses and inhale the fumes. 2) Never move a hit show.

"I'm sorry," I told the producer of *Gypsy* and *Hello, Dolly!* "my mother wouldn't approve."

Merrick was to turn up in 1971, with the same proposal for my next play, *Steambath*, which was performed at the lovely, but modest-sized, Truck and Warehouse Theater in the Village. I said I didn't think so.

"Your mother again?" said Merrick.

"I'm afraid so, sir."

The opinion of mothers, bless them, is not always sound, especially when it comes to the theater. May she rest in peace, it cost me two Broadway hits to listen to mine, which accounts in part for my considering a trailer park in my wintry days.

There were, predictably, a number of film offers. One came from the great Otto Preminger, who asked me to join him at his townhouse. I remember standing face to face with him in his tiny private elevator. His breath was not good. He offered to pay me $50, 000 to write a screenplay based on *Scuba Duba*. If he liked it, he would pay me a quarter of a million dollars for the rights and make the movie. I was offended; he'd indicated that he had no confidence that I could write a screenplay. I shared his insecurity, but that wasn't the issue. I made a counteroffer.

"Pay me the quarter of a million now, make the movie, and if I like it, I'll permit you to release it."

Who was it that had made that proposal? Surely it wasn't the boy from the Bronx who had slept in a kitchen chair. Still, there was no one else in the room, so it must have been me. There was a limp handshake. We said goodbye. He went back to see the play several times, and kept calling the agent, but I'd lost confidence in him. Having a successful play can have a strange effect on the brain.

Warner Brothers ended up with the film rights. Terry Southern was anxious to do the film adaptation and would have been the perfect choice. (With Kubrick directing?) Southern had shown up at our Fire Island rental during the Summer of 1967; as a gift, he had brought along the album of *Sgt. Pepper's Lonely Hearts Club Band*.

When introducing me to others, he would say: "This is Bruce Jay Friedman, if that is indeed his name."

We argued long hours into the night over the relative merits of film versus the stage, Southern, of course, favoring the Big Screen.

"But Grand Guy Bruce," he insisted, "in the theater you can see the actors spitting into the audience."

I assured him that in my plays spitters would be weeded out during auditions.

We remained friends to the end. One of his gifts to me was the trick of blowing into a dog's nose, as a treat.

"They love it," he assured me.

I still do that, as something of an homage to my beloved friend. And when I blow into poor blind Freddie's nose, he shivers appreciatively. Or so I choose to think.

I've always felt that famous last words have been worked on long in advance. As an example, Oscar Wilde's: "Either the wallpaper goes, or I do."

Could even the greatest of all satirists toss that off, with his dying breath?

But I'm convinced that the hospitalized Southern's final words were spontaneous.

"What's the delay?"

I received the biggest laugh of my life in 1995 at a memorial for Southern, given by Virgin Atlantic Records at Elaine's Restaurant.

I told of a scene in Southern's novel *Blue Movie*, in which a starlet is upset about sleeping with a producer – and, afterward, not getting a promised part in his movie.

She complains to her agent:

"That's the last Jewish cock I'll ever suck."

The Virgin Atlantic executives fell on the floor laughing, then got to their feet and offered me lucrative writing deals. I explained patiently that I didn't write the scene. All I did was read it. It didn't matter. They wanted me on the Virgin Atlantic team.

Warner Brothers didn't care for the idea of Southern and chose instead the veteran screenwriter Nunally Johnson, which in turn, led to the saddest of stories. There is no way to avoid the word "charm" in a description of Johnson, a gentle, handsome, impeccably groomed gentleman in his early seventies. He took me to lunch at the fabled 21 Club, a heady experience in itself. Over martinis, of course, he assured me that I needn't worry, he would do nothing "to harm my baby." This was not my favorite expression. The play wasn't my "baby." And do what you like with it. I'd been paid. The play worked. Turn it into a good movie. But this was Nunnally Johnson, with a list of distinguished credits as long as your arm. (The word "distinguished," as related to film, might require an asterisk. In the late David Markson's great, but largely unheralded novel, *Reader's Block*, the novelist says of his central character:

"He had read three hundred novels that were better than any movie."

(At the time, that made sense to me. It no longer does. Not after *The Lives of Others* and *Barton Fink* and *The Easy Life* and a list that would go on interminably.)

But for the moment, I had to deal with the Nunnally Johnson charm. He made what seemed to be an odd request.

"Do you have any scenes that you've discarded?"

Well, of course I did. Dozens. But they didn't work. That's why I had discarded them. Still, would I indulge him and pass them along so that he could have a look at them? Against every instinct, I gathered up a sheaf of discarded scenes and odd patches of dialogue and sent them off to his home in Hollywood. I wasn't on the edge of my seat, waiting for the result. But his screenplay arrived months later. I had assumed the action in the play would be taken out of the single room in a chateau and "opened up," which is what adaptations are purported to do. Johnson hadn't bothered with any of that. What he'd come up with was essentially a copy of the play with my old, discarded dialogue wedged in here and there. And lots of martini-drinking, which his generation did – and mine didn't. I suppose a normal reaction would have been fury. What I felt was sadness. He'd come to the end of a long and distinguished Hollywood career. It was a case, or so I felt, of his need to pick up a check and of the studio throwing him a bone i.e. my poor play, which remains on the capacious Friedman shelf at Warner Brothers.

15

"Clearly it was the work of an irate Camus fan."
>
> The author's reaction, upon hearing that "Crazy Joe" Gallo had been gunned down at Umberto's Clam House in Little Italy

Having Jerry Orbach as the star of *Scuba Duba* almost cost me my life. And it was three words from Mario Puzo that saved it.

The Orbachs had been friends of Joey (Crazy Joe) Gallo who, soon after the play opened, had finished up a sentence of ten years in prison. To help "blend" him into civilian life, Jerry and his wife Marta, old friends of Gallo, held a soiree in his honor each Sunday night at their townhouse in Chelsea. They were sumptuous affairs, "catered" by the Gallos. No expense was spared when it came to food and liquor. Tables were piled high with culinary delicacies. (Foot-long heroes had just come into vogue.) Vintage wines were served. Cocaine hadn't quite brought the city to its knees at that point. But there were bowls of the drug discreetly placed about the apartment for those who were ahead of the curve on addiction. During his prison stay, Gallo had discovered the pleasures of literature, developing strong opinions on the work of Jean-Paul Sartre in particular (adored him) and Albert Camus (a "pussy," couldn't stand him).

Writers were among the guests, Neil Simon for one; also actors – Ben Gazzara and James Caan were regulars. Edsel Ford was there for industry, Tom Guinzburg, publishing. I had a reunion one night with the travel king Arthur Frommer, of all people, who had been a college friend at Missouri. Enthusiastic by nature, he felt, on those Sunday nights, that he had discovered heaven. I felt comfortable enough to invite my family along one night. Gallo looked on with admiration as my 10-year-old son Kipp took a turn at the pool table.

"That kid of yours is a real Jew."

Apparently, in prison circles, this was the highest praise. Observing my estranged wife and the three boys, and missing the mark a bit, he said: "You got a nice tight family."

Gallo family members circulated congenially among the guests.

"What does a person like you *really* want?" was a probing question frequently asked.

There was an implication that our new friends could fill the need, no matter how fanciful. (And no strings, of course.) I said there wasn't much I needed, although a second act for my new play might be useful. In this, they were unhelpful. My (estranged) wife let it be known that she longed for a brick townhouse in the West Village. Gallo called out to an associate: "Don't we have something down there on twelfth street?" Recalling a line of dialogue in *The Godfather* film ("Some day we will call upon you"), I took her aside and said it might be a better idea to contact a real estate agent.

For all of my luxuriating in the evenings, the cigars, the brandy, the poker games, I did notice that every twenty minutes or so Gallo would walk over to a window, pull aside a corner of the blinds and peer out at the streets. There were, I was to learn, more than a dozen contracts out on his life.

We'd all gotten chummy. Gallo was fascinated by Jacqueline Onassis and felt she was royalty, the ultimate in feminine elegance.

I'd met her briefly, having written a story for *Esquire* about Ron Galella, the paparazzi who had stalked her relentlessly. She brought suit against him. I was called as a witness at the trial. ("The worst witness in the history of jurisprudence," according to the *N.Y. Times* court reporter.) I was to teach (literary) Irony at City College for several years in the mid-seventies. As an Irony Man, I found it difficult to answer "Yes"or "No" to questions. When I failed to do so, the judge, who claimed to have admired my books, threatened several times to have me taken from the court in chains.

I suggested to Gallo that the laws of privacy were a wilderness and that Gallela wasn't necessarily a villain. His photographs were lovely and flattering. Onassis was, supposedly, caught offguard – a deer in the headlights – yet she seemed almost complicit in the taking of the photographs. (Or perhaps she was incapable of taking a bad picture.)

Gallo's color changed. His eyes widened. His lips became wet.

"That mutt," he said, making strangling gestures with his big hands. "You tell me about Jackie Kennedy, then you tell me about THAT MUTT."

Here was the "Crazy Joe" of legend. Clearly I'd hit a pressure point and began to picture my body being found in an alley.

"On the other hand," I said, making a sharp conversational turn, "there's no question he behaved poorly."

It took awhile, but eventually he calmed down. Once I was back in the fold, we watched a mobster movie together. At one point, James Cagney, with a gun pointed at him, holds his hands over his head for what seemed like ten minutes.

"You can't do that, you know," said Gallo, who was obviously informed on the subject. "It's impossible."

I was invited along on the historical night he was gunned down at Umberto's Clam House in Little Italy. (Historical, that is, in gangland lore.) Luckily, Puzo called from Hollywood before the fateful night. He was upset about the casting of *The Godfather*.

"They are trying to shove some kid named Pacino down my throat."

I had seen Al Pacino blow the roof off the theater in an off-Broadway play called *The Indian Wants the Bronx*.

"You have nothing to be concerned about," I said, sounding for the moment like Don Corleone. This generally happened when I was in contact with Puzo – a tendency to become Donnish.

"Have confidence in the young man, Mario. He will not disappoint you."

I told him about the glittering Sunday nights, how comfortable I felt with the Gallos.

"Joey is an authentically charming man," I said. "There are a few rough edges, but he has a genuine appreciation of *Middlemarch*. My sons love those nights as much as I do."

He listened, considered, then said: *"That's not intelligent."*

Based on the three-word advisory, I found an excuse to skip Umberto's. Joey was gunned down. Happily (fortunately?) I missed the fireworks.

When I heard about Gallo's fate, I was asked by a reporter for comment.

"Clearly," I said, "it was the work of an irate Camus fan."

Puzo had his own brush with Gallo. Soon after the publication of *The Godfather*, an emissary had arrived at the author's Bay Shore home with a message:

"Joey would like you to write his story."

Puzo said – with respect, of course – that under normal circumstances he would be delighted to write such a book. Unfortunately, his schedule did not permit this.

"And I would appreciate it," he told the emissary, "if you did not tell Mr. Gallo that we had this meeting."

16

OBSCURE, OFF-BROADWAY PLAYWRIGHT
SLAYS AMERICA'S HOPE FOR NOBEL
> The author envisioning a *N.Y. Post* headline as he
> scuffles with Norman Mailer.

The success of *Scuba Duba* led, indirectly, to a fistfight with
Norman Mailer. There have been several published – and many
unpublished – accounts of the incident. In most of them, I come off
as the villain, or at least the instigator, of the piece.

The evening – and I suppose it was fateful – began with a dinner at the Algonquin. Harold Pinter, not yet *Sir* Harold, had
enjoyed my play (though not the direction) and asked our mutual
friend, the novelist Edna O'Brien, if we could all have dinner. I
brought along a new acquaintance, Karen Avakian. After the meal,
each of us took a turn at telling a story. I began with an account of
my drive in from Long Island. Traffic had stopped suddenly.
Along with the other stalled drivers, I was forced to watch a
bizarre fight on the highway. Two men had gotten out of their cars
to confront each other. One was an enormously fat and slovenly
man in shirt-sleeves; the other a young man with the carved body
of an Olympic athlete. They shouted at one another. The dispute

escalated. Light on his feet, the fat man began nimbly to kick out at the other who stood with his muscular arms folded, stoically receiving the kicks as if he welcomed them. Slowly, he dropped to the ground, like a collapsed parade float. A companion lifted his unconscious body into their car. Traffic resumed, and off we went to Manhattan, as if we'd witnessed a brief and violent one-act play. I thought I did well with my story. Then Pinter took over.

He told two of the most word-perfect and exquisitely chiseled stories I'd ever heard, each delivered in the trained voice of an actor, which only added to their effectiveness. Again, the theme (of the evening as well) was one of violence. The first story had to do with a party in London. At the height of it, a huge baronial wrought iron chair had been thrown – impossibly – through a window that seemed to widen in accommodation to its size. The party-goers looked down at the mangled item of furniture in the courtyard below. Then they all raced down to see the wreckage close at hand. After a look around, the narrator was convinced he knew the identity of the offending guest. I have only the dimmest recollection of the second story. It involved two men in a deserted house grappling with each other in a kind of slow and murderous dance. Once again. Violence.

Pinter paused. (A Pinter pause?) So compelling was the story that I took a silent vow never again to attempt one of my own at a dinner table.

A year later, recalling the effect of the evening, I described it to Max Rosenberg, who knew Pinter and had produced a film he had written, *The Birthday Party*.

"Oh, for God's sake," he said, "those stories he 'improvised' are one-act plays. Harold has been trying them out for years at dinner parties."

There went the magic. I overcame my shyness about telling stories at dinner parties.

As for the Algonquin evening, we had all been invited to an after-dinner party at Norman Mailer's townhouse in Brooklyn

Heights. With witch-like prescience, both O'Brien and Pinter decided not to attend and went off to see a movie.

As Pinter left, I noticed that his jacket was several sizes too big for him. It had wide Joan Crawford shoulders and made his legs look short and skinny. It was sad to see the man I considered to be the world's finest living playwright walk off in a bad suit.

I could virtually smell the trouble as we walked into Mailer's townhouse. There were roughly fifty guests. It is no secret that Mailer was not a good drinker. He was well along when we arrived, and was under attack from several S.D.S. members who felt he hadn't been aggressive enough in his stance on the Vietnam war. He was not taking it well. I suggested to Karen that we have a quick drink and leave. Clearly, it was not going to be a convivial evening. We greeted the sportswriter Pete Hamill and a few other friends, then started on our way. Norman, with folded arms, had taken up a position in front of the one exit. I thanked him for the invitation, then, along with Karen, attempted to slide past him. He was not about to let us leave. At this point, I confess to making a contribution to the scuffle (altercation?) that followed. There had been a single Jewish football player at the University of Missouri in 1950 – a stocky linebacker from Jersey City named Bobby Ross. I was in the locker room when a huge Oklahoma farm boy, fists clenched, enraged for some reason, approached him, ready to fight. Bobby, a good-natured soul, chuckled and mussed his hair, as if to say "There, there, mustn't get too excited." The Oklahoma man looked at him with a mixture of fury and stupefaction. Then he dropped his hands; the air had gone out of him. He nuzzled up to Bobby like a puppy. I had always wanted to try that gesture. Here was my chance. I patted Norman on the head, in one account "tousling his hair." He responded with a head-butt to my midsection, which I don't especially recall, though this, too, was reported.

Beverly, Norman's wife at the time, cried out – and I do recall this part – "Kill the bastard, Norman." As if on command, Norman and I dutifully walked down the staircase and out to the street below. The guests all followed. Hamill and José Torres, the light-heavyweight champion of the world, were among them, as was Harold Conrad, Mohammed Ali's boxing promoter. At one point, Torres, though much lighter, was considered a worthy opponent for Ali. At the moment, Torres, who had suffered a torn achilles tendon, was on crutches.

There was a feeling of theater. As if to oblige the crowd, which had formed a circle around us, Norman hunched his shoulders and threw Joe Frazier-like hooks in the moonlight. I held up my end with an imitation of the Ali shuffle.

The crowd seemed impatient. They could take only so much of this posturing.

Richard Adler, the composer of *Damn Yankees* and *The Pajama Game*, came between us.

This was brave of Adler, who was thin-chested and delicately put together.

"You can't fight this man," he said to Mailer. "I plan to do a musical comedy with him."

There was some truth to this. I'd heard the composer had some interest in developing *A Mother's Kisses* for the musical stage.

Someone brushed Adler aside without difficulty. Bernard "Buzz" Farbar, a powerful man who could easily have put an end to the proceedings, made a half-hearted attempt to separate us. But clearly he had no wish to do so.

Mailer began to circle me and to cry out: "*Scuba Duba* sucks. *Scuba Duba* sucks."

His play, an adaptation of *The Deer Park*, had been poorly received and was struggling to stay open. Mine was moving along briskly, and this troubled him. Not that I quite fit into the scenario, but Mailer had always envied Arthur Miller. He had dreamed of having a huge opening night – and a grand success – on Broadway, with Marilyn Monroe thrown in as part of the fantasy.

We threw a few ineffectual punches at one another. Writers tend to be awful as fighters, no matter how fascinated they are about the sport and how much they carry on about it. I threw two punches that landed in Mailer's midsection, taking great care not to aim any higher. I had envisioned a *N.Y. Post* headline:

OBSCURE, OFF-BROADWAY PLAYWRIGHT
SLAYS AMERICA'S HOPE FOR NOBEL

To my great relief, he fell, or stumbled, to his knees. After silently declaring victory, I helped him to his feet, saying graciously (unctuously?)

"We really shouldn't be doing this kind of thing, Norman."

We were both out of breath. For support, we leaned against a wall.

"All you know is belly-punching," he said.

"You have the belly for it," I answered.

He suddenly threw his arms around me in an embrace. Here were two warriors, or so I thought, saluting one another, having behaved gallantly in battle. I felt a tweaking sensation in my shoulder, which I ignored for the moment.

Gathering up Karen, I waved goodbye to the guests and drove off in what was described as "my Jaguar." Actually, we were given a lift by Richard Adler.

By the time we got to my hotel, my shoulder had begun to heat up. I took off my shirt and undershirt, faced the mirror and saw the reflection of a perfect set of human (literary?) bite marks, along with a coating of what I took to be marinara sauce. Karen insisted I go to the ER at Lennox Hill Hospital to have it treated. It did not take much insistence. I was given a tetanus shot. Fortunately, I never began to froth at the mouth.

In the years that followed I continued to admire Mailer's books. I don't know that he was the best novelist of his time, but he was the best *thinker*; he had, in my view, the best mind. And no one was more brave in print. Which accounts for my disappointment that night. I'd always felt he had picked the right enemies. Why me? Unless, of course, he knew something about me that I had missed. I think he felt shabby about the evening and tried several times – with dinner invitations – to make it up to me. It's true I'd contributed to the incident – the alleged hair-tousling – but I remained wary of him. Some might say I'd "won" the brief exchange. The bite impressions may have made the fight a draw. Still, I never quite forgave him for putting me on the spot that way. For the embarrassment.

Puzo and Mailer had a long-simmering feud, dating back to Mailer's attack on William Styron in *Esquire*. ("The Talent In The Room.") Styron was Puzo's hero. He struck back by writing a corrosive review in *Book World* of Mailer's award-winning *March on the Pentagon*.

In later years, I told Puzo I had seen Mailer standing at a urinal in East Hampton after a screening. Actually, with his back turned and the mane of luxuriant gray hair, I thought he might have been Ben Gurion.

"It is my understanding," said Puzo. "that he walks with two canes."

"One cane," I said. And this was true at the time. "I saw only one cane."

"Did you greet him?"

"No, I thought there might have been a sword in it."

After his death in 2007, I ran into Mailer's widow, Norris Church, at a cocktail party.

"I've heard about you," she said. "When Norman was courting me, he said you once picked a fight with him and he was forced to beat you up."

"It didn't happen quite that way," I said. "But I had great admiration for your husband. If that was his version, let it stand."

And so there he was, taking away my one clearcut boxing victory, striking at me from beyond the grave.

Violence. A friend, who'd read much of what I'd written, pointed out that many of my short stories end in violence, either verbal or physical. There was some truth to this, though I hadn't realized it.

What was the source of it? The Bronx in the thirties and forties is often portrayed as a congenial place, with a comfortable ethnic mix of Italians, Jews, Blacks and Irish. And so it was – to a point. There was a layer of violence that ran beneath the surface. The distance from my apartment building to the drugstore was a short city block. It was fairly standard to have a fight or two on the way to pick up some aspirin. My nose took the brunt of it. The fistfights, being flung face-down on the ocean floor at the Rockaways, suddenly cracked across the head in the school cafeteria by a grinning nutcase for his own amusement. There was a popular game in which a boy stood in the center of a circle, and had rocks thrown at him. He was given the lid of a garbage can to defend himself. I wasn't quick enough to be good at the game; on one occasion I had to be carted off to Morrisania Hospital with yet another broken nose. In Southampton, Irwin Shaw introduced me to friends as being a member of the artists' community, "though he doesn't look it."

I had a fighter's face with no particular interest or skills at fighting.

Not the most cheerful situation.

My father hit me just once, which is not a bad score for a Depression boy. The blow was sudden, unexpected. It knocked me halfway across the street. I'd used a slang word, *putz*, though I had no idea it meant penis. Was that it? A fear that he might hit me again? My mother, when angered, would put her fist in her mouth and bite down on it as if to restrain herself from the horrors she might inflict. That fist in the mouth, the eyes popping. Much worse than the actual horrors. So maybe that was it. *Violence.*

More than likely, it's been a literary device.

I'm a story.

Wind me up.

With a bang.

17

"There I was, a short, fat, aging Jewish intellectual, albeit a married one, having an affair with a woman who was – not even arguably – the most beautiful creature on the planet."

> Max Lerner's lament to the author, during a symposium in Caracas, on the political historian's affair with Liz Taylor.

Out of nowhere, at the tail end of the sixties, I received an irresistible offer. Now and then, I'd hear about an academic being sent off by a foundation to be treated regally for a month or so at Lake Como. The closest I'd come to such an offer – and it wasn't close – came from the agent Sam Gelfman who had set up a program in which a Jewish author would spend two weeks living in the home of a wealthy Jewish couple in Beverly Hills.

"And do what?" I wanted to know.

"Nothing. Just be there. They want a Jewish writer in their home."

"Do I get paid for this?"

"No. But you get several days off. And they have a wonderful chef."

Gelfman was surprised when I said I wasn't interested.

"I thought it would be right up your alley."

"It's not. Actually, it's the worst offer I've ever received."

"Fine," he said, irritably. "I'll call Dan Greenburg."

The Caracas invitation was another story. It was not a Lake Como proposal, but it was close.

The idea was to put a group of American artists and intellectuals together with their Latin American counterparts in an attractive setting – the Hotel Avila in Caracas – and to see what came of it. Among those from the States were Lillian Hellman, Ada Louise Huxtable, Arthur Schlesinger, Jr., Elizabeth Hardwick, Robert Lowell, and, as it's put on the television variety shows, "a host of others." I was part of a youthful contingent that included Claude Brown, Jules Feiffer, and Jack Richardson. My play, *Scuba Duba*, was having a strong run in Manhattan, which would have accounted for my being asked along. This was heady company for me. There was a suspicion that the enterprise had been sponsored by the CIA, in an effort to smoke out Cold War chicanery. If so, little profit would have come of it. During one session, a journalist from Brazil took exception to a position the United States had taken on an issue related to Central America. When asked, sharply, by Arthur Schlesinger, Jr., what the correct stance should have been, he said: "I'm not sure."

That was pretty much the extent of the political intrigue.

We got off the ground with what I recall as a solemn processional to a local bordello – as if we were making a scholarly investigation of the local customs and mores. One of our number, an early deconstructionist, got caught up in the sybaritic merry-making and was not seen again for the duration of the conference. Claude Brown, author of the celebrated *Manchild in the Promised Land*, had a reputation as a jazz musician. For the delectation of the ladies, he sat at the piano and played "Heart and Soul." Jack Richardson thought this an odd selection, considering the setting. Brown's performance inspired an economist in our group to sit on the lap of a resident lady, thrust his tongue down her throat, then leap off and call his wife in Manhattan to beg her forgiveness for his transgression.

I chose the most attractive of the women. It was the only time in our long friendship that I was quicker on the draw than Richardson.

For some mysterious reason, I was encouraged to participate in a panel discussion having to do with the pros and cons of Modern Art. The critic Harold Rosenberg, a bearded and fierce-looking man, staked out his position, then whipped his head in my direction as if challenging me to find flaws in his thesis. I muttered something to the effect that Picasso's Blue Period was "a nice little period." Then, falling into the spirit of it, I whipped *my* head around fiercely to the next participant. There seemed to be quite a bit of that going on. Later, at dinner, I was seated beside the poet Robert Lowell. He stared blankly ahead through several courses, then suddenly, in what seemed to be the conference style, did another head-whipper and mystifyingly berated me for personally holding down the Palestinians. The outburst threw me off stride. I tend to be wary of poets generally, afraid I'm going to be quizzed on layers of meaning in *The Waste Land*. Still, I pulled myself together and continued to enjoy the best steak I'd ever eaten.

The panel moved on to a discussion of literature, the critic Alfred Kazin holding forth at length on the wonders to be found in the novels of Herman Melville. I had met Kazin briefly at a book party, was aware of his eminence and was quoted in a local newspaper as having said :

"You're Alfred Kazin . . . and you're just *standing* there, like a normal person?"

After the critic's talk had wound down, something impelled me to get to my feet and say a word on behalf of "our young writers" who had not yet become Herman Melvilles.

"Surely," I heard myself say, as if I were Disraeli, "we did not come all this way to inform our Latin American colleagues that *Moby Dick* has merit."

The comment drew an appreciative chuckle from Elizabeth Hardwick, thus making the moment a high point of my trip. It seemed only fair that I now list the names of the writers who were being slighted, but suddenly I could not think of who they were and took my seat with a certain awkwardness. Further along, I thought of Terry Southern and Thomas Pynchon, among others, but by that time the discussion had moved on to another topic, and I could only whisper their names to a puzzled Jules Feiffer.

There was a reception for our group, given by a wealthy Venezuelan, whose home was filled with major works of contemporary art and sculpture that would have been recognizable to anyone who had only the most glancing acquaintance with modern art. Priceless sculptures were placed casually about the main hall. At one point, as I relaxed, with a drink in my hand, I was told, gently, that I was leaning on a Marisol. Drums could be heard in the hills above us, along with periodic gunshots. An unforgiveably beautiful hostess said that disaffected groups were a stone's throw away.

"When it suits them they will come," she said (noirishly?), and with a shrug. "And they will take everything, including me."

Later in the evening, she said to me: "You're deep, aren't you. Perhaps too deep."

For all of that, I could not pry her away from Richardson. I imagine she felt he was just deep enough.

A poker game started up the next day beside the pool hotel. One advantage of being a poor player is that you can spot someone who is even worse at it than you are. Lillian Hellman, who was such a case, sat prominently at the head of the table, trying to fill inside straights and betting into hands that even a neophyte would recognize as unbeatable. But all the while, she took languorous puffs of a cigarette and gave off the picture of a consummate gambler, which she may have thought she was. It was a costly pose, but seemed worth it to her to be thought of as "one of the guys." Toward the end of our conference, she asked if I would like to spend a few weeks with her, touring the Caribbean and, I would imagine, gambling at the casinos. I thought it was brave of her to ask, and this was one of the few times in my life when I was at loose ends and didn't have much else to do. But I turned down the offer. Though I wasn't familiar with her plays (I was later to enjoy her books, particularly *An Unfinished Woman*), I was intimidated by her fame. Then, too, the prospect of strolling up to the desk of the San Juan Hilton with a woman three decades my senior was unappealing. (I don't need to be told that the reverse situation would have been acceptable.)

But finally, none of that mattered. (I've thought about this often.) She seemed depressed; I had a broken marriage and I was depressed enough for the two of us.

I took a stroll along the beach with the political columnist Max Lerner. He told me at length of his affair with the actress Elizabeth Taylor. (As a lover, in terms of chronology, I believe he was wedged between Eddie Fisher and Michael Wilding.) After tending to the actress in Los Angeles, in 1992, during one of her illnesses, he returned to London, there to endure a lover's agony over the romance.

"I could not believe my situation," he said to himself, as he rolled around in torment on his hotel bed. "There I was, a short, fat, aging Jewish intellectual, albeit a married one, having an affair with a woman who was – not even arguably – the most beautiful creature on the planet. What on earth was I to do?"

As we returned from our talk, we ran into Arthur Schlesinger, Jr.

"You poor man," the historian said to me, "Max has obviously been telling you his Liz Taylor story."

The conference was capped off by a poetry reading. The contribution of an Ecuadorean was essentially a long (metered?) list of infidelities and various cruelties he'd been made to endure at the hands of his spouse. I don't know if it was a good poem – nor did it turn me into a regular at poetry readings – but I can still see his tortured face and hear the anguish in his voice as he cited the woman's horrible transgressions, stopping at intervals, at the tail end of a canto – to raise a clenched fist and to cry out: "BUT SHE'S MY WIFE."

A few years later, Lerner endeared himself to me by saying that my novel *The Dick* – which had been roughed up by the *Times* – was "a *damned* fine book," roaring out this assessment so that it could be heard by every guest at a book party. (Though *The Dick* had sold to Hollywood for a small fortune, the review continued to rankle.)

I doubt that he realized it, but Lerner, in one of his last writings, was to pass along a gift that has become increasingly valuable as I move further along the highway: his re-definition of aging.

"Sixty-five to seventy-five is the youth of old age."

"Seventy-five to eighty-five is the middle age."

"Eighty-five and what follows is. . . . oh, well, whatever you make of it."

Lerner died in 1992 at the age of eighty-nine.

I'd seen him at a party, seriously ill, but bluff, jovial, carrying on gamely. Now and then he glanced in my direction, inviting me – with his eyes – to come and join him. I stayed away. Though he admired my books, I'd always been intimidated by his great erudition. And there was an absurd fear that I might catch his cancer. I don't have too many regrets in this life, but not embracing Lerner, saying goodbye to this exceptional man, is one of them.

A psychiatrist once told me that guilt was a waste of time.

But where would we be without it?

Some years later, at a restaurant, I ran into Arthur Schlesinger, Jr. and asked if he missed Max. "No," he said. "He liked Reagan."

18

"Friedman here is our new irony man."
> Chairman of the English Department, presenting
> the author to his new colleagues at York College.

Technically speaking, the last of the sixties should have been a glorious time for me. I'd written a hit play, a flock of short stories and two novels: one, *A Mother's Kisses*, a substantial bestseller. Manhattan was awash with the much commented upon sex, drugs and rock 'n' roll. It was all there for the taking. I felt a little long in the tooth – at thirty-five – but take it I did. My only regret is that I never got to know the women I slept with. And, of course, that there weren't more of them. Still, all of the roguishness was half-hearted. My life was a scenario badly in need of a rewrite (And yes, I did write that sentence.) I had tried the hearth, in Oscar Wilde's phrase, and failed at it. Perhaps I'd tried the wrong hearth. Still, there I was, not married, not divorced, existing in some uneasy twilight area, not knowing quite where to put myself. It was probably no accident that my next play was about a capricious and unreliable deity who reveled in creating such disorder.

I can't say there was a line snaking down the street, but there was no shortage of directors in 1970 who wanted to take on

Steambath. My first effort in the theater, *Scuba Duba,* had worked out so well. Or perhaps it was the theme of the new play: A man (TANDY) wanders into a steambath which turns out to be a way station between life and death, heaven and hell. God purports to be a Puerto Rican towel attendant. Through various feats, some trivial and absurd, others impressive, he establishes his divinity.

Though I still had one foot in the family home in Great Neck, I'd written the play quickly, in a series of hotel rooms along Lexington Avenue. Unlike *Scuba Duba,* it was mounted with barely a line changed.

Jacques Levy was my first choice as a director. We'd had such good luck before. He reacted to the play by saying "I loved it and I hated it," quoting a line of dialogue from *Scuba Duba,* which was designed to amuse me and didn't quite. And why, he wondered, did the characters in the steambath have to be dead, a question that struck at the heart of the play (Why did Cyrano have to have a big nose?). Perhaps more of an issue was that he had signed on to direct Kenneth Tynan's review, *Oh! Calcutta!* I'd met the fabled British critic, who had asked me to do a sketch for his production. We got off to a poor start.

"I would not hesitate," he said, "to mention you in the same breath as Neil Simon."

This was flattering – to a point. In my ego, which was towering at the time, I would vastly have preferred a comparison to Harold Pinter, or Edward Albee for that matter.

He explained his concept.

"Surely, Bruce, you've had a longing now and then to bind and gag a housekeeper, for example, dress her in a corset, spank her with a fish and send her tumbling down a flight of stairs."

"Well, actually," I said, "I've never had quite that particular fantasy."

"Very well then," he said, giving me a curious look. "But how about being shut up in a motel room with a one-legged Eskimo hooker . . . No doubt you've had that one. . . ."

"Doesn't ring a bell," I said.

Parents Irving and Molly,
Coney Island, 1920.

BJF's parents, in the sixties, on a railing
at Joyce Kilmer Park in the Bronx.

BJF with sister Dollie, left, and mother Molly. Monticello, N.Y., 1941.

Comedian Jackie Miles with a 10-year-old BJF—at Amateur Night, Laurels Country Club, Sackett Lake, N.Y., 1940. BJF sang "I Understand."

BJF in his early twenties, as Air Force officer and photojournalist for *Air Training* magazine.

BJF with three sons and first wife Ginger at restaurant in San Juan, Puerto Rico.

Bruce at Magazine Management Company, 1950s.

BJF and Mario Puzo, soon after the explosive
publication of *The Godfather*.

Award-winning
cover of BJF's first
novel, *Stern*.

Mademoiselle magazine had the
brilliant notion of pairing up
first-time novelists and Swedish
models.

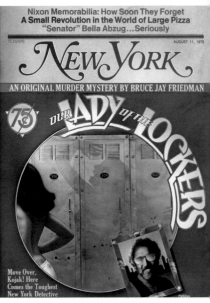

New York cover, August 11, 1975.

BJF, c. 1971.

Jerry Orbach starred in BJF's play
Scuba Duba, which launched the
actor's career.

From left: Tony Curtis, director
Jacques Levy and BJF at rehearsal
for *Turtlenecks*, 1972. Photo
appeared in *Vogue*.

From left: BJF, Elliot Gould, Anthony Newly, Carol Channing and
Laurence Harvey in the seventies.

BJF and Elaine May, who directed
The Heartbreak Kid (based on BJF's
Esquire story "A Change of Plan").

BJF and Steve Martin on the set of
The Lonely Guy—an adaptation of a
BJF book.

Woman with arms around BJF is Patricia J. O'Donohue
before their marriage in 1981.

The Friedman boys.

From left: sons Josh and Drew, BJF, and
Pat O'Donohue in the late seventies.

BJF and Molly Friedman, about age one.

BJF dancing with 4-year-old daughter Molly, Water Mill, 1988.

In front of BJF's shack/office, Water Mill, N.Y., 1990, from left: BJF and daughter, Molly; Sandy Morse, film editor, and son Dwight; Robert Brown, Samuel Johnson scholar; Carl Gurevitch, film producer; David Newman, screenwriter (*Bonnie and Clyde*); playwright Jack Richardson; screenwriter Leslie Newman.

BJF, Joseph Heller and Christie Hefner at a *Playboy* party.

BJF had cameo roles in three Woody Allen films (*Another Woman, Celebrity,* and *Husbands and Wives*). BJF: "Beats the hell out of writing."

Elaine Kaufman, BJF and Jack
Richardson, c. 2000.

James Salter at BJF's 75th birthday
party at Elaine's, 2005.

BJF and a bearded Speed Vogel, Joseph Heller's collaborator
on *No Laughing Matter*.

George Plimpton and BJF at
Water Mill, c. 2000.

Tom Hanks and Meg Ryan with BJF
on the set of *You've Got Mail*.
BJF had a cameo role.

Mario Puzo, Carol Gino and BJF at Water Mill, 1990.

On the set of *You've Got Mail* with director/writer Nora Ephron.
BJF had a cameo role.

Sketch of BJF by LeRoy Neiman, 1996.

Book-signing for Andre Dubus, center. Standing from left: Joseph Heller,
Jay McInerney, BJF and Speed Vogel.

A tanned BJF in Miami Beach, 2000.

BJF standing next to daughter Molly with sons Kipp (left), Josh (center), and Drew (right), and sister Dollie.

Freddie, family Tibetan terrier, Greenwich Village, 2000.

Granddaughter, Chloe, at Charles Dickens's desk in the Berg Archive, where BJF's papers are archived.

From left: Herman Liebovitch; BJF; Skip Erwin; Ted Cohen and Monte Safron.
Reunion of BJF's Missouri University college mates.

BJF's 80th birthday party, from left: Kipp Friedman, BJF, Chuck Messing
(nephew), Molly Friedman and granddaughter Chloe Mae, Josh Friedman
and Drew Friedman.

BJF signed to do the screenplay of *Stir Crazy*, forgot about it, and was horrified to receive a call from Columbia Pictures saying cast and crew were assembled—all they needed was a screenplay.

BJF was managing editor of Martin Goodman's entry into the brief bite-sized magazine craze of the fifties

BJF thought Brian Grazer was an office boy, and didn't realize he was the film's producer.

Early issue of the short-lived *Swank*, the first title "thrown" to BJF by publisher Martin Goodman. Chip Goodman, the publisher's son, was later to flag the title on to pornographic glory.

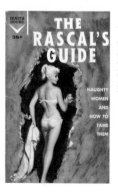

An absurdly innocent anthology of "naughty" pieces, edited—and moonlighted—by BJF in 1959.

Ticket to *Scuba Duba*.

And so it went until he as much as declared me hopeless and we parted company. Nor did I think much more about it until a friend, the screenwriter David Newman (*Bonnie and Clyde*) treated me to an acccount of the handsome royalties he received each month for his contribution to *Oh! Calcutta!* of a five-minute sketch.

Bob Fosse seemed anxious to stage the play, although you would never have guessed it based on his behavior. He was not yet the Fosse of *Chicago* and *All That Jazz*, but I'd seen his work on *Redhead*, for example, and knew how good he was. I can't recall his having much to say about the play. What he did was prowl (gracefully) around the producer's office, chain-smoking and throwing off the impression that we were in awful trouble. And this, before we'd begun. I was a novice in the theater (best always to be a novice) and felt I needed a steadier and more encouraging hand at the controls. (Actually, his concerns about the second act, in particular, were well-founded. Though the play had a good run and a healthy life afterward – a film, a TV series, many productions – I feel it would have been stronger if we'd chosen him as a director.)

José Ferrer was next. Though I knew little of his directing skills, I had seen him on the stage in all his magnificence, as Cyrano de Bergerac. It was his idea to play the part of the Puerto Rican steambath attendant and to direct the play as well. It all made sense. We shook hands. He left. And we never saw or heard from him again. I'm not sure that anyone did. There was something about central Mexico.

And then Anthony Perkins came by. He was fresh, cheerful, confident, in love with the play, ready to roll up his sleeves and get started. In an instant my play was no longer a disaster in the making. It occurred to me that it might even have a chance of succeeding.

Perkins had starred or played in more than fifty films, yet it was as the character Norman Bates that he was widely known. He had a recurring fantasy in which he was at the end of his career, about to perform in a small roadside inn, singing and accompanying himself on the piano. The emcee introduced him:

"And here he is, ladies and gentlemen, Mr. Tony 'Psycho' Perkins."

At the time I knew him, he was what is now called "openly gay," living with the choreographer Grover Dale. I did not see how anyone, man, woman or cow, could fail to adore him. I soon found out how wrong I was.

The film actor Dane Clark auditioned for the lead role of Tandy. As a boy, I'd seen him in dozens of movies at the Fleetwood theater in the Bronx, playing opposite the film gods Humphrey Bogart and Cary Grant. (Clark had been born Bernard Zanville. It was Bogart who gave him his screen name.) And here he was, astonishingly, trying out for a part in my play. A Southampton doyenne had once stopped me in my tracks, saying, "My, we've had a spotty career, haven't we." In terms of the theater, she was on to something. But oh, those spots. Dane Clark's mesmerizing, *chilling* reading was one of them. I'm sure that more than one playwright has had an actor come along who has made his work seem three times (make it ten times) better than what existed on the page. (Perhaps not Edward Albee.) In any case, such was my reaction to Clark's reading. He had done the work. After listening to him, *I* was the one who was exhausted.

He lit a cigarette, sat beside me and asked "Who is directing the play?"

Still feeling the effect of his reading, I pulled myself together long enough to tell him it was Anthony Perkins.

"That faggot," he said, in disbelief. "You expect me to work with that Hollywood *faggot*?"

With that, he stormed out of the theater and, like José Ferrer, was never heard from again. I began to think there was something about my work that caused people to storm off, never to be heard from again.

Or perhaps there was something about that lead role. Over the course of several weeks of previews, at least three more than capable and often brilliant actors (Dick Shawn, Charles Grodin, Rip Torn) played the part and never quite lived up to Perkins' specifications. It never occurred to me, until long after the run, that Perkins had always wanted the part for himself. He did step in, at the last minute and agreed (graciously?) to do the role, seamlessly, as if it had always belonged to him.

Casting the part of the Puerto Rican steambath attendant, i.e. God, was tricky. God is always a tough nut to crack. We received death threats – actual bloody notes pinned with a knife to a dressing-room wall – stating that someone would die unless the part was given to an actual Puerto Rican. We shook this off – to the extent that one can shake off a few death threats – and looked at at least sixty actors. There were high hopes for Raul Julia whose audition was disappointing. I began to feel that I'd written something awful until Hector Elizondo showed up a bit late and said he had a cold and had just returned from making a film with *"Mister* Kirk Douglas, and *Mister* Burt Lancaster."* The two Misters were annoying and I thought – there goes another one. As if to be even more irritating, he began to mumble his lines. (The result of the cold.)

This time it was Perkin's turn to be outraged. I hadn't seen that side of him.

"You show up here late and you dare to mumble at me!"

He stormed out of the theater (dramatically) and I stormed out after him.

"Tony, I know he was mumbling, but I listened carefully. They were brilliant mumbles."

Perkins agreed (deigned?) to have him back again. He was magical on stage; his performance led to an Emmy and a rich career in Hollywood. (Elizondo, it should be noted, was half Puerto Rican – his father was a Basque. The mixed heritage got him past the important Puerto Rican benchmark. None of us were knifed to death.)

Was it possible that Perkins was fearful of playing opposite Elizondo? To be fair about it, God was the flashier role. (In the Bible as well.) It would have been easy for Perkins to be outshone. A seasoned veteran, he did not allow this to happen. "Brilliant" is a word that is often thrown around casually: but Perkins was crisply brilliant in his way.

This being the theater, there was more than one crisis to come. The ingénue has a brief nude scene. She appears in the steambath, takes a brisk shower and disappears. Was a brisk nude scene becoming my trademark? I "defended" the moment by saying it was only a touch, designed to enhance the strangeness of the environment. But it was quite a touch. And she was awfully nude. The scene was a big hit with my three sons who showed up regularly to catch a bit of the first act, then disappeared. I wondered about this – that sudden interest in at least a few moments of my work – then realized of course that it was the "touch" that so fascinated them.

Just before the opening, the actress and her agent asked to meet me. To move things along, I'd cut a few lines of hers. She threatened to leave the show unless they were restored. I thought about this. My integrity was at stake, a ridiculous concern. After all, this was the theater. Creating greater pressure was the understudy, who hovered seductively in the background, then called me aside and said:

"My roommate and I do sandwiches."

"In a deli?" I asked, then quickly realized the reference was an extremely naughty one – though not necessarily for the sixties.

Ignominiously, I caved in and restored the actress's lines. My integrity would have to wait and be tested at a more convenient time.

(If only the understudy had been more attractive. Or brought the roommate along for a quick look.)

A final crisis came about when the producer disappeared on the day of the opening. Beset by personal and theatrical demons, he had gone off to chop wood in the Colorado mountains. One of David Balding's skills was to assemble the perfect opening night audience, each seat filled with "a friend of the production" and hearty laugher. This, of course, is especially helpful when the play is a comedy. With Balding gone, the stage manager and I were reduced at the last minute to calling in people from the streets. The show opened with an audience made up primarily of nurses who cared for terminal patients in a hospital nearby. Many were on call. They were, understandably, somewhat despondent, and not the ideal group for a comedy. Still, they turned out to be a decent enough audience. The critical reception was almost unanimously favorable, with only Clive Barnes dragging his feet a bit, still miffed over being scolded for calling *Scuba Duba* a hit before it became one. And, of course, taking it out on me. Audience members reported him sleeping through an entire performance of my 1995 play, *Have You Spoken To Any Jews Lately?*, snoring loudly into the bargain, then trashing a play he'd never seen in the *N.Y. Post*. Vincent Canby, his replacement at the *Times*, loved it.

Soon after *Steambath* opened, a man showed up in Robert Lantz's office with a check for $75,000, as an advance (along with percentages) for the film rights to the play. I had no idea of who he was and told Lantz I wasn't interested.

The agent kept calling me. He spoke in the Berlin accent that he clung to, decades after he'd escaped from Hitler's clutches.

"Bruce, the poor man is sitting here in my office with his check. He is quivering with anxiety. We must give him an answer. The check, incidentally, is certified."

"Tell him to be patient,"I said.

What could I possibly have been thinking? I hadn't gone entirely berserk. Jerome Hellman had just seen the play and expressed interest in acquiring the film rights. Once again, snobbery prevailed. Here was a situation that was much more to my liking. Hellman had produced two Academy Award-winning films – *Coming Home* and *Midnight Cowboy*. The unknown man had only money (cash) to offer. The nerve of him. And to compare the two was absurd. Hellman came to see the play a second time. I never heard from him again. In the meanwhile, the man with the check had given up, slunk away, and was nowhere to be found. For all I know, he may have been "fronting" for Fellini.

We had such a lovely group – and a winning team – in The New Theater. Had it held together, I might have – in my dreams – become the resident playwright and taken up the theater as a career – actually boning up on *Hedda Gabler* and *The Wild Duck*. But the key figures were after what they felt was bigger game. Balding, after wood-chopping in Colorado, turned up in Europe as the impresario of a traveling circus. Jacques Levy had *Calcutta*, and cleverly insinuated himself into Bob Dylan's life as co-lyricist on the album *Stone Pony*. David Merrick's offer to move the play to Broadway was tempting, but here again I came up against my mother's advisory – never move a play, never move *anything* – furniture, an apartment, nothing. (Don't change wives, either.) With Balding gone, it fell to me, in 1973, to take over as producer of my own play. That meant writing ads (I didn't mind that) and balancing box office receipts (in this I failed miserably). My skills at business affairs were laughable. The Chinese are said to save one quarter of their income for the future. I've generally set aside most of mine for living beyond my means.

Unguided by steady hands, *Steambath* quietly languished away after a highly respectable run, then came vividly to life with a controversial PBS production a y ear later. The producer sent me a long list of actors who were anxious to do the lead role. Among them were James Franciscus, Dennis Weaver, David Janssen and Bill Bixby. I knew none of these actors and said I'd have to speak to my people before making a decision. My "people" consisted of my 12-year-old son Drew, a serious television watcher. Without hesitation, he said:

"Bill Bixby is your man, dad." (He had admired the actor in *The Courtship of Eddie's Father*.)

"I've consulted my people," I reported to the producer, Norman Lloyd. "They all feel that Bixby is the right choice."

And Bixby it was.

Soon after I'd published a first novel, I met the novelist James Baldwin (*Go Tell It On The Mountain*) who suggested it was too early to get carried away.

"You're not a writer until you have a shelf."

I do have a shelf now, a fairly substantial one, but the entity (bound copy) that's had the longest life is *Steambath*. The PBS film, a television series, multiple productions including an all-lesbian one, an all-black production and one in Jerusalem in which the Puerto Rican God shows up as a Palestinian. I haven't seen any of them. Once I know the story, once I know what *happens*, I tend to lose interest. There are those who will dash off to see a Canadian, any Canadian, do *Lear*, but I'm not one of them. I know *Lear*. I've had enough of *Lear*.

There is something about the essentials of *Steambath*, the randomness of life, the absurdity of divine behavior (God as a quirky novelist?) that continues to appeal to audiences (if not the playwright), even if many of them are in Texas. Still, *Steambath* was merely a play, which by its very nature, *Lear* to the contrary, wasn't serious enough. Or so I'd been led to believe. It was only the novel, and its often-ignored cousin, the short story, that was *sufficiently* serious. I could see my editor wagging his finger at me – "Let's get back to work" – which was odd, since Gottlieb admitted to loving *Steambath* and published a handsome hardcover edition of it. (As an homage to my editor, God's second-in-command is named Gottlieb.)

After my play closed, I went back to writing short stories, returning to my base, in a sense. There are those who feel it's necessary to travel to Kathmandu in search of stories to tell. I've always found that the good ones drop into my lap when all I've done is get up in the morning and go about my business, such as it is. A story called "Detroit Abe" is one such example.

In 1975 I was asked to be the Distinguished Visiting Professor of Irony at York College, a division of the City University of New York. The moment I showed interest, the word "Distinguished" was dropped from the title, and my compensation was equivalently reduced. No matter. Here was another means of shoring up my serious side. Always, that need to be serious. (Were the Coen brothers eavesdropping on my life when they filmed their master-work, *A Serious Man*?)

The chairman of the English Department presented me to his colleagues.

"Friedman here is our new Irony man."

Few showed up for my classes and I can't say that I blamed them. I had inherited the syllabus of my predecessor whose focus was on Congreve. I knew little about the playwright and didn't know what to say about him other than that he suffered from gout and was easily stung by criticism. Once I'd established this, and ten minutes had gone by, I told my little band of students that I needed a break and left the classroom. A fellow teacher, Joan Klein, reported seeing me in the corridor, pounding my head against the wall and chanting:

"I have nothing more to say about Congreve."

I found teaching – if that is indeed what I was doing – to be exhausting. For relaxation, I would stop off in the evening at one of Manhattan's many ethnic restaurants. One night, at Gaylord's, which pioneered Indian food in Manhattan and had just opened, I noticed that the fellow in an adjacent booth was struggling with the menu. I suggested he try the tandoori chicken. He thanked me, placed his order, and we began to chat amiably. I told him about my irony work at the college. In turn, he said he was in what he described as "the pimping profession." His name was "Silky." There had been a coffee-table book published in which he declared (unwisely) that he earned half-a-million dollars a year and never got up before noon. We struck up a casual friendship. Soon after-ward, a story appeared in the press saying that my new friend had been indicted for income tax evasion and faced a jail sentence of several years. What if he approached me, I wondered, and asked me to look after his "stable" while he was in prison? (The question *What If?* is always a good starting point for a story. *What if* I had married a different person? *What if* a psychiatrist consulted *me*?)

I tried out the concept on Robert Gottlieb who had reserva-tions about it. One of them was that he hated it. Discouraged, but undaunted, I wrote a story about the episode, in which Irwin Abrahamowitz, a professor of irony, does indeed take over his new friend's stable of women and becomes "Detroit Abe." The story was published by *Esquire* and bought much later by the movies. It was released in 1983 as the execrable *Dr. Detroit*. Surprisingly, it has fans. *Ishtar* has fans as well. There will always be fans.

In the *what if?* department, there was a moment at the start of my Florida honeymoon in the early fifties that became the basis of a small cottage industry. After a long drive from Manhattan, Ginger, my first wife, decided to take a nap at the hotel. Overtired, unable to sleep, I struck up a conversation with a young woman at the pool and found her intriguing. So much so that I wondered: *What if* I'd made a mistake and married the wrong person? The thought died, for the moment, and I sailed right back into the marriage. The rest is a kind of bleak history. Some years later I was challenged to write a short story in two hours. I thought back to the honeymoon incident and came up with "A Change of Plan" (I met the two hour deadline . . . and how I wish I could do that now). In my fictional version, Leonard Cantrow falls in love with another woman on the first day of his honeymoon, "calls off" the marriage and goes off in pursuit of the swimming pool woman in Minnesota. The story was published in *Esquire*. There was immediate film interest. Neil Simon was brought in to write the screenplay, changing the title to *The Heartbreak Kid*.

Soon after the film was released, the producer told me that Simon had called him from Majorca and said he couldn't find a single redeeming feature in the central character. Therefore he was unable to continue with the screenplay.

"Did he return the money?" I asked.

"No."

"Then you had nothing to worry about."

That question – *What if?*

As for the two hours it took to write "A Change of Plan," Puzo had a story that would top mine. The producer, Sidney Beckerman, had earned a fortune with *two words*. As he was leaving Dan Tana's restaurant in Los Angeles, he stopped and whispered into Mario's ear: "*Earthquake. Puzo.*"

Mario wrote the film – *Earthquake* – and received a "mere" half-a-million dollars for his screenplay. Beckerman received four million for a whisper. This infuriated Puzo (although one could argue that it was the *right* whisper). It wasn't the money (although it was that, too). But the very idea of it. One again, a writer, in his view, had gotten the short end of the stick.

Beckerman was a bit of a legend himself. During one of my frequent trips to Hollywood in the seventies, I was sitting in a lounge chair beside the pool at the Beverly Hills Hotel (I spent a great deal of time in lounge chairs) reading an obscure Evelyn Waugh memoir – about the novelist's mild adventures in World War II. Beckerman came by, snatched the book out of my hands and circled the pool, holding the slim volume under one arm. Before he got to the diving board he had received film offers for the rights to the book. To feel they own something, producers need to hold something in their hands. It doesn't mattter what it is. That is why so many books are optioned – and never made into films.

So much happened beside that pool. Bob Guccione, the publisher of *Penthouse* magazine, showed up one day, surrounded by bodyguards. After sunning himself for a bit, he sent over an aide in a fedora and a raincoat, no less. The man had the look of a subway flasher; in the films, he would have been played by Peter Lorre.

"Mr. Guccione is planning a matoor film," he said, "and wants to know if you'd be interested in penning it."

I said I was awfully sorry, but I had a full plate at the moment and wouldn't be able to take it on.

The "matoor" film was made. It was called *Caligula* and was penned by Gore Vidal, who had found room on his plate.

Though "Detroit Abe" had a healthy afterlife as an *Esquire* story and was later sold to the films, it nagged at me that Robert Gottlieb had rejected the concept as a novel. I suppose if I had a powerful belief in it I would have gone ahead and written the novel all the same. Still, I felt I had to "win back my publisher," and at the same time strengthen my credentials as a serious man (writer). In the early seventies, my estranged wife and my family lived in Great Neck. I had taken a one-room flat on Sixty-Fifth Street, just off Madison Avenue. There was nothing shoddy about it. It was a lovely room with high ceilings, on the first floor of a brownstone. I seemed to be the only available man in the neighborhood and received much attention from a group who called themselves "the 65th Street girls." One was more attractive than the others, although they did compare notes on their romantic escapades, a fact that had eluded me. I dated each one. By the end of the following day, at the cocktail hour, the others had been filled in on every detail of what had transpired. (How I'd measured up?)

At this point, there was no marriage to speak of. My wife was happily occupied with her new friend. (I can't quite bring myself to say "lover." It connotes someone who goes around "loving" all the time, starting at the crack of dawn.) The only intelligent option was to end a marriage that had ended long before. With this in mind, I had gone to see a divorce lawyer, carrying a Gristedes shopping bag filled with my documents. He spread them out on his desk.

"I don't see any difficulty here. There's a third of your income for your wife, a third for child support and a third for accounting and legal procedures."

"But what about *my* third?" I said.

"Oh," he said, taken aback. "That might present a problem."

To manage all those thirds, I set about in a fury (and a panic) to write not only stories but a new novel, drawing on the weeks I'd spent as a journalist at a Chicago Homicide Bureau. After my *Saturday Evening Post* piece was published, the smell of violence continued to follow me. In the novel I had in mind, Kenneth LePeters (ne Sussman) is a public relations man attached to the most violent homicide bureau in the country. His "baby badge," which is much smaller than the official one, greatly amuses his detective colleagues. He yearns (in the style of Pinocchio?) to become "a real dick" with a real badge. I showed a hundred pages or so to Gottlieb who said: "That's more like it."

The pat on the head was helpful. I returned to the flat, determined to press on with *The Dick* and discovered two gentlemen, waiting for me on the doorstep. One was Richard Adler. I'd met the composer before, the night of my scuffle with Norman Mailer. The other was Gene Saks, the director of many if not all of Neil Simon's successful Broadway plays. Along with a producer, Lester Osterman, they had acquired the rights to *A Mother's Kisses* and were planning a Broadway musical version of the novel. They were most anxious to have me do the libretto. I enjoyed musicals. Has anyone ever loved *Gypsy* as much as I do? But I had no special interest in writing one – or returning to *A Mother's Kisses*, for that matter. Moving forward was the ticket. One of my favorite characters in history is the World War I figure, Marshal Joseph Jacques Césaire Joffre. No matter how dire the battlefield situation ("*Mon generale*, both our flanks are compromised, our center has collapsed") he had a single strategy: *J'Attaque*.

Still, my new friends were persuasive.

"You are the only one who can pull this off," they said, almost in unison.

Easily distracted (promiscuous?) I fell victim to theatrical seduction, of which there is no more potent force. I agreed to give it a try. Here, as well, was a chance to get out of my one-room flat, to do something a little different with two gifted new friends. Also, the producer had it put in the contracts, that if the show succeeded we would each be given a race horse.

Setting my poor novel aside for the moment, I patched together the libretto in a series of delicatessens, the Carnegie on Seventh Avenue chief among them. Some of the better scenes were written in the kitchen of a favorite restaurant called Dinty Moore's. It was all casual and leisurely. I felt blessed by my new situation until Adler tapped me on the shoulder and said we were off to Philadelphia.

"Why?" I asked, setting aside my corned beef sandwich. "It's so comfortable here."

"But we're trying out the show in Philadelphia."

This came as a surprise. I thought it was a little game we were playing and that I'd be permitted to continue to while away my time in Broadway delicatessens.

The show had tryouts in Philadelphia and Baltimore and never quite came together. For this I take full responsibility. Sort of. The score was exceptional. The lyrics, in which I helped out, seemed fine. The libretto? I thought it could be tossed together with my left hand, never realizing that it was a form (an art form?) unto itself. At any given time there are only a few who can do it well, and even that small group can't do it consistently. Additionally, I'd always felt that Bea Arthur, for all of her skills, was miscast in the leading role. The mother in the novel is rough-edged and street smart. I thought the edges should be softened a bit by a more, shall we say, feminine actress. (Does anyone remember Rosalind Russell?) In Arthur's case, you had tough on tough, which was hard to take. And we never found a boy who could play opposite her. (At a Friar's Club Roast, the comedian Jeffrey Ross said, memorably, of Joan Rivers: "I wouldn't fuck her with Bea Arthur's dick.")

Al Pacino showed up to audition. I had seen him in an off-Broadway play and knew how powerful he was. Easily a match for Arthur. Yet, through no fault of Pacino's, his audition was a disaster. Gene Saks, the director, had a theatrical *bête noire*. He would tear his hair out when an actor used "Luck Be a Lady" from *Guys and Dolls* as an audition piece. (It was a favorite at the time.) At the conclusion of the song, the actor would fall to his knees, blow on imaginary dice, and hurl them out in front of him. Which is what Pacino did. The piano accompanist, the song, the dice, the roll, all of it capped off by a cry of *tah-DAH*.

Saks held his head, as if being tortured.

"Why," he asked the fates, "do they do this to me?"

"He's a wonderful actor," I said. "You've got to trust me on this."

All to no avail. The part of a 17-year-old boy went to a (depressed) thirty-year old actor who sang and danced routinely.

The show expired quietly, disappointing some who thought the package (composer, director, librettist) was irresistible. I wasn't one of them, although I felt the show did hit the mark on a single night in Baltimore. In the show, the boy attends a social function and is upset by an anti-Semitic remark. His mother (Bea Arthur) sings a dark and malevolent song called "Wait, Baby, Wait." It might have been written by Kurt Weil. The implication is that the slur is nothing compared to what awaits the boy further along in life. The heat in the theater seemed to rise. The atmosphere created by this dark Brechtian song was suffocating. Theater-party ladies, expecting to see a variation of *Mame*, headed for the exits. (They were flagged on by a rival producer, Alexander Cohen, jowls quivering, as if he had been personally affronted.) The scene – and the song – hit exactly the note I had hoped for. Bea Arthur refused to sing it again. The director insisted, weakly, that she do so. Arthur prevailed. Such is the price of hiring a director whose wife is joined to his hip as a leading lady.

David Merrick flew down to inspect the rubble and see if there was anything worth salvaging.

"What this show needs," he said, "is one sonofabitch to pull it all together."

Stephen Sondheim showed up to see if he could lend a hand. After watching a performance, he graded the show with a twenty (on the scale of one hundred). He did feel there was a certain "sweetness" to it. And he became attached to one of the songs: "There Goes My Life," in which the mother expresses her love for her son – who is "a little upset" because he can't get into a college. (*There goes my life . . . there goes my stocks and bonds . . . Is that a doll? Is that pure gorgeousness?*) Ouch. Sondheim thought of beginning the show with that song, the trouble being that it was the whole show in a capsule and there didn't seem to be any way – or need – to go on from there.

So that was it. None of us were given race horses, although some years later, in a time of momentary affluence, I actually bought a horse, a jumper, for my new wife, Pat. And then, when my fortunes declined, I was forced to sell Robby.

I told Mario Puzo that I had fallen on hard times, and the measures I'd had to take to stay afloat.

"If you're looking for sympathy," he said, "never say that you had to sell a horse."

Theater professionals applauded me for hanging in to the last, for never abandoning the musical until it was safely dead and buried. This was considered unusual. When a show begins to falter, there are participants who have been known to slink away in the night. In truth, I was happy to get out of Baltimore and be done with it. *A Mother's Kisses*, the novel, was in print, alive and well. That was all I ever needed. Still, the episode may have been a bit more bruising that I let on. Along with my friend Karen, I took off immediately for Bermuda and wrote a fictionalized version of the experience. A retired homicide detective with a flair for writing is hired to do a musical about violence in, where else, a homicide bureau. (Once again, milking the time I spent covering detectives in Chicago.) *Violencia* was completed in two frenzied weeks that included time out for romantic activity with my faithful companion. Such things can be done when you're young, lucky and not so much committed as committable. I set *Violencia* aside to "marinade" for three or four decades, before it was eventually published in 2000 by Grove Atlantic.

19

"I'm sorry," she said. "You're stuck with me. I am your secretary."
Natalie Wood, to the author, the day the screen star became his assistant on *The Owl and the Pussycat*.

Some find peace in the Himalayas. Others, in a Buddhist temple. The most tranquil moment I can recall experiencing – and what does this say about me? – was on the outdoor dining-room patio of the Beverly Hills Hotel.

I'd been hired by Ray Stark, the producer of *Funny Girl*, to write a screenplay based on the Broadway comedy *The Owl and the Pussycat*. Stark had read that *A Mother's Kisses* had packed it in after a brief try-out in Baltimore. Assuming I would be beaten and bloodied by the experience he thought I would be ripe picking, eager to lap up anything that was offered to me. He was wrong. Still, it was freezing in Manhattan. There was the lure of sunny California. So many had succumbed to it. Why should I be different?

Once again, and much too readily, I set aside my poor novel, *The Dick*, and took up Stark on his offer, joining a long line of New York writers who had allowed themselves to be seductively "flown out to the Coast," many never to return. I refused to let that happen to me. Like Douglas MacArthur, forced to evacuate WWII Phillipines, I made a a solemn vow: "*I shall return*" (to New York, that is). I succeeded to an extent, although I did run back and forth quite a few times.

Short days after Stark's offer, I was having lunch on the patio of the Beverly Hills Hotel, luxuriating in the California sunshine. I had ordered melon and prosciutto and a glass of Pinot Noir at a time (the early seventies) when California wines were not taken seriously. Still, Frank Sinatra had recommended the wine, and, in such matters, he was my guide. My ex-wife, too, felt a connection to the singer. Years back, a remark she'd made about Sinatra had circulated widely. He had arrived unexpectedly at a party she'd attended. In a state of high excitement, she called out:

"Frank Sinatra is here. What should I do?"

All was tranquil. It was the start of a perfect summer. Whatever domestic difficulties I had were three thousand miles away. I could find nothing to dislike about Los Angeles. The temperature, of course, was ideal. Food tasted better than ever before. A simple glass of orange juice took on a new meaning. I was struck by the easy commingling of races at upscale Los Angeles restaurants; this was something new to a Manhattan resident. The women, predictably, were exquisite. Mario Puzo, a small man, had been startled by them.

"They're like Amazons," he said. "A separate race."

I thought of staying on forever, but was dissuaded by a producer-friend.

"You're a New Yorker. That gives you some cachet. If you move here, you'll just be another member of the club."

The agent Sue Mengers put it another way to Clay Felker, the distinguished editor of *New York Magazine*. It puzzled him that the film people who had courted him in Manhattan ignored him when he moved to the West Coast.

"You were a big deal in New York," she explained. "Here, you're just another schmuck."

There were times when I wondered: "What would be so awful about being a 'club' member?" And then I'd recall the story of Daniel Fuchs, author of the brilliant *Williamsburg Trilogy*, who had moved to California and stayed on and loved it, loved the movies, the movie-making process, the easy way of life. And, of course, the money. And yet, as described in his book, *The Golden West: Hollywood Stories*, there was a glum moment each day when the sun went down in the late afternoon. He felt a hollowness in his stomach as he became aware of all that he'd left behind – the literary promise that had been broken in exchange for sunshine and a few screen credits. I did not want to experience that glum moment.

Stark had made it comfortable enough. Greeting me in the hotel lobby, he handed me an envelope stuffed with "walking around" money – though there were few who walked around in Beverly Hills. Jerry Rubin, of the famed "Chicago Seven," tried it once and lost his life jaywalking on Wilshire Boulevard. (I had met him in Haiti and did not like his swimming style. When he died, I regretted having such feelings.) Stark had arranged a palatial suite for me at the hotel; it was filled with gift baskets containing enough fruit to feed my old neighborhood in the Bronx. He liked me then. Later, when I fell out of favor, he made a dismissive remark that had great appeal to the novelist Kurt Vonnegut. (And when will this man stop name-dropping?)

"You know what your trouble is, Friedman? You will always be one of those hundred thousand dollar guys."

This, to a man whose father brought up a Depression family of four on thirty dollars a week.

On Broadway, the roles in *The Owl and the Pussycat* had been played by Diana Sands and Alan Alda. It was Stark's idea to have Barbra Streisand and Sidney Poitier star in the film, thereby reversing the color or race or ethnicity, or whatever the phrase of the moment is. Before leaving the hotel, Stark tossed me a copy of the play and said:

"Do anything you want with it. Shit on it if you like. Just keep the basic premise: *Intellectual Meets Hooker.*"

"And by the way," he said, as he left, "the playwright is blind."

The implication, *Stark's* implication, I now realize, was that the poor playwright (William Manhoff) would be unable to read or see whatever desecration was visited on his work, and that I was therefore free to trample all over it. But what kind of swine would change a word of blind Manhoff's play. Gritting my teeth throughout the process, I did what I could to hold on to every bit of what I felt, quite frankly, was his pedestrian dialogue, blind or not. A big mistake. Paying a fortune for a property, and eliminating every trace of it, was fairly standard at the time. No doubt it still is. It's *expected*. After all, the original was a play or book, which was clearly an encumbrance. Someone might have asked J.D. Salinger about the Hollywood approach to his story, "Uncle Wiggly in Connecticut," which was unrecognizeable in the film, *My Foolish Heart.* That was the last of his works he allowed to be adapted. (Not to be perverse about it, but I recall enjoying the movie. Of course, it wasn't my story.)

Though I had no need for a secretary, Stark insisted that I have one. (Sometime earlier, I'd had a meeting in Manhattan with a noted screenwriter named Leonard Speigelglass, who had been hired to write a play based on *A Mother's Kisses.* From time to time he would excuse himself and call the West Coast to rearrange the timing of his sessions with a personal masseur. If I swung over and became a screenwriter, would I be assigned a personal masseur? And did I want one? What happened to the sensitive and aspiring young novelist from the Bronx?)

The secretary (that I didn't need) had a horrible cold. I had a fear of catching it, which was not what I had in mind for my stay in Los Angeles. (That she was not a babe, it must be stated, was unhelpful. After all, this was Hollywood.) I called Stark and told him I knew what he was getting at in his choice of a secretary. He did not want me to be distracted.

"But this is distracting me the wrong way."

The producer said he understood entirely. Would I come out to his home in Malibu? By the time I arrived there would be a new secretary waiting for me. Crossing the lawn in front of his property, I recall tripping over giant Henry Moore sculptures that hadn't quite been unpacked and were half out of their crates. Apparently, a great tidal wave of money had come Stark's way from the box-office grosses of *Funny Girl*. What does a producer do with all that money? He buys Henry Moores.

I met Stark at his vast swimming-pool area. Warren Beatty was on hand, entertaining (charming) the dancers of the visiting Royal Ballet. The producer summoned my new secretary. Natalie Wood, a reigning goddess of the screen, trim in a two-piece bathing suit, walked out of a dressing room. She approached me and introduced herself. I tried to remain composed. Stark was known to be a prankster, but I felt he'd gone too far.

"This is amusing," I told the producer, "but I can't possibly have Natalie Wood as my secretary."

"I'm sorry," she said sweetly. "You're stuck with me. I *am* your secretary."

And so she was. In the week that followed, I would pick up the star of *Splendor in the Grass* and *West Side Story* at her home in Malibu and drive her back to the Beverly Hills Hotel, pretending to be relaxed and trying my utmost to stay on the highway.

I kept mumbling to myself: "I don't believe this. I have Natalie Fucking Wood in my car."

There are several explanations for all of this. She was in her late thirties at the time, between marriages to Robert Wagner, and wasn't being offered major roles. A psychiatrist may very well have suggested that she try something different for a while. (Become Friedman's secretary? Unlikely.) There is yet another explanation, which is self-serving. I had seen her for a split-second at a party the previous night. Joan Collins was there, hands on her hips, eyes flashing, daring someone, anyone, to do something, anything. Warren Beatty was another guest. So was Steve McQueen. (I had collided with him in the lobby of the hotel and been embarrassed when a hair-dryer fell out of my luggage.) I sensed that I was out of my depth. I *was* out of my depth. Still, always reluctant to leave a party, I was among the last to thank the host and say goodbye. The producer, Jack Haley, Jr., a man I'd never met before, said to me with a sneer:

"Alone again, eh Bruce?"

All this before I'd written *The Lonely Guy*. He must have seen it coming.

Was it possible that Natalie Wood had noticed me? And liked me? Great wonders have been known to transpire in the long march of human events.

I would enjoy reporting that our week in the hotel was a passionate one. It was less than that. There were a few mildly amorous interludes. But, for the most part, I felt I was locked up in a hotel room with a wounded bird. She *was* a wounded bird. I treated her as such, and spent a great deal of time with a comforting arm around her shoulder. There were hugs. Warm supportive embraces. This at a time when I would have rolled around lubriciously with a mop.

It's possible that screen goddesses should remain where they belong – on the screen.

She was, incidentally, an excellent secretary. If only I had needed one.

I did what I could to cling to every word of poor blind William Manhoff's play. The novels I had written required that I deliver my insides, hot and smoking, on a table. By contrast, screenwriting, or at least the ones I was offered, seemed light and fluffy. A soufflé comes to mind. There didn't seem to be a way to put any passion into them. There might be a flash of opportunity in a single patch of dialogue, and then it was off to another scene. Usually there were one hundred or so. At the writing end, it was like sex with no release. Puzo became untypically heated on this subject.

"Screenwriting is *not* writing. It's something else. They should give it another name. The screenwriter is the dopey kid you put in right field, because there's no place else to put him."

Manhoff's play was on the fluffy side. I tried to darken it up a bit with an opening scene in which Streisand's character clings to a rooftop, legs flailing, and threatens suicide. The scene never made it into the film.

Poitier had some reservations about the script, although Marty Baum, his agent, loved me. He told the producer:

"You got a guy here who writes fast, doesn't make any trouble. Don't let him get away."

Apparently this was a rarity in Hollywood.

Streisand was interested in (had a crush on?) Oskar Werner. Would I consider tailoring the script for him? Of course I would. I had no interest in leaving. I had the hotel, room service, adventurous nights. I took up tennis and played each day at a court alongside Anthony Quinn. I'd been told I bore a slight resemblance to the actor. Apparently Quinn agreed and kept glancing over at me. It's possible he'd never seen anyone whose backhand was worse than his. (I've noticed that writers have a tendency to think they resemble movie stars. Joseph Heller was convinced he was the image of Paul Newman. Puzo thought he looked like Brando. Oddly enough, in his late years, when poor health caused Puzo to lose weight – and Brando gained quite a bit of it – the two actually did become lookalikes.)

I saw Puzo at the hotel. He'd been given a master suite and hired a secretary who wore the shortest skirts (and had the longest legs) of any woman in Hollywood. I never felt they were having an affair (though such things are not unheard of). Naked to the waist, proudly flaunting his flipper arms, hairless chest and big belly, he enjoyed watching the effect she had on visiting friends. He wrote (pounded out) scripts on the little Royal typewriter on which he'd written the *Godfather*, and which he continued to use until the end.

On weekends Puzo would entertain friends at a Malibu estate he was to rent from the actor Burgess Meredith each year for the next decade. The annual rent was a quarter of a million dollars.

"It would have made much more sense," he complained later, "if I had bought the fuckin' place."

Some of his visitors were hard-looking men from Vegas. I recalled the producer Sidney Beckerman telling me: "Your friend is hanging around with 'the wrong people'" (i.e. mobsters).

"I never worry about them," Puzo told me. "They only kill each other. "

He loved tennis and though his weight limited his movement, it was a mistake to underestimate him on the court. His forehand was a stiletto. Any ball within his reach was dead on arrival.

Also interfering with his pleasure, though only slightly, were the illnesses that continued to plague him. When he suffered one of several heart attacks I visited him in the ER. To cheer him up, I brought along a pretty young Asian woman who'd become a friend. She was instantly delighted by him.

"Oh, Mario," she said, "You're so cute."

And she began to tickle his belly.

"She was charming," he said to me later. "But it could have gone either way."

When Oskar Werner lost interest in *The Owl and the Pussycat*, Streisand thought it might be fun to work with Michael Caine. Would I change the script once again and make it irresistible to the British star? Of course I would. It seemed a pleasant and painless occupation, writing different versions of the play for Streisand's favorite (crush) of the moment. As long as I had my beloved room service. And my new friend, Warren Beatty. And the dancers of the Royal Ballet.

One lazy afternoon, on Stark's patio, Beatty selected the prettiest – and leggiest – of the ballet troupe and went frolicking off with her. I noticed a thin and bedraggled young member of the company, off by herself, and hunched over as if she was in hiding. She had the look of a girl who had never been asked to the prom. As an act of compassion, I introduced myself and told her I planned to see *Swan Lake* that evening at the civic center. Perhaps I could drop by after the performance and take her out for a hamburger. She said yes and seemed terribly grateful.

Congratulating myself on this gesture of kindness, I showed up at the theater that night and took a seat that had been provided by Nora Kaye, who was married to the director Herbert Ross, and had herself been a prima ballerina. (Thick Brooklyn accent and all.) She'd had a previous marriage to the legendary violinist Isaac Stern.

She recalled: "All I ever said to him was 'Practice, Isaac, practice.'"

The auditorium was at capacity. When Odile took the stage, thousands got to their feet and greeted her with a thunderous ovation. The mousey-looking woman I'd pitied at the pool was Antoinette (later Dame) Antoinette Sibley, one of the most celebrated classical dancers in ballet history.

I had to fight my way through a throng of well-wishers to get to her dressing room.

"Why didn't you say something?" I asked as she removed her make-up.

"About what?"

"About who you are. Were."

"It didn't seem terribly important."

"Still want the hamburger?"

"Of course."

Off we drove to a diner.

Everything seemed scripted. A week in a hotel suite with Natalie Wood. Hamburgers with the world's most famous ballerina. None of this led to romance. I had an affair with a woman who played supporting roles in the company – but that would have led the script in a listless direction and it wouldn't have worked. Possibly years later, with the Coen Brothers in charge.

*

Warren Beatty was the most agreeable of men. He had the capability of making anyone he spoke to feel that he or she was the total center of his interest. I'd watched (stood by) and saw him juggle affairs on the phone with three different women at the same time, making each one feel she was the only one in the world he cared about. He was awfully busy at it. You would have felt that juggling affairs was his full-time job. I don't see how he found time to make movies. He'd seen my play *Scuba Duba* several times, stroking his chin as he watched it, no doubt riddled with doubt as to whether it would make a good film. He came across as always being riddled with doubt. Somehow he was convinced that I had been a professional fighter; he seemed to be on his guard the few times we spent together, as if I might lash out at any moment and punch him.

"How many fights did you have?" he wanted to know.

I got tired of the question and finally said I'd had a few.

"I'll bet," he said, convinced that at some point I'd won a title – and was being modest about it.

I've never seen anyone have the effect on women that he had. A popular club at the time was called The Garage. It was central headquarters for the most beautiful women in Hollywood. The idea of women falling at someone's feet is generally a metaphor. But when Beatty made his appearance, you would swear that they actually did fall at his feet. Or at least grow weak and melt and call out: "Oh, Warren."

There was a night, at the club, that I now think of as a tiny dim flash of what was later to grow into what we know as "The Women's Movement." Or at least the Beverly Hills branch.

Warren looked around for his date and spotted a small exquisite woman (child) who more than caught his fancy. He introduced himself, chatted with her for a moment, then asked me if I would be a good friend (sidekick) and wait outside with her while he found his date and told her he'd been called away on business. (He wasn't misrepresenting. This was his business.)

It was raining heavily. I found an umbrella and held it over Warren's new friend, who could not have been more than eighteen. She told me that she'd had twins with Tony Curtis who were being looked after in Marin County. And that she'd just come back from Las Vegas, where she had "been with" Frank Sinatra.

"He was nice, but I didn't care for the people around him."

The wait for Beatty took a little longer than each of us had expected. She grew impatient and seemed to be having a struggle of conscience. Finally she said: "I'm not going to fuck Warren."

Then, after consideration, she said: "I'll give him head. Because after all, he *is* a movie star. But no fucking."

I became restless. Los Angeles was a toy store. The real world, i.e. the literary world, was in Manhattan. I found it annoying, if not offensive, when a Hollywood agency claimed to have a "literary" division – when all of its clients were screenwriters. If there was something literary about writing for the films I was unaware of it. If all this sounds snobbish, it's intended to be.

This is not to suggest, incidentally, that there aren't gifted screenwriters. I felt that Harold Pinter was the best of them. But was it literature?

Streisand, for the time being, had run out of favorite actors. As a result, there was little for me to do. George Segal eventually starred in the film. But by the time he came on board I was long gone. My contribution to the film, such as it was, went uncredited. Nor was I unhappy about this. As strange as it may seem today – when every third person you meet is enrolled in a film school – I was still uneasy about being "branded" as a screenwriter, thinking it might sully whatever reputation I had as a novelist. Nor was I being entirely paranoid. My (literary) agent, Candida Donadio, told me that my name came up from time to time in her talks with publishers.

She reported, ominously: "But I keep hearing 'movies,' Bruce."

Back I went to Manhattan to press on with *The Dick*. As I was leaving Los Angeles, the producer Marvin Worth virtually headed me off at the airport and asked me to write the Lenny Bruce story.

(One way to get a writing job in Hollywood is to be spotted racing for the airport.)

It was easy enough to say no. Though I had never seen the comedian perform, I was aware of his legendary standing and his importance to friends I cared about. I did not want to be the one who ruined (fucked up) the Lenny Bruce story. That task would fall to others. (Some years later, Bruce's monologue, 'Frank Dell at the Palladium,' became the touchstone for me of all comedy, the finest – and most heartbreaking – half hour, of *anything* for that matter, either written or spoken.)

Worth was undeterred. I was the man for the job. He needed someone who was fundamentally out-of-control, but presentable at meetings. (Such individuals evidently were in short supply during the early seventies.) On the tarmac, he offered me a fee of $50,000 to "stay interested" in the project for a month. Fifty thousand was fifty thousand. It was then, it is now and it always will be. I thought I might be able to pull this off, but I insisted that I had to "stay interested" on the East Coast. He agreed. Off I went to Manhattan.

As a reasonably honest man, I took the assignment seriously. For weeks I walked about with a grim expression and a furrowed brow.

"Is anything wrong?" friends would ask.

"Not at all. I'm staying interested in the Lenny Bruce story."

When the month passed I immediately lost interest, collected the money and went about my business.

Paying someone a large sum of money to maintain interest in a notion is not uncommon in Hollywood. Or at least it wasn't at the time. Some years later, I was paid yet another tidy sum and flown to St. Tropez. Once there, I was to "stay interested" in a Peter Sellers film in which he would play a gay fashion photographer. The actor, in turn, had already been paid $200,000 to "remain enthusiasatic" about the project in France.

Sellers seemed puzzled by my sudden appearance. He told his lovely fifth wife:

"I believe Mr. Friedman and I are intended to form some sort of comedy team."

Nonetheless, for several weeks, in the lobby of the Byblos Hotel, we sat opposite one another, exchanging glances now and then, to ensure that the other's interest in the film was unflagging.

"You still keyed up about this?" I would ask.

"Of course," was his answer. "You?"

"Terribly."

And then we took walks. Separately.

Sellers died soon after. Which is not to suggest that it was from the strain of having constantly to remain interested in our project. Staying up to conjugal speed with that angelic fifth wife may have been a factor.

A bit later, the producer arranged for me to meet Vittorio Gassman, who was, in my view, the greatest comedic actor of his time. (This was only evident in his Italian films.) The Sellers role was up for grabs. Gassman gave the impression that he wasn't terribly interested in it. After swanning around for a bit on Fifty-Seventh Street, nodding graciously to those who recognized him, he suddenly clutched at my lapels and asked me, pleadingly, and yes, heartbreakingly, "Do you think I'm right for the part?"

I thought he was, although there was no part, at the moment, for him to be right for. The studio had little interest in him. In their wisdom, they wanted him only for gangster roles. And as for Gassman's heartbreak, who knows. After all, he was a great actor.

As a coda to the *Owl and the Pussycat* story, I ran into Barbra Streisand at Elaine's restaurant a year after the film had been released. She had just come in from the rain and was a bit bedraggled. She looked like the young waif from Brooklyn who had astonished the world with her first public performance on the Ed Sullivan show. I recall my wife Ginger calling me in from another room.

"Come in, come in. You've got to listen to this person."

She was rained on at Elaine's, wore no make-up; I had never seen her look more appealing. She put her head on my chest and said she should have used my script, or at least one of them. This may have been standard Hollywood procedure, but she seemed sincere. I had a fantasy in which I agreed to live with her, on condition that she keep singing to me round the clock.

It should be noted, incidentally, that Buck Henry, the most agreeable of men, and a *real* screenwriter, was quite properly awarded the credit on the film. Evidently, he had been working "behind" me, that is, doing his version of the screenplay while I was doing mine. Evidently, this was not unusual. There may very well have been someone working "behind" Henry.

20

"Was it like this? Is this what he did to you?"
> The critic Anatole Broyard, falling to the floor
> and kicking up his legs, while mimicking the
> character Stern's reaction to a sexual assault on
> his wife.

I returned to work on *The Dick* with a vengeance, stepping down hard on the gas, as if to atone for my wastrel summer in Los Angeles. Gottlieb was more than satisfied with the result, though he did ask me to lop off a final section of the novel.

"Do we really need a 'Flying Down to Rio' chapter?" he asked.

We didn't. The book was published by Alfred Knopf. I looked forward to smooth sailing in the review area. Up until then, I'd had it all my way. I'd been scuffed up a bit as a musical comedy librettist, but this was of minor importance to me. My novels and plays and stories had all worked out well. For more than a decade, I'd thought of myself as a Jewish Golden Boy. And then Anatole Broyard's review of *The Dick* appeared in the *N.Y. Times* and I felt I'd been in a ten-car collision. The review was vicious. It implied, though never stated, that I was a racist. To make it even worse, Broyard had gotten my age wrong, tacking on an extra year, which

I felt was unnecessary. Gottlieb read the review to me on the phone. Half-way along, he stopped and said: "I can't go on . . . ," suggesting that it was all too awful for him to deal with. Fair enough. He'd read wonderful reviews to me in the past. Why not let him, for the sake of variety, read a dreadful one.

There are writers who can shrug off a nasty review. Or so they claim. I wasn't one of them. It was the racist insinuation that stung. My area of reference for the novel had been the weeks I'd spent as a journalist at a Chicago homicide bureau in the sixties. It was racist the second you walked in the door. Some of the banter was just that, banter. Some wasn't. But racism was built into the DNA of the bureau. I felt, when I could feel anything, that Broyard had made a horrible misjudgment, confusing the attitude of the characters with that of the author. The kind of mistake made by an amateur critic. But he was no amateur.

Virtually the same day the review appeared, the film rights were sold to Warner Brothers for a small fortune. Add to this a handsome deal for me to write the screenplay (in which, as usual, I had little interest). At roughly the same time, my play *Steambath* was picked up as a television film, and a bit later as a *Showtime* Series. Other plums were dropped into my lap. *Book World*, a *Herald Tribune* rival to the *Times*, was enthusiastic about *The Dick*. William Buckley's *National Review* was as well. Nelson Algren and *Steely Dan*, of all people (groups) were among the admirers. There were substantial foreign sales. None of this meant anything. I was numb. It was the implied racism charge that stung. Was there any truth to it? As a freshman at the University of Missouri I recalled having fierce, even bloody, civil rights debates with young klansmen-in-the-making. Yet somehow I had never noticed that there wasn't a single black student on the campus. Did that make me a racist?

For years I flashed back on the review; infuriatingly, it pushed me into taking up a "Some of my Best Friends" defense. I never said any of this aloud (nor was I asked to) but hadn't I discovered Cleavon Little in my play *Scuba Duba*? Written *Stir Crazy*, Richard

Pryor's highest-grossing film? Cast David Chapelle as the lead in a television show (*Legionnaires*) before he became David Chappelle? Fought to have Alvin Hollingsworth signed on as the first black illustrator to work for the Magazine Management Company? It disgusted me that I had to even think of these efforts as "achievements." They were as natural as breathing. And yet. And yet. Why did I take such comfort in the song "Everyone's a Little Bit Racist" in the Broadway musical *Avenue Q*?

Clearly Broyard had pushed some buttons. And the novel had pushed some of his. He'd loved *Stern* and *A Mother's Kisses*, and seized me up for dinner parties, wanting to be my friend, pursuing me so aggressively that I began to think that his interest extended beyond the literary. It was important to him that I meet Ralph Ellison. The three of us had dinner together. Throughout, the author of *Invisible Man* referred to me as "Mr. Stern." The intent was to be amusing. I found it irritating. After dinner, with Ellison looking on, Broyard acted out scenes from *Stern*; his favorite was an episode in which Stern re-enacts an alleged sexual assault on his wife. Mimicking Stern, Broyard fell to the floor, kicked up his legs and said to his wife in a high-pitched voice:

"Was it like this? Is this what he did to you?"

To Ellison's delight, he ad-libbed, with horror: "And no panties? You weren't wearing panties?"

Later, Broyard became "outed" as a black man. He had fooled a great many people into thinking he was white, but not Charlie Parker. According to a book by the educator Henry Louis Gates, Jr., the legendary "Bird" took one look at the critic and said to a friend: "He's one of us."

Some say Broyard served as the model for the main character in Philip Roth's *The Human Stain*. As for his being a "closeted" black man, I had no idea of what he was and could not have cared less. I recall only that he did indeed love books, was taken with mine and followed me down the street, insisting that we meet again. It was nothing personal, but I had no particular need for a new friend. It was no accident that I was to write *The Lonely Guy*. I did not enjoy being fawned over.

For all of the hurt feelings about the review, I was not about to switch professions.

"When you are going through hell," Churchill once said, "keep going."

My situation was far from hellish. With my mother dying of cancer at Lennox Hill Hospital, I had been able to sit in the waiting room and write a piece about a group called "Earth Artists" for Harold Hayes at *Esquire*. Was it any good? I didn't think so. Hayes did. It was published. Did this make me a monster? Not especially. I was a writer. I had a deadline. And this is what writers do. At a literary conference, Jack Richardson said:

"I don't know anyone like you. You're a writer. And you actually write."

I had no idea what he was talking about. But apparently there are people who identify themselves as writers – and don't write.

Though I hadn't set the world on fire in Hollywood – at least not at that point – there had been a residual benefit to my West Coast trips. I invented a character named Harry Towns, a kind of second-rate screenwriter, and wrote two stories about his adventures. F. Scott Fitzgerald's Pat Hobby stories had always been favorites of mine. (Shamefully, I enjoyed them as much as I did *Gatsby*.) Hobby was also a fringe player in Hollywood. At one point he had served as a minor executive and, after a poor decision, had been "reduced back to a writer." Did the Hobby stories influence me? I don't expecially think so – and who cares. What I generally take from writers who interest me is courage. (He or she did that? What am I afraid of? Maybe I can do it, too.)

Perhaps that's influence of a kind.

Gottlieb read The Harry Towns stories and said:

"You will do more with this character."

I did. Perhaps because he expected me to. Two novels, *About Harry Towns* and *The Current Climate*. And half-a-dozen more stories. There is a question that is asked of authors, almost reflexively. "Are your books autobiographical?" Of course they are. All writing is autobiographical. Harry Towns was a bit closer to the bone than the usual. Now and then I would put on my Harry Towns hat and become Harry Towns. I'm a bit more intelligent than he is; Harry is the reckless one. One of the early stories went to *Esquire*, the other to *Harper's*. I doubt that either one of the magazines would take my call now – but at the time I felt I was acting out of largesse, spreading the wealth. Poor Willie Morris at *Harper's*. Why not give *him* a story. How the mighty, etc. . . .

Lee Eisenberg, who had taken over from Harold Hayes at *Esquire*, called me down one day to exchange ideas with several editors. I threw out a few half-hearted notions. Theirs were even less inspired than mine. As I was about to leave, I mentioned that I had recently tried my hand at cooking. What about "The Lonely Guy's Cookbook?" (Forget one and a half tbs. of coriander. . . . You just throw in hunks of things.) Five suddenly enthusiastic editors leapt to their feet, crying out "That's it, that's it."

I wrote the piece. It was published. Most magazine stories are glanced at. A few get some attention. Most are quickly forgotten. And every now and then, a story hits a chord. Such was the case with *The Lonely Guy's Cookbook*. I can't say that it made readers dance in the streets. But Norman Mailer (my old boxing partner) stopped me on Fifth Avenue to congratulate me, although he did make a correction on the preparation of chicken breasts: I was wrong in suggesting that the skin be removed before baking.) Here was evidence that he had read the story carefully. Perhaps of greater importance, there were offers to write a book based on The Lonely Guy – his Business Affairs, Grooming, Sex Life . . .

McGraw/Hill won the day. The book was published, then sold and re-sold, to NBC as a special (which made no sense), then to CBS as a series (it did make sense), and finally to my "adapter" Neil Simon as a film vehicle for Steve Martin. How easy it seems when it all goes well. One forgets the vomiting. I asked Simon how he planned to approach the film.

"That's easy," he said. "Lonely Guy meets Lonely Girl."

I congratulated him.

"That's why you're Neil Simon and I'm not."

Still, a faint alarm went off. Suddenly, the Lonely Guy didn't seem all that lonely. When I read that Charles Grodin had signed on as a friend, the alarm became more insistent. A friend. A girl. What happened to the loneliness? When I asked Steve Martin who the director was, he'd said, without enthusiasm, "Arthur Hiller is photographing it."

The film worked out decently. It has some fans. There is a curious sidebar to the story. I was asked to do publicity for the book and appeared as a guest on several television shows. Without fail, the host would assume that I was a single person, leading a wild life. (It's unlikely that he had actually read the book.) Irritatingly, I'd be asked: "What's it like, Bruce, TO BE A SWINGING BACHELOR?"

David Susskind had one of the leading talk shows at the time. He asked me to join a panel on Loneliness in America. Each of my fellow guests had been let out of a nursing home for the occasion. Susskind was impatient.

"Oh, c'mon, Bruce. You're not a lonely person."

"But I am, David. Honest. What you see before you is a façade."

In truth, I had met Patricia J. O'Donohue almost the very day the book appeared in the stores, and I insisted, when we met a second time, that we live together. (One of her more attractive features is that she was not writing a screenplay.) Try as I might to cling to my loneliness, I was unsuccessful. I'm happy to report that slowly I fought my way back to loneliness, a condition that seems to be a requirement for practicing this strange monk-like profession of ours.

21

"Take a right at Michael Caine."

> The restauranteur Elaine, upon being asked for
> directions to the men's room.

Before I met Pat, my second wife-to-be, in 1976, I was sustained
throughout a ragged patch of my life by Elaine's on the upper East
Side. The restaurant, when it all began (in 1963), was a scruffy
gathering place for ragamuffin novelists, playwrights, and a stray
poet or two, who were on the cusp, in some cases, of strong careers.
Though many remained on the cusp, none starved. Elaine saw to
that, often "carrying" failed novelists for decades. Little money
made it to the cash register. Most of the receipts were safely tucked
away in Elaine's enormous décolletage. When a writer was down
on his heels and needed a financial boost, Elaine would reach a
bejeweled hand into the pillowy "bank" for a quick withdrawal.

I was in love the moment I walked in. I had never dared to
dream that such a place existed. Here was safety. Here was comfort. Here was a haven I could turn to each night – which I did in
the early days. If there had been rooms in the back I might have
moved in. The lighting was warm and inviting. (I'd always felt it
was a secret to the restaurant's longevity – over fifty years.) One

night, Norman Mailer's date felt the light was unflattering. She reached up and unscrewed an overhead bulb. This was unacceptable. Elaine, a large woman who often served as her own security, belly-bumped the woman into the street. Mailer was deeply offended and wrote Elaine an almost book-length letter expressing his discontent. Elaine marked each page "Boring, Norman" and returned the letter. They became friends again.

Jack Richardson, who introduced me to the restaurant, was himself one of its main attractions. A gifted playwright (He'd won an Obie for *The Prodigal*) he was/is one of the most rakishly attractive men I've ever known. Linguist, musician, classics scholar, he gave off the impression that he could have made his way – and excelled – in any profession or enterprise, legal or not, that caught his fancy. It is a great sorrow that he never pressed on with a life in the theater that had begun in such triumph. A tall slender graceful man, he wore clothes that were fitted in London and was so off-handed about it that it took years for it to sink in that he was the most deceptive of fashion plates. I don't think he was ever seen in short sleeves. You would not want to see him in short sleeves. The actor he most resembled was John Carradine, although a case could be made that there was a touch of Peter O'Toole in the mix. He could easily have stepped in and taken the place of the Duke in *Huckleberry Finn*. I once watched him disarm a deranged person on East Eighty-Sixth Street at four in the morning. He could not keep his hands still, which made driving a car out of the question. Yet he was the most graceful of men. Barely moving his feet, and with couples gyrating wildly all about him, he became the center of attention on the dance floor of Studio 54. In the back room of Elaine's, he casually picked up a guitar as if he'd never before held one, and seamlessly accompanied an appreciative Paul Desmond, the fabled jazz saxophonist. He was invited by Elaine to join a visiting Iranian who had come into the restaurant alone and was in need of company. Within minutes, Richardson was conversing with the man in highly passable Farsi. The visitor tested him by switching to Pushto. Richardson more than held his own.

Gambling was his passion. (I feared for him when online investing became possible.) Not even arguably, his *Memoir of a Gambler* was one of the best books ever written on the subject. He waved off the reviews, which were uncommonly good.

"The little ball came out in my favor."

He had seen it go the other way.

He was at his tableau-creating best in the restaurant one night, playing high-stakes poker and sipping his beloved (and lethal – to me) Fundador. When the sideline kibbitzing of the journalist Tom Buckley got out of hand, Richardson broke a wine glass on the table, gently lifted the jagged side and said: "Make your move."

Confused as to whether this was theater or real life, Buckley chose to race out the door.

Richardson could be ice-cold. The critic Stanley Kauffman had been rude to one of his plays. Richardson was later given Kauffman's book to review for the *New York Times Book Review*. Not even thinking to recuse himself, he savaged the critic back. I saw him show fear only once. Passing our table, the producer Sidney Beckerman stopped to say a few unkind words about Mario Puzo.

"Mario is my friend," I said. "And I'd prefer not having him spoken about that way."

Beckerman considered this and moved on. In the meanwhile, the color had gone out of Richardson's face. Didn't I know who that was? Beckerman was the most dangerous man in Hollywood. He had served time in prison and once been a feared enforcer for the mob. No, I did not know that and yes, if I had, there was a chance my behavior would have been more measured.

It was no secret that Elaine had her favorites – Willie Morris, Irwin Shaw, Lewis Lapham, John Barry Ryan, George Plimpton, Bobby Short, Nick Pileggi, Tennessee Williams. (Before he left the restaurant one night – and toward the end of his days – Williams scribbled a note for Elaine that was written in Gaelic. She had it translated: "I have lost my way.")

In the order of her affections, I put myself, with some presumption, in the number eleven position, if for no other reason than the frequency of my appearances. (Over years, and with the thinning out of the ranks, I may have moved up a few notches.) But Richardson far and away had always held the number one spot. Some envied Jack. Most of us loved him. From time to time I'd run into Peter Falk at Dan Tana's restaurant in Hollywood. Richardson could have served as a prototype for the villainously suave types Columbo fenced with in each of the show's episodes. Each brief conversation with Falk began with a single fond question, "How's Jack?" and ended when I reported that he was fine.

More than once, Richardson and I ran into the rough weather that most every writer eventually encounters. We hit upon the idea one night of leaving the city ("pulling up stakes") and going off to live in Mexico. But after picturing ourselves on a veranda in Guadalajara, wearing jockey shorts and preparing martinis, we abandoned the plan.

Jack had been seeing a young editor and had abruptly broken off the affair, essentially disappearing from her life. When she called the restaurant late one night and asked to speak to him, he was at a loss as to what to say to her.

"Tell her you've been following your star," I said.

He spoke to her, then returned to our table, looking as if he had been through open heart surgery.

"If you don't mind," he said, "no more suggestions."

My first visit to the restaurant could have served as the pencil sketch for a fully-realized portrait of the nights to come. A scholarly-looking woman with a short skirt and incredibly beautiful legs danced atop a jukebox adjacent to the front door. Off in another world, at the back of the restaurant, the novelist Frank Conroy (*Stop-Time*) played jazz chords on a piano, making tortured faces as if the music was being wrenched out of his soul, which it may or may not have been. From time to time, he would join the literary gypsies at Table Four and wave a cautionary finger:

"Nobody monkeys with my prose."

It was as if there were editors among us who were anxious to get their hands on it.

Alongside a bank of phones a craps game was discreetly under way presided over by a heavy-lidded man named Mosely, whose specialization was to make loans to writers who were short of funds and had exceeded Elaine's generous limit. He was in no rush to be repaid.

"I never worry," he would say, "so long as they don't avoit my eyes."

Seated widely at the bar was a large man with big ears and huge hands known only as "Bob." A 50-year-old man, he lived with his mother in Brooklyn. Affecting the doltish look of a small-time rube, he was a skilled card shark, banned from every casino on the East coast. Later on, I was to come upon his photo on the cover of a tabloid. Handcuffed and grinning widely, he was being frog-marched out of a casino in Haiti with guns at his throat.

The celebrities would come later, but it was the irregulars in those early days who made the place fascinating. Chief among them was Anthony J. Tuttle. Born into genteel New England poverty, he spoke with a lock-jawed Groton accent and was vocal about his impoverished state. When offered small amounts to tide him over, his language, in its disdain, became elevated, almost Shakespearian.

"You offer me tens? What need have I for tens? I HAVE NO MONEY."

Shamed, we all reached deeper into our pockets – in clear violation of Elaine's iron-clad rule – *Never borrow money from a writer.*

Only Richardson was unphased.

"Oh, do shut up, Tony," he would say and shuffle the cards.

Tuttle was not a novelist of the first tier. There may not have been an appropriate tier for his work. His great gift was not so much in writing but in applying for grants. He probably received more of them than any other writer on record. This turned more than a few of us against government funding of the arts.

When I first met Tuttle, he was working as a waiter at a nearby restaurant. It was his night off.

"What a pleasure it is to meet you, Mr. Friedman. I just finished *Stern* and flung it across the room."

"Did you like it?"

"Oh, babe," he said, and clutched my shoulder, his eyes watering over. "Oh, babe."

He never quite finished the sentence.

"I've completed my own novel," he then said, cheerfully. "Tonight, I plan to put in layers."

He accompanied this last with little shoving gestures as if he were a baker, adding layers to a cake.

A bit further along in our friendship, Tuttle asked my opinion of a passage he'd written in a play. He read it aloud.

"Jew," one character says to another. "You with your belly bursting with lox, your fridge overflowing with scallion cream cheese. Oh Jew, open your eyes to those less fortunate – to a tenement-dweller, for example, who stands before you and is forced to draw his electricity from the toaster of a kindly tenant in a neighboring apartment.

"Jew. Eater of knishes. Cease stuffing your face with chopped liver and in the name of the Holy Father, Open thine eyes."

"I thought I'd call the play *Jew*. What do you think?"

"I don't know, Tony. Sounds a little anti-Semitic."

"It does?" he said in surprise. "Oh, babe, that's the last thing I had in mind. What if I inserted layers?"

"Can't hurt," I said.

He actually found a publisher for a novel about golf, my least favorite subject, and asked me for a quote. Unable to think of a suitable one I came up with the following:

"This novel is filled with energy."

It seemed to please the publisher.

A year later, Tuttle completed a second novel. About this, I wrote:

"Tuttle's new novel has even more energy than his first."

Though Tuttle had a murky and perhaps nonexistent sex-life, he was the favorite of a nest of depressed flight attendants. (Then called "airline stewardesses.") Now and then he would say to me, wincingly: "Let's go visit the stewie downers." We spent evenings listening to their tales of biological mishaps and broken love affairs while Tuttle fried up the tarragon chicken of my dreams. Such were my nights. Small wonder that my next book was *The Lonely Guy*.

He confided in me a bit more than I would have preferred.

"Oh, babe," he said once, remorsefully. "I got stoned and passed out last night. It's a lucky thing I woke up. I would have been found with my arms around a blow-up doll and a vibrator up my ass."

The Russian poet Yevgeny Yevtushenko, visited Elaine's one night. Something of a literary rock star, he had brought along two adoring grad students. Discreetly, he took a table in the rear. Tuttle smoked him out and introduced himself.

"Hi, Mr. Yevtushenko. I'm Anthony J. Tuttle. I have two novels under my belt, I'm inserting layers in a third and welcome to America."

The Russian was stunned, as were his two companions. Richardson felt that the incident seriously threw off-kilter the poet's dream of unbridled sex in the Free World.

The last time I heard from Tuttle he was in the psychiatric ward of a hospital. Electroshock treatments had been prescribed.

He said to me: "Volts, babe, they're talking volts."

I attended his memorial. Throngs of people showed up. I had no idea he had so many friends.

"They're all from A.A.," said Richardson.

His spirit was disorderly, perhaps a bit more than ours. But he was a decent soul. He was a fixture at Elaine's. He was one of us.

Elaine had greeted me that first night with open arms and a kind of cheerfully-understated *bonhomie*. (I've tried but can't find another word for it.) She seemed to be asking: "Where have you been all this time?" She adored writers, though she put them in separate categories – those who wrote – or at least attempted – literature, and others who didn't and were virtually in a different profession. With murder in his eyes, a huge man who wrote television sitcoms confronted the novelist Irwin Shaw one night and said: "Elaine tells me you're a so-called 'real' writer," then emptied a drink in his lap.

She showed me to the (literary) gypsy table. I sat beside Paul Desmond, who'd said he had enjoyed "When You're Excused, You're Excused," a story I'd written that I thought no one had noticed. This of course became the basis of an enduring friendship. On stage and off, Desmond dressed fastidiously and was thought to sleep in a suit and tie. He described his unique sound on the saxophone as being "the equivalent of a dry martini." The great black musicians thought of him as "The Rick Barry of Jazz" and included him in the Pantheon. The second room at Elaine's was named after him. His influence was far-reaching. A decade after his death in 1977, I stopped in for a bite at the only café in a tiny village at the northern-most tip of Iceland. A waitress suggested I try the seal testicles, a specialty of the house.

"I love 'the balls'," she said. "You will, too."

While I waited to be served, I heard Paul Desmond's signature "Take Five" on the jukebox.

That first night at Elaine's, I ordered a dish that was highly satisfying and that I was to enjoy many times – though it led eventually to an annual query from my accountant:

"I don't understand this $18,000 item for veal piccata."

Over the many decades, I've had only a single bumpy experience with the food. One night, I noticed that kidneys, a favorite of mine, were listed on the menu. I'd always had them breaded. These were on the rare side and prepared in a vinegary style that I found to be unusual. I had trouble getting past the first bite and thought I would discreetly deposit it in my napkin. Elaine, who had been watching, said:

"A Frenchman could've kept 'em down."

Elaine was always being teased about her food, which I found highly decent and occasionally exceptional. In the latter case I was always quick with my praise. I thought, one night, she'd served a superior veal osso buco.

"Are you kidding me," she said. "They fly in from all over the world for that dish."

I imagined Silvio Berlusconi in Rome saying to a female companion:

"You know what I'm in the mood for, darling? Elaine's osso buco. Warm up the jet immediately."

Elaine, incidentally, objected fiercely to having the establishment referred to in the press as "a watering hole."

"It's a restaurant. What the hell is wrong with them."

Jack Gelber, who was having a success with his play *The Connection*, introduced himself that first night. Some years later, when I'd been ill, he endeared himself to me by trekking out to York College in Queens to cover my seven in the morning class in Irony. When I'd asked a few other friends, they'd replied, almost as a chorus: "Are you insane?"

Arthur Kopit came by with the hopelessly beautiful artist Priscilla Bowden. As a couple, they were unbearably attractive. To compound the felony, Barbara Harris, another heartbreaker, was starring in Kopit's hit play *Oh Dad, Poor Dad . . .* I found all of this perfection inexcuseable. For solace, I plunged into a blackjack game with a young investment banker from Southampton. Within a short period of time I had won several thousand dollars, which normally would have been cause for celebration. But I did not know if gambling debts, cavalierly incurred at Elaine's, were honored (some were, some weren't) and could not see myself sending "representatives" to break my new friend's legs. As a result, I could not relax until I had lost it all back.

Egos in Elaine's were large, easily bruised. The combination of wine, women, gambling, and Mediterranean waiters who outdid the writers in sensitivity – was combustible. There were indentations that marked the spot where Norman Mailer and the lyricist Jerry Lieber ("Hound Dog") settled a disagreement by flinging themselves against a wall in a tight ball of fury. (With some pride, Elaine showed off the famed crack in the wall.) A giant of a man named "Pinhead," who felt he'd been treated poorly, flung an ashcan through the front window. Revealing a gallant side, he sent a bouquet of flowers to Elaine the following day. (He was found, years later, lifeless, and hanging from a hook in a cell at Riker's island.)

Individuals as well as large objects were thrown through the front window with some regularity. Bernard "Buzz" Farbar, who saw it as his function to protect writers, once hurled an advertising executive through the window after the man had insulted a poet. To drain off energy that had not gone into the day's (or month's) output of prose and poetry, there were arm-wrestling and competitive midnight sprints down Second Avenue. When the director James Toback ("The Pick-Up Artist") began to lag behind in a push-up contest, Elaine said: "Put a broad under him."

Jack Richardson shocked the group by winning a 100-yard dash competition along Second Avenue. This, on emu legs, after drinking a fifth of his beloved Fundador.

At times, the locker room byplay took an intellectual turn. A journalist from England seated himself at the "writer's table" one night. Thinking to establish his bona fides, he began showering the group with a stream of erudite references, most of them having to do with Cromwell. He soon found himself sitting alone. The scholarly and even-tempered Robert Brown had to be pulled away from an advertising man who made a comment about Shakespeare and "that other classical shit." Violence peaked one night when a trio held up the restaurant, forcing Elaine and the staff at gunpoint to lie face down on the floor while the register was emptied. The take was pitiful. Had it been "an inside job," they would have known about Elaine's monied décolletage.

One waiter's plea was heart-rending:

"I have three kids," he cried out, then pointed to a coworker. "Shoot *him*."

Late that first night, I was still out of sorts and only slightly pacified when I was served scrambled eggs, prepared with excellence by yet another waiter, Nicola. Then, as if by heavenly intervention, I found myself taking home the woman who had danced so invitingly atop the jukebox. Though she was never to repeat the performance, I no longer doubted that I had found the ultimate hangout.

There may be those who don't require bright lights and attention and for whom the writing itself is its own reward. I may have even run across one or two such strange individuals. Most writers do not insist on having benefit-dinners thrown in their honor, but there is a need now and then – when the circumstance warrants it – to come out of the darkness and take a discreet bow. A strong review, a book contract, a film sale, each was cause to go racing swiftly to Elaine's. But not too swiftly. It was tacky to show up on the very day of a triumph. Better to slip in without ceremony some time afterward and pretend to be taken aback by all the fuss, assuming there was some. (*"The Manchester Guardian?* Don't tell me you actually *saw* that review. Nice of you to mention it.") Waiting too long before basking in the glow of a victory had its risks as well . . . After a few weeks, there might not be a glow in which to bask. I can recall a moment of glory – a strong review in the *NYTBR* – when I was trapped in Miami, and had to search for adulation at Joe's Stone Crab's.

Some showed up to celebrate. The brave came to lick their wounds. When the writer Sidney Zion was under attack for revealing the source of *The Pentagon Papers*, Elaine seated him – or more accurately propped him up – beside her at a table near the front door, folded her arms – a terrifying sight – and defied anyone to look at him crossly.

People tended to burst into the restaurant with important news.

David Halberstam charged in one night, holding up four fingers and announced: "I'm four for four with Lehman-Haupt." (Chris Lehman-Haupt being the daily book-reviewer for the *N.Y. Times*.)

Representing the Hollywood faction, the film executive Diane Sokolow, burst in soon after, crying out:

"*Tootsie* just broke into profits."

A much more baleful announcement came, through tears, from Anthony Tuttle. Getting to his feet, his fists clenched, he shouted: "I have never had a blowjob" – causing us all to feel we had to rush out and arrange one for him.

The nights all seemed glittering and carefree. There wasn't much literary content to them. Presumably some writing transpired during the daylight hours. But how remarkable that such a safe haven existed. To know that there *was* such a place. That there would always be a party, one to which there was a permanent invitation. Where there was no need to slink around nibbling at hors d'oeuvres, and wondering snobbishly if anyone spoke the same language. Was there a downside to all of this, an *Anna Karenina* that went unwritten because of those dissolute midnight hours? Those who saw such a danger went off to teach writing workshops in the MidWest. Others stayed behind, stole some bleary-eyed pleasure after a good day's work – or as often a bad day's work. Many published. Few perished. The output from the virtuous hinterlands was less than torrential.

It was the beginning nights – like any first act – that are most vivid. Everyone seemed young and either strong or formidably dissipated. The cast slowly began to change. Or did this happen overnight? William Styron gave way to George Steinbrenner, Irwin Shaw to Harvey Weinstein. There was less of Mailer, more of Miramax. A wave of film-people appeared, many of them named "Marty." Being in what they thought of as a literary atmosphere made them *feel* literary and spared them the trouble of actually reading literature. Or perhaps they solved the mystery of how writers got by with so little. And devised plans to pay them even less. Models, actors followed in their wake. Al Pacino, thinking I'd be flattered, stopped at the bar and said he'd read the "coverage" of my new novel. I promised to review the coverage of his next performance. (Actually, and in retrospect, the actor meant well: how many novels was he supposed to read?)

The restaurant caught fire with law enforcers. It raised a question. Was it preferable to spend an evening with a poet or a homicide detective? A second room had to be added, which led to some grumbling about the change in the very character of the restaurant. Had the faith been broken? Why couldn't Elaine's have remained a secret hideaway for sensitive and for the most part impoverished fiction writers? But there was always the fascination of the front door. Who would be the next to slip through? Even the most jaded contributor to *Lingua Franca* snapped to weary attention when Frank Sinatra came barreling in, with Truffaut slipping in quietly behind him. Legendary figures actually became directional guideposts.

Elaine: "The men's room? Take a right at Michael Caine."

For all the muttering about the new and supposedly unwanted notoriety, there wasn't anyone who didn't have a celebrity threshold. (Jack Richardson might have been an exception, although Umberto Eco would have captured his attention.) Elaine herself, who had entertained royalty, came girlishly apart when Marlon Brando appeared – or materialized – before her. It was the sports stars who threw me off stride. *Would you mind if Dominguín joined you? Can you make a little room for Jim Brown? . . . Hi, I'm Derek Jeter.* Yet there was never an icon on hand when you needed one. I took my starstruck niece to the restaurant on an uncommonly slow night. A book editor was there, along with some set designers and the comedian Alan King. He was wearing his trademark tuxedo and had been tipped by some tourists who assumed he was the headwaiter. I introduced my niece to A.E. Hotchner, "a friend of Paul Newman's."

"Who's Paul Newman?" my niece wanted to know.

Elaine came over and said we had just missed Bette Midler. I was reduced to pointing out Woody Allen's chair.

The party threatened to get out of hand in the frenzied seventies. The pre-Giuliani city was something of a crime scene. There were drug and disco casualties and some of us stepped away to catch a breath. I went off to pursue a romantic fantasy of not just visiting but actually living at the beach. We found serious lovers. Elaine herself had a brief highly-charged marriage. Her husband, who was abusive, received a visit from a private eye (a serious man) and was told it would be best for his health to change his address. To a foreign country. He did. A decade and more disappeared. A play, some stories, logs on the fire and still no *Daniel Deronda*. One by one, we came straggling back, to see if we could catch an echo of what now seemed a lost and enchanted time. We were sharply aware that others had lost a step ("That can't possibly be Lewis Lapham"), failing to notice that we'd fallen off a bit ourselves. Strangers had taken over our tables; incredibly, they behaved as if they belonged there. We set up a frail beachhead all the same, attempting to blend in with the new troops. We watered our drinks and listened to heavily embroidered stories of our early victories. As much as the warm lights and the pretty girls, it was the stories that had always brought us there. It was as if we had sat beside an invisible campfire, listening to exquisitely manicured tales, lovingly burnished over time and told by such masters of the form as the great Frederick Morton (*A Nervous Splendor*) and the reticent pipe-smoker Robert Brown. (Occasionally, Brown would push the envelope by reciting interminable epic poetry.) We came back to make sure Elaine was there, her shoulders, if needed, ready to be cried on, though still damp with the tears of a thousand novelists. Keeper of uncountable secrets, a reluctant Scheherazade, she spoke only in one-liners ... "You're breaking balls ... Where'd you get the Jewish Princess? Make them (the publishers) spend ..." And for those unfortunates who came in late – and had stopped to get a bite elsewhere, the accusatory: "Where'd yez eat?"

The columnist Sidney Zion said that if you had Frank Sinatra for a friend you didn't need anyone else.

If you had Elaine, you didn't need Sinatra.

One night, a woman at the bar failed to recognize her.

"Who are you?" she asked.

"I'm Elaine," she said, pointing outside. "From the sign."

I doubt that Elaine's has ever been named as a co-respondent in a divorce suit, although the restaurant has been accused here and there of breaking up an occasional marriage. It's unlikely that the charge has substance. If anything, the hangout that became an institution probably shored up more than a few shaky marriages. Many a wife or mistress took comfort – or was relieved – to hear a restless soulmate announce that he was going to spend a few hours "uptown." And it remained "uptown" for me. When I lived at the beach, in the eighties, the nineties . . . and felt the urge to drop into a local pub, I would say to my second wife Pat, automatically, "I think I'll go uptown for a bit."

Though the restaurant was often thought of as a "boys club," the description – or charge – never quite fit. Dani Padwa, China Machado, Jackie Rogers, Mary Ann Madden, Judy Gordon, Jessica Burstyn, all of them handsome and accomplished women, were every bit as "regular" as the regulars. There were always beautiful women in the mix. A waiter not too long ago told me I would show up now then with a pretty girl. I'll take his word for it. But the women I admired – with apologies to some bad lyricist – were always (dancing?) with someone else. Silent liasons were possible. But there was an understanding that it was bad form to approach a woman who had arrived with an escort – or at least to do so in the restaurant itself.

"What happens after that," said Elaine, "is none of my affair."

On one particular night, when the restaurant was crowded with exquisite women, the British director Michael Rudman shook his head woefully and said:

"In all these decades, I've never gone to bed with a woman I've met here."

I have a feeling his experience was not unique. My own history as a rogue was uneven. But after a night at Elaine's there was, if nothing else, a *feeling* of sexual achievement.

There was a moment that seems out of time when I walked the midtown streets at night and stopped to look in, or actually to peer in, through the great windows of several gentleman's clubs. I admired the chandeliered ceilings, the wood-paneled rooms, the affluent-looking pipe-smoking men in overstuffed chairs, sipping brandy, appearing to read Thackeray, or, more likely, the *Financial Times*. I wondered why I had no such club of my own. And then I realized that I was on my way to Elaine's and that I had an unofficial membership in the most unique and convivial club the city has ever known.

Elaine died in December of 2010. The restaurant petered out under the stewardship of her assistant, Diane Becker. People, many of them not regulars, made reservations long in advance to be there on the last night, May 26, 2011, crowding out the faithful. I could barely get in and managed to land a seat in the back room, where I was joined by Carl Bernstein. In my more than forty years as a patron I had never sat in the "second room" and found it pleasant. I had scribbled down the lyrics of Auld Lang Syne, but when I started up a chorus of it, no one joined in and I gave up, since I wasn't about to do it solo. I left on the early side and was almost trampled by a curious crowd, waiting outside for admittance. A common refrain was: "Where were all these people when Elaine died, and the restaurant was struggling?"

I suppose it should all have been sad, but it wasn't especially. The closing was inevitable. Half-hearted attempts were made to buy the place and keep it going. All were unsuccessful. There wasn't any Elaine's without Elaine.

22

"I know it doesn't come out of a faucet. But where is the goddamned screenplay?"

> An agitated Columbia Pictures executive to the author who had forgotten he'd agreed to write *Stir Crazy*.

After presumably living the carefree life of an unattached novelist, I showed up with a date at a wedding reception and met my second wife-to-be Patricia J. O'Donohue. We spoke awkwardly for a total of a minute-and-a-half. Though I was too shy to call her (the great ladies' man), there wasn't a day that passed in the year that followed that I didn't think about her. (Actually, this was progress of a kind. It had taken me four years to work up the courage to call my first wife.) Pat and I met again, entirely by chance, at a cocktail party on a Sunday night, an evening almost religiously set aside for dinner with my three sons at a Chinese restaurant. Happily and miraculously, the fates ordained that on this night of all nights they would each have made other plans and had to cancel. When I recognized Pat – which took a puzzled minute or two – I told her I had been in love with her for the past year. She said she had been away in Ireland – and that she had often thought of me. (As often as I thought of her? I'll never know.) But from that moment on, we became inseparable. It's my favorite love story (My sister and brother-in-law's WWII romance notwithstanding). On the down side, I keep recycling it, disguising it in my fiction, but it remains resolutely the same love story, the only one I know, the only one I care about. I can hear the ghost of Norman Mailer saying: "For God's sakes, in the interest of forging ahead as a novelist, have a few affairs." (In his case, a few dozen.)

There have been temptations. If there are none, in a twenty-seven-year marriage, something has gone horribly wrong. Undying love and devotion spared me. And, not incidentally, naked fear.

We lived together on Manhattan's upper East Side for several years. The producer Hannah Weinstein came into our lives in 1979 with an idea for a film she was anxious for me to write. I knew a little bit about her. In London, during the House Un-American Activities investigation, she had found work on British television for writers who were victims of the Hollywood blacklist. Some called her a "limousine liberal." This may have been so. She did like the high-life. But she averted more than one suicide. No taller than a tabletop, she and her closest friend, the playwright Lillian Hellman, had been scamps as young girls and continued to be scamps in their seventies. (Do they still have scamps?)

She told me about a prison in Huntsville, Texas, where the inmates – some of them serial killers and child molesters – got to compete in an annual rodeo.

"Is that it?" I asked.

"That's it."

"It's a nice concept," I said, though it hadn't yet reached the level of a concept. "Let me think about it."

The agent Robert Lantz called the next day and said that Hannah enjoyed meeting me.

"And she thought you were very handsome."

"She did?" I said. "Why that little scamp. But all right, tell her
I'll do the movie."

And then I forgot about it.

A month later, I received a call from David Chasman, an agitated Columbia Pictures executive.

"We have an empty lot here. We've signed Gene Wilder and
Richard Pryor. I know it doesn't come out of a faucet, but where is
the goddamned screenplay?"

"Oh, that," I said. "Well, just relax. I have it in hand."

Then I panicked. Apparently, I'd accepted some money from
the studio and I didn't have a thought in my head.

My friend Jacques Levy, a theater director and former psychol-
ogist, told me the best idea in a troubled circumstance is to take a
walk. So I took one. I passed a bank on Fifth Avenue and saw two
actors singing and dancing in front of a small gathering. They had
been hired to entertain passersby as a means of encouraging them
to open a checking account. (In a playful bank?) I thought that
might be a way to begin the movie. Have Wilder and Pryor play
out-of-work actors who travel South and get a similar job. Two
hoods steal their (chicken suit) costumes and rob the bank. The
actors are accused of the crime, taken into custody and given long
sentences in prison. One shows skills at riding bulls.

I told my idea to Chasman.

"That's fine," he said. "But it's two minutes of screen time. We
need the whole movie."

I told him I was just about to wrap it up, but for authenticity, I
needed to visit the Texas prison.

He arranged for me to do so. I received full access to the facility and the prisoners and got to meet ex-inmates in Houston who
were able to speak freely. The power of the studios. The director
Sidney Poitier accompanied me on a walk through the grounds. A
black lifer, who was scrubbing the floors of a false teeth factory,
saw the director coming toward him and could not believe his
eyes. Poitier, for many years, had been the only black film star of
any consequence. The man, who must have been ninety, got off his

knees, as if for the first time, and whispered, "Hallelujah." He might have been staring at Moses reborn. Later in the day, Poitier complained to me about the price of fame: there wasn't a place in the world he could go and not be recognized. How fortunate I was that no one knew who I was. (A nobody?) I wondered if he would want to trade places.

The prisoners made their own clothing and had a garden in which they grew their own food and then cooked it. I had never tasted such delicious vegetables and asked the warden if I could take some back to my hotel. (He arranged for me to have a container of them.) At one point, I saw a huge inmate being led through the grounds by a small cortège of guards. Apparently, he was so violent that it took an entire team to keep him under control. I used him in the film as a model for the character Grossberger. In real life, he was a Jewish axe murderer. Score one, in a sense, for the Jews, who are always in need of heroes.

I mailed off the screenplay and had no idea if the film would be made. On an earlier trip to Hollywood, the producer Ray Stark had approached me and James Baldwin in the Columbia Pictures commissary.

"Boys," he said, with what can only be described as a shit-eating grin. "You both have interesting projects. I certainly do hope the cameras roll."

Translation: There isn't a chance in hell that this will happen.

Until then, I thought people only spoke that way in a mini-series.

The cameras did not roll on either project, *Your Basic Lousy Marriage*, or Baldwin's screenplay version of *Malcolm X* – until much later. They rolled almost immediately on *Stir Crazy*.

Gene Wilder, who had read and enjoyed my novels, wondered how he ought to approach his character. I told him to think *Candide*. In the prison yard, his character marvels at a sculpture and asks the guard:

"Is that a Kandinsky?"

The guard's response is to hit him with a rifle butt.

I visited the set only once and saw Wilder pat a mechanical bull on the head before mounting it and whisper "Nice horsey" into its ear. I did not write "Nice horsey." Nor would I ever write "Nice horsey." Bed-wetters say "Nice horsey." I started to walk off the set and was stopped by Richard Pryor. Early on, he had asked the producer: "Is Friedman black?"

"I never met a writer like you," he said. "Take the money. Don't take no shit. I have fifty in cash. I might just do the same."

He had sensed that I was upset and turned the situation around to make it a victory for me.

We walked toward his trailer.

"Ever get high?" he asked.

"There was one time," I said, borrowing some dialogue from the film. "It was in the spring of '57. It was a very good year."

Then I gave him three reasons why there were no (or very few) Jewish junkies.

• Jews need eight hours of sleep.
• They must have fresh orange juice in the morning.
• They have to read the entire *N.Y. Times*.

"Ergo. No Jewish junkies."

Undeterred, he led me into his trailer. It was filled with wicks and pipes and odd-looking vials and jars. I was no stranger to drugs, but this was a different world. The air was thick. I had a feeling that if I lit a match, we would both go up in flames. And several weeks later, he did. And miraculously recovered and based a stand-up routine on the experience.

We were saved for the moment by Hannah Weinstein. He was terrified of this tiny woman, who treated him like a loveable but occasionally unruly son.

"Oh, Jesus," he said. "It's Mrs. Weinstein. You (Uncle) Tom her while I get rid of this shit."

He started to shove all the paraphernalia under a bed.

She stood outside the trailer and said sweetly, "Richard, are you all right?"

"I'm fine, Mrs. Weinstein."

"Good. And can we expect you on the set tomorrow morning, all refreshed and ready to go?"

"Of course, Mrs. Weinstein. I'll be there bright and early."

Soon afterward, he disappeared for a few days.

What struck me about his performance in the finished movie is that he didn't change a syllable of the dialogue as written. It was hardly scripture, but he treated it as such. Wilder, who thought of himself as a writer, used the dialogue as a jumping-off point. As far as he was concerned, the trinity was Faulkner, Fitzgerald and Gene Wilder. Ironically, it was Pryor who was considered the wild man.

A rough cut of the film was shown in Manhattan to a group of ex-prisoners who were in a recovery program called The Fortune Society. Poitier saw me coming and crouched down as if protecting his back.

"You're going to stab me, aren't you, Bruce?"

"No, no, Sidney. I enjoyed the movie."

Which I had. I liked it, but I didn't love it. After seeing it several times, in the years that followed, I started to like it a lot more.

There was a small riot that night. The recovering prisoners had not quite recovered yet. Lillian Hellman was in the audience. Her eyesight was failing and she could not find the ladies' room. Pat, who was in awe of her, offered to help out. When they returned, Hellman thanked my wife.

"Think nothing of it," Pat said.

And then she added a comment that became a favorite of mine.

"It was the least I could do." (. . . 'the least I could do, Mr. Einstein, for your Unified Field Theory of the Universe . . .')

"And you wrote the movie, didn't you?" she said to Pat.

Hellman had given Dashiell Hammett more than a little help on his work. She assumed it always worked that way. And there was enough truth in the remark to make me squirm a bit.

Later, we went off to Hannah's new apartment to celebrate Richard Pryor's birthday. We were joined by Patti LaBelle, Mary Tyler Moore, and Warren Beatty, who seemed to be everywhere.

When a cake was brought out, LaBelle sang "Happy Birthday" a capella and full out, as if she was performing at Carnegie Hall. Richard hung his head. It was wonderful and embarrassing and moving.

Still, I was uneasy about the film. How would it be received? The comedy seemed so broad on the screen – much more so than on the page. I enjoy broad comedy, as long as I'm not responsible for it.

I was already making up excuses.

"I'm a novelist. This is just something I do once in a while . . . to pick up a check . . . and to get out of the house."

One of Poitier's friends was reassuring. A slender black man in a pin-striped suit, he punched me lightly on the shoulder and said: "Right on time, brother." (An old railroad expression.)

Stir Crazy became the biggest-grossing comedy – at the time – in Columbia Pictures history.

This, of course, should have been an exhilarating time for me. To have written a blockbuster movie was every screenwriter's dream. Except that I was not a screenwriter. And somehow this reduced my claim to being a serious novelist. So naturally, I was depressed. And not just because I'm Jewish.

The agent Robert Lantz called in a state of high excitement.

"I *told* them that you had broad appeal and that you were more than just a cult-writer. But they wouldn't listen."

Who had he told such things? And why wouldn't they listen?

Actually, yet another Hollywod agent had introduced me as a writer with a cult-following.

I had to take him aside and tell him never to do that again. It would cut my price in half.

As for *Stir Crazy*, Lantz said: "You will make a million dollars."

"But will I be happy?"

"This I cannot assure you," he said.

Later that night, the producer Sidney Beckerman passed my table at Elaine's and said:

"You will never see a *dime*."

He made a mean and sadistic face when he said this. He was wrong. I did see a dime. Quite a few, actually.

A psychiatrist who had treated me briefly in Long Island stopped me on the street and said he had seen and loved the movie.

"This is a perfect time for you to go back into therapy."

I didn't see the connection. With a hit movie, why would I need more therapy? But just to make sure, I did go back for a few sessions.

A young lawyer and a movie fan – at Greenbaum, Wolff and Ernst – had been assigned to oversee my affairs. Looking up from a contract he said:

"Do you realize that at this moment you are the hottest screenwriter in Hollywood?"

The very thought sickened me. It was the last thing I wanted to hear, a total betrayal of my (serious writer) dreams. It was as if someone who aspired to be an NFL quarterback was told; "You are the finest bowler in Peoria, Illinois." Though offers to write movies began to pour in, I rushed back home and turned off the phone. A young film school graduate in 2010 would think I was committable. But this was another time. And in this area, I was a little on the rigid side. In the film I had written, Skip, the Gene Wilder character, at first declines to ride in the prison rodeo.

"Are you sure?" the Warden asks.

"Yes, sir," Skip replies. "I'm afraid I have only have one speed."

That was the author talking.

23

"Never get a disease with someone's name on it."
Mario Puzo, after learning that Joseph Heller had
come down with Guillain-Barre Syndrome.

I had always had a fantasy of living at the beach, or in the country, as a year-round resident, and not just vacationing for a week or two during the summer. Books, dogs, logs on the fire, solitude. At long last, A Writer's Life For Me. Pat had the same fantasy – or at least said she did. She enjoys books, devours them, often three a day. Although she does have a tendency to skip to the last pages – to make sure that none of the characters have been harmed. We moved to Long Island in 1982. A justice of the peace presided over our marriage in 1983.

Pat had found a friendly old barn for us in Water Mill, which is sort of a Hampton but isn't called one. No one knows quite what the boundaries are – it kind of drifts and floats. In terms of location, it can't quite be pinned down. For a sense of place, which I'm told is important for a novelist, I had to refer to Manhattan and my old neighborhood in the Bronx. All of which is by way of a limp explanation as to why – in the eighteen years we lived on the East End – I was never able to pull off the equivalent of *The Mill On the Floss*. (Joe Heller, who became a neighbor, would ask: "Who has?")

Writers and artists were drawn to the area. I missed out on meeting Truman Capote, but my old friend Irwin Shaw was there to greet me and took me off to eat his favorite dish, the fried oysters at Herb McCarthy's. He had left the area because of an anti-Semitic incident in Quogue. Now, decades later, he returned to a tightly controlled little cul-de-sac of half-a-dozen houses that smacked, frankly, of what Terry Southern called "anti-Sem." John Knowles, author of *A Separate Peace*, was a regular at Bobby Van's, the literary gathering place in Bridgehampton. Soon after I met him, and after a civilized moment or two, he inquired about my penis size.

Kurt Vonnegut had bought a house in the area. He'd been annoyed at me for mentioning him in the introduction to an anthology called "Black Humor" and, unforgiveably, not including one of his stories. I met him on the street in Bridgehampton.

"Can you teach me how to hang out?" he asked.

He was a shy man, but still, it seemed a strange question to be asking the author of *The Lonely Guy*. But apparently he thought of me as some kind of boulevardier. We became friends, although from time to time he would refer to me dismissively as "one of those script writers."

After we'd lived in Water Mill for some time, Joseph Heller came out from Manhattan to have dinner with us. He was recovering from Guillain-Barre Syndrome, having violated his friend Mario Puzo's dictum:

"Never get a disease with somebody's name on it."

He'd recently been divorced. According to his confidant Speed Vogel, co-author of *No Laughing Matter*, when Heller's wife asked why he was leaving he replied:

"It is because you are old and fat and ugly."

Anyone who doubts this needs only to refer to the narrator of *Something Happened*, the novel he considered his best. I felt it was a masterpiece, although as a 500-page harangue (kvetch) it had no *right* to be one – but it was.

We served mako-shark for dinner. It had been caught that morning off the coast of Montauk and was a novelty at the time. After one bite, Heller made a comment in the manner of his stylistic opposite Ernest Hemingway:

"This is a good fish."

A short time later, he bought a house in East Hampton and behaved as if he had been a long-time resident. Soon after he unpacked, he called me and said "I can get you invited to *good* parties," implying that until his arrival I had been attending only shabby little wine-and-cheese affairs. Though I came to love him, he could be infuriating.

Mario Puzo began to show up. Though he lived in baronial splendor in Bay Shore, he bought what he called a "throwaway" house, alongside Route 27 in chic and fashionable East Hampton. He would look out the window and watch the traffic whiz by.

"It reminds me of Eastern Parkway in Brooklyn."

We scheduled a regular lunch at Bobby Van's, then switched to Barrister's in Southampton where the waitresses were prettier. The core group was made up of Puzo, Heller, Speed Vogel, Mel Brooks, when he was in the area, and the screenwriter David Zelag Goodman.

From time to time we thought of inviting others to join us. I proposed the novelist James Salter.

Puzo objected. "He is too good a writer."

There was a feeling that the novelist William Gaddis would fit in. A gentleman of the old school, he was the winner of the MacArthur Genius award. I'd met him several times. The man who had been compared to Melville and Joyce wanted to talk only of how to break into movies. But he did wonder why I bothered to write short stories.

"Write novels," he advised me, "and throw it all in."

He wrote novels. And throw it all in he did.

There was some hesitation when it came to inviting him to join us. Some unease, and perhaps guilt. None of us had read his books.

A call was put through to Candida Donadio, who represented each of us and had been Gaddis' agent for five decades.

"Don't worry about it." she said. "No one has read his books."

(There is, incidentally, a typo on poor Gaddis' tombstone in East Hampton. His acclaimed novel, "The Recognitions," is chiseled in as "The Recongnitions.")

Heller vetoed Peter Matthiessen because of his continual reference to his membership in the Institute of Arts and Letters:

("As I was saying to my colleagues at the Institute of Arts and Letters . . .")

"It's an organization," said Puzo, "for guys who can't get screen deals."

We stayed with the core group, though George Plimpton would drop by now and then and treat us to an anecdote. (Robert Brown, a Samuel Johnson scholar, said that whenever George spotted a gathering of any kind he was unable to resist addressing it.) Plimpton told us one day he'd been playing tennis with George H.W. Bush at Camp David when the red phone went off, signalling that something horrible must have happened. Fearing the worst, the President dropped his racket and ran over to the netpost to pick up the receiver. After listening anxiously, he smiled and handed the receiver to Plimpton.

"It's for you, George."

Willie Morris would have been happily piped aboard, but he had recently fled to Mississippi as a result of a single remark made by a Southampton doyenne.

"Willie Morris? Oh yes, I remember. You never did pan out, did you?"

"Not to the unlettered," would have been an appropriate response. But before he had time to think of it, Morris was back home in the deep-South.

Almost without fail, a summer visitor would approach Puzo for an autograph, then ask if he had made up *The Godfather*, or did he have some connection to the mob. Puzo replied patiently, as he had all along, that he had read *The Valachi Papers*, and used

some characters and events from his childhood. The rest was
fiction.

"The closest I ever got to the Mafia was when I saw three
studio executives huddled together in the Warner Brothers
commissary."

Now and then I had some doubts about his purported innocence. A terrifying look would come over his face when someone
dared to suggest, as an example, that French cuisine was superior
to Italian food. Even *Northern* Italian food was suspect. Pavillon, at
the time, was considered the leading French restaurant in
Manhattan. Puzo dined there once. From then on, to show his contempt for the menu, he referred to the restaurant as *The Pavillyun*.
You would not want to hear him pronounce Anna Karenina (*Anna
Karaneeneeya*?).

One day he came running into Barrister's in a state of agitation
over an item he'd read in the press about a support group for sex
addicts.

"I can't believe it. Those people should get down on their
knees and thank God they have such an addiction."

When it came to sex, he was generationally trapped. To an
extent, all of us were.

"I picked up the phone by accident one day and overheard my
teenage daughter discussing boys with her friends. It took me
years to recover from what I heard."

I mentioned that I had read a letter to the editor of a popular
magazine in which the correspondent identified himself as a ter-
minally jealous lover. After years of anguish, he realized suddenly
that he had thrown away countless days and nights of his life, tortured by thoughts of what his lover did – or did not do – with her
genitals. Once he saw this clearly, his days of torment came to an
end.

Second-to-none as a jealous lover, Puzo said:

"That is the wisest and most useful insight I've ever heard."

As an afterthought, he said it puzzled him that vice was considered shameful.

"The only fun I ever had was with my vices."

Heller had learned that women now looked for mates – and offered their intimate services – in magazines. He claimed (you could never be sure in his case) that this was all new to him. I confirmed that it was true and referred him to the Personals in *New York* magazine. (The Internet was in its infancy.) A friend, who had been a long-time bachelor, found a woman in one such listing. He fell in love with her, got married and his once grim life became blissful. The sex was beyond anything he'd thought possible.

"What kind of women advertise?" Heller asked.

"All kinds."

"Girls with big bushes?"

"They have their own section."

Heller was delighted. In return, he told me about reduced rate bus passes for seniors in Manhattan. Though I didn't need one at the time, I thanked him. And that was our exchange. Big bushes for bus passes.

Goodman returned one afternoon from the West Coast with news of a victory. Sophia Loren was delighted with a screenplay he'd written for her.

"She was so pleased that she personally cooked a bowl of spaghetti for me."

Heller said: "It would be a better story if she gave you a blowjob."

Mel Brooks came by. He'd been pricing real estate in the area. After vigorously defending the grosses on his Dracula movie, he fell uncharacteristically silent and seemed to be humming to himself. We couldn't know it at the time, but he was composing the score of his landmark hit-musical *The Producers*. Soon after it opened, I saw the show and sent him the following telegram:

"I don't care what anyone says. I loved it."

The conversation, as it did now and then, turned to literature.

Puzo said: "I don't get this guy Borges."

But then he brightened a bit.

"I've figured out the reason for John Grisham's success. He writes so that a 10-year-old can understand him."

"I can't read light fiction," was Heller's response. "It's too heavy."

The 1984 Nobel Prize for literature was about to be announced. No matter how lowly a writer's standing, no matter how preposterous the thought, there is always a fleeting dream of winning the coveted award. On a fishing boat, off the coast of Iceland, I met an ancient poet with a long beard and the weary eyes of a prophet. He claimed to have read my books.

"You are in contention for the prize," he told me. "I have influence with the judges. I'll speak on your behalf, but there is one condition."

The story was absurd. Still, such was my ego that I showed interest.

"What's that?" I asked,

"You must arrange a meeting for me with Michael Ovitz."

(Ovitz, at the time, was the chairman of CAA, the most powerful entertainment agency in Hollywood.)

Who knew that there were Nobel Prize hustlers.

Heller felt he was a shoo-in for the prize. His novel, *Catch-22*, had been awarded the Number Seven position on the *N.Y. Times* list of the *One Hundred Greatest Novels of the Twentieth Century.*

"I should have been Number One," he said. "And let's not forget, I'm the only *living* novelist on the list. As for the Nobel this year, it's definitely me, although Gore (Vidal) has a slight chance."

The winner that year was Jaroslav Seifert, a relatively obscure Czech poet.

Puzo returned from California one day and joined us, as mystified as ever by the ways of Hollywood. The producer Bob Evans had spotted him at the Polo Lounge of the Beverly Hills Hotel and said: "Mario. What a wonderful coincidence. I've been looking all over for you."

On the spot, he offered Puzo a million dollars to write *The Cotton Club.*

Said Puzo: "If you're interested in writing for the movies, you have to *be* in Hollywood. If I hadn't run into him that day, I would never have heard from the man."

They went to work on the screenplay. At one point, Evans said:

"And here the sidewalk explodes."

"Why is that?" Puzo asked, a reasonable question, since there had been no build-up to the scene, and no particular need for it.

"Because it just does," said Evans.

"And that was the end of it," said Puzo. "He was the producer. And for all I know, he may have been right."

(Though Puzo was given a screenplay credit, not a single word he had written was spoken on the screen.)

Some years before in 1972, soon after the release of the first *Godfather* film, the press had been filled with accounts of Puzo's dust-up with Frank Sinatra. There were many versions of the encounter. We'd never before heard Puzo speak about it.

It was no secret that there was bad blood between the two. The singer was reported to be infuriated that the character of Johnny Fontaine in *The Godfather* had been modeled after him. He was further offended when the role in the movie was offered to another actor. Puzo was dining at a restaurant in Santa Monica and spotted the crooner at another table. To impress the woman he was with he decided to approach Sinatra and perhaps smooth things over.

"Maybe I was showing off a little, but I saw instantly that I had made a mistake. He was surrounded by bodyguards with big necks. Just in case, I picked up a fork and put it in my pocket."

He introduced himself. Sinatra cursed at him for what seemed like five minutes, using every foul expression in the language.

"I said nothing in response, though I noticed that he stared straight ahead and never once looked me in the eye. And I was amused. The idea of a Northern Italian daring to threaten a man from the South was laughable.

"Still, I was happy that I had brought along the fork."

At Barrister's I asked the waitress for a cup of decaf coffee. Heller, our health-expert, canceled the order.

"There's more caffeine in de-caf than there is in regular coffee. And make sure you drink a lot of water after a meal, in case you get itches."

I appreciated his concern. Puzo wasn't surprised.

"That Guillain made Joe a much nicer guy."

Mario's eldest son Tony came to pick up his father. Like a wheelman, he always waited outside in the car, sometimes in the bitter cold. He thanked the group for "taking care of Mario."

All five Puzo children referred to their father as "Mario."

Puzo signalled an end to the gathering. He'd always been concerned about his smile, thinking it wasn't charming enough. I'd seen him practicing variations in a mirror. But his concluding statement was made with a wolfish lear:

"Gentlemen. We are old. And we are going to die."

There was silence in the restaurant. It was as if everyone at Barrister's had heard him.

As the youngest member of the group, I asked for a temporary dispensation.

Mario nodded his approval.

Heller said "Forget it."

Then Puzo said to Speed Vogel: "It's still early. Let's go shoot some golf."

"No, no, Mario, you shoot pool. You *play* golf."

Mario's style was infectious.

That night I spoke to Pat in the style of a Don.

"It is my wish that we have lamb chops for dinner."

And to my young daughter: "You have dishonored me by not making your bed."

24

"You are a perfect candidate for hair transplants."
> Tony Curtis's first remark, upon meeting the author and agreeing to play the lead in his play *Turtlenecks.*

To atone for my wastrel-ways in Hollywood, I began to write a novel in 1984. Japan had always fascinated me. I had read a great many Japanese novels, with a particular focus on the books of Tanizaki and Kawabata. It was my idea to set the new book in Japan. All seemed pure and serene there. I thought of Japan as a nation of Lonely Guys, which would be right up my alley. Before visiting the country, I planned to find out all I could about Japan and then make the trip – even though Oscar Wilde insisted there was no such country. ("The whole of Japan is a pure invention.") I became a regular customer at Kinokuniya, a Japanese book store in midtown Manhattan. Once a week, I would load up with books on Japanese history and culture and bring them back to Water Mill. I worked in a little shack next to our barn. It was filled, floor to ceiling, with books about Japan. I had street maps of Tokyo pasted to the wall. Every now and then these days, I stare at my computer in wonder. Everything I needed to know at the time could have been accomplished with a few clicks. But as with many of us, I worked on a Royal typewriter. Only Joseph Heller used a computer. He was forced to because the Guillain-Barre disease meant he could only apply a light touch to the keyboard.

Pat was pregnant. She came into the shack one morning, tapped me on the shoulder and said she had gotten the results of an amniocentesis.

I said that was fine, but I was busy boning-up on the Meiji Restoration.

"All I know so far is that it was 'enlightened.' I need a little more before I can run with it."

"The baby has female chromosomes."

She said it with the little smile that had put an end to my life as a bachelor. Puzo had called her "the girl with the laughing eyes."

I was stunned by the news and forgot about the Meiji Restoration. The Meiji Restoration could wait. I had three sons and had assumed the next child would be a boy as well. There were boys in my family as far back as the genealogy could stretch. Pat wanted a child. I loved her. Fine with me. Put another one on the team. *But a girl?* I had no idea I could contribute to such a child. I jumped up and hit the ceiling and never came down. (Well, maybe a few times – in her teens and during the current recession.)

There was no way I could take off for Japan and leave Pat in this condition. I decided to wait until we had the baby. Then I would head for the airport. Lamaze was in vogue at the time. I enrolled in the program and was assigned the part of a vulva.

I saw no harm in *starting* the novel. It would give me a jump on writing the whole book. I knew what a Japanese airliner was like. And I had read a hundred descriptions of Mount Fuji. It was easy enough to imagine my hero, Mike Halsey, befriending a Japanese passenger, and the fellow inviting Mike to stay at his home – rather than one of those cramped "cigarette" hotels. And no one could describe the interior of a Japanese apartment better than I could. The shoji screens, that kind of thing. So I wrote all that and kept going, and before I knew it, my daughter Molly was on board and I was finished with the novel. Much as I had admired Japan from afar – there was no need actually to visit the country. At least, not at the moment.

Donald Fine was my publisher at the time. We had a mild disagreement over a chapter I'd written about a Penis Parade on the remote island of Hokkaido, one in which a long line of penis worshippers and enthusiasts carry penis replicas aloft (with anti-penis protesters harassing them along the way). Donald had a fastidious (prissy?) side and wanted it removed. I insisted there was such a parade. My orthodontist, who had served in the occupation army following World War II, had observed such a spectacle on the island of Hokkaido. Fine said all right then, as long as my orthodontist could testify that he saw such a thing, that was good enough for him.

The book was published in 1985 as *Tokyo Woes* and received more than seventy-five reviews, which was not considered a great number at the time. (Now it is.) Most were favorable. What amused me is that not a single reviewer guessed that the author had never been to Japan. That included Michiko Kakutani of the *Times*, who liked the book and who is Japanese-American. One television interviewer in the MidWest was closing in on me, but I was able to escape before I was unmasked.

David Letterman had asked me to appear on his show in full Samurai costume and to go hissing about the stage making warrior-like gestures. I had always held up the novelist William Styron as a model of correct (literary) demeanor. In such situations, I asked myself: What would *Styron* do? (With Styron gone, I now rely on James Salter.) I decided Styron would politely decline. Not serious enough. I declined as well. (And who knows, had it been offered to him, Styron might have jumped at the chance.)

An executive at American Airlines learned that I had written an entire novel about Japan and had never visited the country. He arranged for me to fly to Japan and write a story for his in-flight magazine, comparing my imagined version of the country to the real thing. After two weeks in Japan, I decided that my version was the accurate one.

Soon after the publication of *Tokyo Woes*, I decided that I wanted to write a play. I still hadn't made up my mind as to whether I wanted to be a playwright or novelist (or journalist or actor, for that matter.) Why not try them all? There was no law against it. Then, too, life in Water Mill, for all of the fresh air and pristine landscape, could be confining. Puzo had called writing "a monk's life." But even monks get restless and need to get out and about and, in my case, to be with other people such as pretty girls and the like. Which is why theater was born.

And I imagine I missed being roughed-up by the theater, which in most cases was inevitable. My last experience with the stage had been a train wreck. I had written a play called *Turtlenecks* which was produced by David Merrick and tried out at the Fisher theater in Detroit. It was a small play. Watching it in the 2000-seat emporium was like sitting off in the distance and peering at a postage stamp. The central character creates half-time shows for the National Football League and suspects – and fears – in his middle age that he might be gay. (This was before gay-themed plays virtually took over the theater.) Tony Curtis was cast in the lead role. The ingénue was played by an actress who had been spotted by Jacques Levy, the director, in a toothpaste commercial.

When I met Curtis, his first remark to me was:

"I've never seen anything like it. You are a perfect candidate for hair transplants."

He then asked me to shake hands and promise that we would do the play as written and not a word would be changed. I agreed, although I knew this was impossible. "Plays are not written, they are re-written." So says a plaque above the desk of the great theater coach Wynn Handman. Still, Curtis was a star and I did not want him to walk out before we began. He confided in me that he only wore a certain type of underwear that had to be shipped to him from Sweden. I had no idea why he told me that. He hadn't worked in the theater for decades. He may have felt that as the playwright it was my responsibility to replenish his underwear supply. It's possible that writers were assigned that function in Hollywood. We had lunch. He had the most unusual way of telling a story. If it concerned a man who had dropped a veal cutlet on the floor, Curtis would – by way of illustration – drop an actual veal cutlet on the floor, and let it lie there. My guess is that – as a film star – there would always be a lackey around to pick up veal cutlets that had, in the telling of anecdotes, been thrown on the floor. Though the producer David Merrick was generous, there was so such individual provided for in the budget.

As the previews were about to begin, Merrick called me into his office for a meeting. He was unhappy about Curtis' co-star, William Devane.

"Audiences do not like William *Doo*vane," he said. (His pronunciation.)

He turned to his lovely wife.

"Do they, Etan?"

"No, they do not, David."

"See that, Bruce," he said.

I said I felt Devane was brilliant.

"And we can't fire him. We'll lose the director, who thinks that Devane is the only one who can do the part."

Merrick let that sit for a moment.

Then he asked: "What's the play about, Bruce?"

"It's about a middle-aged man who produces half-time shows and fears that he might be gay."

"I won't do a gay show, Bruce."

"But you optioned the play, David. There are two thousand people waiting to see it in Detroit."

Then I reminded him that the last half-a-dozen shows he produced had gay themes. Among them, *A Patriot For Me*; *Norman, Is That You?*; and *Sugar*, a cross-dressing musical based on the film *Some Like It Hot*.

"Those were different, Bruce. There will be no gay shows for me."

I appealed to a reasonable side of him, which was, of course, nonexistent.

"Surely, David, at some point in your life you've had a homosexual fantasy. Every man has."

"Well, *I* haven't, have I, Etan?"

"No, you haven't, David."

"There you are, Bruce."

After a moment's reflection, he said: "Can we say the play is about 'Entertainment'?"

"I suppose we could do that."

"Then let's open the sonofabitch."

The director, Jacques Levy, had developed an affection for marijuana and smoked it all day long. As a result, his pacing, crisp in the past, had become a bit sluggish. Merrick's motto had always been:

"If it's a comedy, I want them back in the car in ninety minutes."

The play, as it stood, ran for around five-and-a-half hours. Merrick was furious.

"For God's sakes, Bruce, the ushers can cut the damned thing."

He wanted to fire Levy, but this was impossible. In a weak moment, and out of friendship, I had agreed to give him half the author's credit. (He had always yearned to be an author.) In return, I was awarded half the director's credit, which was of no interest to me. We were joined at the hip. In order to fire Levy, David Merrick would also have to fire me. Which would have left him with nothing but a gay-themed play that he pretended was about entertainment.

In addition, Curtis had difficulty with his voice. In films he could speak at a conversational level. In the theater, he would have to project and he could not be heard beyond the second row. With a mic, the sound was dreadful. Levy had called him "a hoarse *latke*." As a result, the show continued in Detroit and ended its "try-out" run in Philadelphia. We all went down together. And I was determined to do my next play in a cozy little three-hundred-seat theater where it belonged. And then move it to Broadway, no matter what my mother had said.

So there I was in lonely Water Mill, with a need to stretch my legs and make a triumphant return to the theater. Or a return, of some kind. *What if?* That question again. The most valuable one a storyteller can ask himself. So *what if* two friends, in some remote and abandoned resort area, (Montauk in the winter?) began to suspect that they were the last two Jews left in the world? And in the course of the first act, this became established? The clues mount. The Carnegie Delicatessen doesn't answer. A Jewish lawyer doesn't return calls. Israel, they learn, has moved to Miami Beach. What are they to do? They are consigned to a Long Island version of Auschwitz in the second act.

This is the play I had. This is the play I wrote. It was called *Have You Spoken To Any Jews Lately?*

A co-producer of The American Jewish Theater loved it.

"Just what we've been looking for," he said. "An angry play."

His colleague was lukewarm. The AJT subscription audience was made up largely of Holocaust survivors. They wanted to see *Milk and Honey*, even though they'd seen it many times. Give them singing and dancing, preferably in Israel. Never mind about the last two Jews.

The passionate producer who had wanted an angry play died soon after. I was left with his partner, who had gone from lukewarm to ice-cold. (Vomiting, which occurred in each of my theater experiences, had begun earlier than usual.) He laid down a condition which he considered impossible to fulfill. There was only one director in the world he would consider: Michael Rudman, a Brit, a member of the Royal Shakespeare Academy and the husband of Felicity Kendal, a reigning goddess of the London theater. Only if Rudman agreed to direct would he produce the play.

Rudman loved it and agreed to fly to Manhattan immediately and direct the play. This was great news except that no one had ever told me about it. So he sat there at the phone in London, waiting to hear from me and calling "that sonofabitch" Friedman every name under the sun for making him suffer. Finally, I asked the theater agent if anyone had heard from Rudman.

"Oh, yes," I was told. "He called last month and said he loved the play and was anxious to direct it. He's been waiting to hear from you."

I called Rudman immediately. He said:

"Well . . . you're quite the little prick, aren't you."

I explained that no one had told me of his interest. Not for a second did he believe me. (We became friends. Years have passed, and he *still* doesn't believe me.) Nonetheless, Rudman agreed to fly over and begin casting. My next concern was the theater. It was a sweet little space, but it was no Helen Hayes. Additionally, it sat beside a supermarket. The rasping sound of shopping carts could be heard through the walls. As a Royal Shakespeare man, would he take one look at our modest little theater and take the next plane back to London?

The first day of casting, he arrived before I did. When I got there, he was sitting beneath a single light bulb in the darkened little semi-circle of a stage, with a pile of notes on his lap.

He said: "This is quite the loveliest space I've ever seen."

I was moved, and even more so when he added:

"There will be no squabbling beween us over actresses, Bruce. They all belong to the playwright. I've held to that in each of my productions."

Though I was not on the prowl for actresses, I had noticed several of them, waiting to audition. And I was, as I said, moved.

We began casting. I'd arrived in a driving rain, wearing sneakers. My socks were soaking wet.

"You'll have to excuse me, Michael. I need to run out and find a dry pair."

He reacted as if this was the most outrageous statement he'd ever heard.

"We're about to begin casting your precious play, the actors, with limited time, are waiting to audition, and you're concerned about your bloody *socks*?"

Apparently such behavior was unheard of in Royal Shakespeare productions.

I mumbled something about grandmothers in the Bronx who warned boys about wet socks and the risk of pneumonia. Rudman, having survived The Blitz, was unimpressed. And so I soldiered on, wet feet and all, unable fully to concentrate on the casting. It's entirely possible we might have had a different set of actors if my feet had been dry. As it was, we ended up with a good selection.

Yet even with his coveted Rudman on board, the lukewarm producer kept us twirling about in doubt as to whether he would allow the play to open.

"Either I take another valium," I told Rudman, after one confrontation, "or I strangle the little shit."

"Take the valium," said Rudman who had been through many a backstage war.

In his defense, the producer claimed that after a first preview, some of his Holocaust subscription people, expecting to see Jews joyously singing and dancing, were outraged.

"They tore up their season tickets and threw them in my face."

After the final preview, the producer decided not to open the play after all. All that work. Up in smoke. I was fully prepared to slaughter him and spend my life on Riker's Island. (Assuming I would be allowed a pen and writing paper.)

The producer placed great stock in the opinion of the playwright Jack Gelber and had invited him to the final preview:

"Open it," he said. "You will do well."

Gelber took me aside:

"And I finally figured out what you are. You're a spritzer."

A spritzer, as I understood it, is a house entertainer who "spritzes" (sprays) one-liners at the guests of hotels in the

Catskills. It wasn't quite the way I saw myself, but if that's what he thought I was, it was fine with me. The play would open. And Gelber became my hero. I began to like one of his early plays that I hadn't much cared for.

Vincent Canby, writing in the *Times*, was ecstatic about what he called a "fever dream" of a play. Never mind that he'd been unenthusiastic about *Stir Crazy*. The play was a sell out for its (unfortunately) limited run. My brother-in-law, who is in finance, brought a colleague to see a performance. He fell in love with the play and offered to write out a check and move it, cast, sets and all, to another theater. The producer, who had never before had a major review in the *Times*, refused to let this happen. He was still upset about his Holocaust subscription people throwing tickets in his face. Nonetheless, I declared the experience a successful one and went off happily to Water Mill. The first one to comment was a gas station attendant who sneered in at me through the driver's window and said: "Have you spoken to any *Jewzzzz* lately?"

Welcome home.

Two productions of the play followed. One was produced and directed by a mailman. I thought that was charming. A man who delivered the mail and had his own theater company. The production was insufferable. An actor-friend said:

"What did you expect? The guy is a mailman."

Another unsettling note was to follow. A hopeless Anglophile, I'd always (snobbishly) longed to work with a British director. Rudman, for all of his Royal Shakespeare background – and his Noel Coward accent – turned out to have been born in Houston, the son of a Texas oilman. So I had my British director – but with an asterisk.

25

"Would you mind exchanging my meat for your vegetables?" . . .
The Nobelist Isaac Bashevis Singer to the author,
who was expecting a disquisition on Spinoza.

The trick to living year-round in Water Mill is to get out of there whenever possible. I had the trips to the Coast, and for the family, there was Sanibel in the winter, on the West Coast of Florida. The "Redneck Riviera" was seashells and more seashells and silence after ten at night. Even Molly, at nine, grew weary of this. And then along came Miami. The city, which had long been slumbering, was suddenly, in the early nineties, alive, rested and vibrant with life. Sweeping out of the driveway of the Alexander Hotel at night, in search of adventure, was every bit (well, almost) as exciting as sailing out of the Beverly Hills Hotel and onto Sunset Boulevard in Hollywood. I began to think of moving the family to Miami permanently until a friend in the fashion industry raised an eye-brow and said: "Rollerblades, Bruce?"

Still, it was Miami every winter, where the models were as tall and striking as the actresses in Hollywood and everyone seemed to be a rogue of some kind, escaping from a dark past – a perfect stewpot for a writer, as the novelist Carl Hiaasen would be the first to acknowledge. For company, there was Dan Wakefield, a favorite novelist (*Going All The Way*) who taught a heavily-subscribed course at F.I.U. based on his book *New York In the Fifties*. He had shoehorned me into the book, even though I was off in Missouri when everyone from the MidWest was discovering the wonders of Greenwich Village. Also in residence was Tom Harris (*The Silence of the Lambs*), who had left the Hamptons and bought a palatial home on the Gold Coast of Miami (I like to think at my urging). Shy and reclusive, he was the most affable of men. "Courtly" was a description that suited him. Still, having read his books, it was discomfiting to see him eat a bowl of clams linguini and then lick his (plump) glistening fingers. Once he'd become a Miami resident, he took great pride in introducing me to a favorite restaurant, Miyako's, on Washington Avenue. I had eaten there several times, but decided not to mention it. Why spoil his pleasure? Still, when we walked in, the captain's greeting was embarrassing.

"Mr. Friedman, how nice to have you back."

I was delighted, perhaps by way of small compensation, to tell Harris that Mario Puzo was one of his biggest fans.

"That Lecter character? He should take those publishers for every penny they've got."

In later years, had I been in touch with Harris, I would have told him that Harris' *Hannibal* was the last book that Puzo read before he died.

"At the end of the novel, he tries something very daring," Mario had told me, "and just about pulls it off."

A few weeks, or a month in Miami, provided that perfect change in routine that a writer seems to require. No doubt accountants do as well. I completed several novels in Miami, and more than a few short stories. Always beckoning were the sybaritic pleasures of South Beach. I played tennis with a Brit who was able to beat me with sickening regularity. I had the feeling that if we played on into the next century I would never be able to win a single set. Too young, too strong. He did say, in admiration – and puzzlement:

"You're always around the ball, aren't you."

The trick, of course, was to know what to do with the ball once I was indeed around it.

On an impulse, I decided to make a literary pilgrimage to the Miami home of the late Isaac Bashevis Singer. It was my first literary pilgrimage. I'd driven past the home of Ernest Hemingway in Key West, but it was only because I was on my way to the zoo.

I knew Singer, though I can't say that we were buddies. He did not have buddies. If anything, he had "cronies." Most lived on upper Broadway in Manhattan or had been left behind in Cracow. Still, it intrigued me that he was the only Nobelist who had used his $250,000 in prize-money to buy a condo on Miami Beach. I needed to see that condo.

It did not take much effort. Drive north on Collins Avenue. Keep an eye out for "Isaac Bashevis Singer Boulevard."

It was my mother, in the early fifties, who had first called my attention to Singer. He had been a speaker at her temple, the Young Israel of the Concourse in the Bronx. I don't recall her ever being so taken with a writer, or at least the physical presence of one. Normally, it was stage people who had that effect on her. (Maurice Evans, the Lunts, Gertrude "Gertie" Lawrence.)

"He was as big as a second," she reported, "and he didn't have a hair on his head. But he had the most beautiful eyes, and he could undress you with a single look. We gave him fifty dollars. He was tickled to death and never stopped thanking us."

I met Singer a decade later at a University of North Carolina Symposium sponsored by *Esquire* magazine. The theme was "The Novelist as Journalist" or "The Journalist as Novelist." I'm not clear on that. I do recall that "The New Journalism" was much in the air. I now see it as a category designed to make journalists feel better about themselves. Half-a-dozen of us, including Jack Richardson and Norman Podhoretz, editor of *Commentary*, flew down from New York City. Podhoretz took one look at the campus and the pretty co-eds, and remarked (more or less) famously:

"*Another* college where I won't get laid."

Singer came down by bus, a small, somewhat frail-looking man who seemed never to have been exposed to the sun. My first impulse was to rush forward and put a protective arm around him, as if he were a Holocaust victim – a wildly misguided notion if ever there was one. Fortunately, Richardson restrained me.

"For God's sakes, the man's as strong as an ox – and he's never been near a concentration camp. He's a notorious boulevardier."

The thrust of my talk – I was the first speaker – is that I wanted always to be placed at the center of events. ("Action, action, give me action.") Richardson followed and asked some phantom body (the fates?) that he be permitted to do his work. ("Let me write.") We became good friends and in the years that followed teased each other about our passionate *cries des coeurs*, which somehow don't seem as absurd now as they did then. I was seated opposite Singer at the mid-day lunch break, aware at this point of his growing reputation, and properly in awe of him. When he leaned forward in my direction, I waited apprehensively, expecting some Spinoza-like insight or observation.

"Mr. Friedman," he said, "would you mind exchanging my meat for your vegetables?"

Later, Singer was to say of Spinoza:

"A brilliant man. I agreed with half of what he wrote."

He charmed the audience a bit later on with the story of a staff writer for the *Jewish Daily Forward* who was a shameless plagiarist, but one with a difference: he always added a personal touch to his thievery. In one article, which dealt with the composition of the sun, the writer copied the following word-for-word from a major publication:

"At its center, the sun is twenty million degrees centigrade."

Then he added a touch of his own.

"And there the heat is unbearable."

Singer held forth as well on a favorite – and for him, an exasperating – topic: translation.

"If you're going to be translated, you have to be one hundred and fifty percent good, because at least fifty percent will be lost."

As for Franz Kafka:

"I admired him, but one Kafka every century is enough."

Singer spoke of a fellow writer who – along with his mistress – barely escaped Hitler and the Gestapo and made his way to London, only to remember that he'd left the manuscript of his new novel behind in a Berlin apartment.

"Not to fear," his mistress said. "I will retrieve it for you."

She made her way through the German lines, evaded the Gestapo, returned to a burning apartment building and plucked the pages from the flames. After another nightmarish journey, she reached London, starved and bedraggled. Expecting gratitude, she handed her lover the precious pages.

Waving her off, he said: "You didn't do me such a favor. I found another copy."

As a speaker, you did not want to follow Isaac Singer.

That evening, at a cocktail party, I asked him if there were any contemporary writers he admired.

"I don't read the moderns," he said, "only the classics."

The comment came across as being elitist, but seems less so to me now as time begins to peter out. Saul Bellow, incidentally, who was entering his sixties, was considered by Singer to be a 'modern.' It was Bellow's translation of Singer's "Gimpel the Fool" that was credited with introducing Singer to an American audience.

"To be honest with you," he said, "the translation wasn't so terrific."

Nor was he delighted by Barbra Streisand's film version of *Yentl*.

"Why was it necessary to make Yentl, whose greatest passion was the Torah, go on a ship to America, singing at the top of her lungs?"

He was skeptical, generally, of turning stories into film.

"As my Aunt, also named Yentl, used to say to my Uncle Joseph, 'In a pinch, I can make from a chicken soup a borscht, but to make from a borscht a chicken soup, this is beyond any cook.'"

As he listed his complaints, I could hear Richard Pryor, whispering in the background: "Did you take the money?"

Later in the evening, this great man approached me with a modesty and shyness that was almost painful to observe.

"Tell me, Mr. Friedman, do you know of a place in Manhattan.... maybe a restaurant ... where I could be with writers?"

What I felt he had in mind was the equivalent of a coffee house in Cracow where bearded intellectuals debated free will and the pessimism of Schopenhauer. I thought of, but didn't mention, Elaine's in Manhattan, where writers did, indeed, gather, but rarely discussed serious matters, heatedly or otherwise. The topics were generally book advances and pretty girls; everyone, while drinking, kept an eye out for the latter.

As to Singer's inquiry, I didn't push too hard for him to try Elaine's, and I regret this. All that chatter about book advances, film sales – and a possibility, at the restaurant, of meeting pretty girls – that may have been exactly what he was looking for.

Richardson assuaged my guilt:

"If he'd ordered one of his vegetable platters, Elaine would have thrown him out on the street."

I met Singer again, in the mid-seventies, at the Sophomore Literary Festival, an annual event sponsored by the University of Notre Dame. Among those invited were Joyce Carol Oates and the actor and playwright Jason Miller (*The Championship Season*), who caused a stir by arriving, seriously in his cups, with a *Playboy* bunny on each arm. At a reception for the participants, I was introduced to Oates.

"Well, I'm not *funny*," she said with some pique, then disappeared in the crowd before I could respond. (What would my response have been? You're funnier than you think?) A bit later, she returned and apologized – I didn't think one was necessary – and said that with the publication of my novel *About Harry Towns* my writing had taken a turn for the better.

Each of us was given an evening to do a reading or some form of literary presentation to the students and faculty. Out of laziness, or perhaps intimidated by the Jesuits, I ran a tape of the PBS production of my play *Steambath,* and lurked in the background while it was being shown. Evidently, it had touched a chord in the Theology Department and resulted in my being invited to the festival. Singer and I sat together in the front row for a poetry reading by Joyce Carol Oates. When I remarked on how huge the turn-out was – people literally hanging from the rafters – Singer, the future Nobelist, shrugged and said: "Well . . . she has a name."

Halfway along in the program, he turned to me.

"So tell me, Mr. Friedman," he said, "why does she wear such a little skirt?"

It was always "Tell me, Mr. Friedman," as if he'd appointed me his guide to an alien culture.

In the years that followed, I was to run into Oates from time to time. She always seemed skittish when I was near her. My wife reminded me that a character in my novel, *A Father's Kisses*, wakes up terrified in the middle of the night. In the dream he's just had, he is locked in a library and all of the books have been written by Joyce Carol Oates. Still, for all of the teasing, I feel that some of her short stories, in particular, are among the best in the language. And there is no finer – and more generous – literary critic.

In an image I have of him, Singer sits alone in the Notre Dame cafeteria, and writes in a notebook, oblivious to the deafening lunchtime din and clatter of a huge student population. Sealed off from the world, he is, no doubt, pushing on with one of his celebrated stories. On upper Broadway in Manhattan, he was known always to be available to friends, relatives, strangers, baffled new immigrants, every sort of petitioner. He would listen patiently to their stories and grievances, perhaps comment, then put down the phone and get on seamlessly with his work – until the next call which he did not regard as an interruption. All of this seemingly a rebuke to writers who feel that for inspiration, it's essential to be in

St. Tropez, staring at the Mediterranean. Singer alone seemed to have the gift of working no matter what the circumstance, of canceling out the most clamorous environment. Or so I thought. Years later, I took some comfort in coming across a published interview in which he said (complained) that in his long years as a writer, he had never once found "a peaceful situation."

As to that moment I recall at Notre Dame – there is another possibility. (There is always another possibility.) It was no secret that he adored women. The list of his female translators seems to go on without end – Ruth Shachner Finkel, Mirra Ginsburg, Martha Glicklich. There was virtually a different one for each of his many stories. Predictably, he had charmed the female student body at Notre Dame. Does it reduce or increase his humanity to think that as he sat alone in the cafeteria, he was not – as I imagined – barreling ahead with the next *Spinoza of Market Street*, but scribbling down the names and numbers of fresh new translating prospects?

I kept in touch with Singer through his books and stories. My pattern was to read *The Magician of Lublin* or *A Crown of Feathers* then to forget it and to wander off, as if in search of a new literary romance. This would last until the next Singer arrived at the bookstores. And I would be seduced back into the fold. What remains with me is not any particular story or character – but a giant stewpot brimming over with knaves and scoundrels, innocents, schemers, the faithful and faithless, a great broth of humanity all of it stirred up with wonder and stubborn insight. I wondered why he hadn't written at any length about the Holocaust. In an interview he removed this concern with a single reference – to the Nazi officers who played croquet "with the skulls of Jewish babies."

Mario Puzo described the Canadian novelist Robertson Davies with a word out of children's books and not much in vogue now – "learned." Singer was a learned man. And there was the sheer volume of his work which was stupendous. Books and stories continuing to appear posthumously – with no reduction in quality – as if he were impishly tossing them down from on high.

Still, it would be a misrepresentation to say it was Singer's genius that sent me off on my first literary pilgrimage.

It was that condo he'd bought with his Nobel Prize money.

I was staying at the Alexander Hotel, a few miles south of my destination, so the whole pilgrimage business involved a drive of about fifteen minutes. Miami Beach – South Beach in particular – had just been rediscovered, but the rejuvenation process hadn't quite extended that far north on Collins Avenue. The area I drove through seemed generally to be in need of an overall paint job. I was disappointed when the Singer building did not stand out with any distinction along a strip of shabby and slightly forlorn high-rises. A saving grace is that the sun shines just as brilliantly and democratically on this section as it does on the sleek new hotels along pricier South Beach. A doorman confirmed that yes, indeed, I had come to the right address . . . and that I had just missed Mr. Singer's widow, Alma, who had gone up to her apartment. He arranged for me to speak to her on the intercom. While he rang upstairs, two women, neighbors of the Singers, who had overheard our brief conversation, joined me in the lobby.

"Izzy Singer?" said one. "Of course I knew him. He told stories at the synagogue that were filled with such *schmutz* it could make your hair stand on end."

"And he had a crony, too," said the other, "don't forget *him*. He had a mouth on him that was even worse than Izzy."

The doorman signalled to me that he had Mrs. Singer on the intercom. I told her that I was a writer and a great admirer of her late husband, and that I had gotten to know him at several literary gatherings.

"If it's not inconvenient, I was hoping I could come up and chat for a while."

I could barely make out her response. There was something about limos coming and going after her husband had won the

Nobel prize. As to the condo itself, it had not worked out as well as
they had wanted it to.

"In the last years, I couldn't do a thing with him here. We
should have stayed on upper Broadway."

And I had picked a poor time for a visit.

"Maybe tomorrow. I just came back from shopping and
frankly, my feet are killing me."

I said I'd call again, but I knew it was unlikely. No doubt it
says something about me that a quick look at the building and our
garbled conversation on the intercom was enough of an homage.
When I got back to my hotel, I decided, sacrificially, to forego the
fleshly pleasures of South Beach for an evening and to read the
posthumously published (and unfortunately titled) *Scum* – as satisfying a novel as any he'd written – and to go back once again, to
A Friend of Kafka, the collection that had always been a favorite.
And that was my pilgrimage.

26

"I didn't know you were a writer. But I loved your acting in 'Husbands and Wives.'"

> A young woman to the author, who had been expecting praise for one of his novels.

Mario Puzo pulled into the Barrister's parking lot in a Pontiac Grand Marquis, a car favored by the help in Southampton and the local police. I arrived in a BMW convertible I'd leased for the summer of '97. When Kurt Vonnegut saw me driving along Main Street, he had jumped up and down, shouting "I know that man."

I parked alongside Speed Vogel's Alfa Romeo. Mario took note – with envy – of Speed's car and mine.

"We're supposed to be rich," he said to Tony, his son and chauffeur, now fifty. "So how come I'm not allowed to have that kind of car?"

Inside the restaurant, he slipped a waitress a fifty and said:

"See to it that I am given the check."

There was a note in his voice indicating that something unfortunate might happen to her if she failed to follow his instructions. We joined Speed Vogel and David Zelag Goodman at our usual table. Heller hadn't yet arrived. Goodman reminded me of someone who should have been – but wasn't – one of the writers on *Casablanca*. He really *looked* like a screenwriter. The last time I saw him he was sniffing exotic fruit at the Farmer's Market in Beverly Hills. There are three signs that a screenwriter has achieved success in Hollywood. He carries only one hundred dollar bills, has a house with white floors and sniffs exotic fruit. Goodman took some pride in having written – and been paid handsomely – for seventeen straight unproduced screenplays.

Ever optimistic, he said: "I'm confident that the one I'm working on now is a winner."

He had maxed out his Writer's Guild pension at more than one hundred thousand dollars. (Per annum.)

Vogel took his hat off to Goodman.

"Now *that's* an achievement."

Puzo's health had been slipping. Doggedly, he put in what had become his standard order of 'runny eggs,' knowing that it would be rejected by the chef, who objected to a dish prepared in this manner.

"Maybe if you called them something else?" Vogel suggested. "'Softly scrambled,' for example. He probably doesn't care for the word 'runny.' Reminds him of a runny nose."

As it did me.

Puzo refused. The chef wouldn't budge. Never once did Puzo get what he'd ordered. True to form, the eggs were served well done, forcing him to nibble at everyone else's food.

Puzo, with the exception of my wife Pat, read more books than anyone I knew. I have a picture of him in my mind at lunch time, back at The Magazine Management Company, with half-a-dozen novels in his lap, taking little "tastes" of each one. Yet for all of his love of literature, he was not what you would think of as an "officially" cultured man. He had once told me of his single visit to the Guggenheim Museum.

"I checked out the first few paintings. Then I looked at some more. I started looking faster and faster until I was racing through the corridors. I could hardly wait to get the fuck out of there."

He had been up late the night before, wading through Norman Mailer's *Harlot's Ghost*.

"I was halfway finished with the book when I became aware of a heaviness on my chest. Surely, I was having another heart attack. I was about to call 9-1-1 when I realized it was the weight of the novel."

I asked him how he dealt with it.

"I cracked it in half."

It said something about him that he could read the work of a (literary) enemy. I could never do the same. Not that I can think of any I know of – but this has been costly.

Clearly, the long-time feud with Mailer was still simmering. I'd had a recent – and brief – chat with Mailer and found myself praising Mario's gift for storytelling.

Mailer shook his head sadly.

"If only I could write as poorly as he does."

The two had been having dinner at Elaine's one night, at separate tables, of course. Elaine, a large woman, daintily tiptoed over to each of the novelists and asked if they'd like to sit together at one table and have a nice chat. The reaction from both was chilling, even to the usually unflappable Elaine. She had brought lifelong enemies together in harmony. It was one of her strengths. And only once before had she failed miserably – when she tried to make peace between Puzo and Sinatra.

We noticed, at Barrister's, that Mario had lost some weight – in the nick of time, we all felt. More than once, after shoveling in a bowl of linguini, he had looked up at me and said:

"I take in a lot of pasta."

His look at those moments bordered on the ghoulish.

It was Weight Watchers, he claimed, that had saved his life.

"All of their dinner selections were so terrific that I ended up eating every one of them. It was only when I quit being a member that I started to get skinny."

The outfit Puzo wore – a handsome cream-colored blazer and well-tailored off-white slacks – was a far cry from the green velour "leisure suit" that was his gambling uniform in Las Vegas. I'd run into him one morning in the casino of the Sands Hotel, with a huge pile of hundred dollar chips folded up in the velour jacket. He was the picture of delight, like a child in a toystore. He had been playing blackjack all night. For him, Las Vegas – and not New York – was the city that never sleeps. A few hours later, I saw him again and the chips were gone, gambled away. Still, he was jolly as ever. I looked for him later and feared for my friend when I saw that he had a special section cordoned off for him to play baccarat. To further protect his privacy, he was referred to by the casino bosses as "Mr. P." He'd made huge "deposits" at the casinos. For all of his millions, he supported an army of relatives. And there were loans to his friends. With my back against the wall, I'd once borrowed ten thousand from him. He sent me a check immediately with a note attached that said:

"Your credit is still good."

I paid it back almost as soon as I cashed the check. John Bowers had worked beside him at The Magazine Management Company. When I told him about the loan, he said:

"You could have done much better. The going rate for a Puzo loan is twenty-five thousand."

Still, it bothered me that he might die penniless.

As for his nights at the casino, he told me not to be concerned.

"Gamblers like me always age out."

I had my doubts.

For all of his new finery at Barrister's, he still refused to wear socks. (As had Albert Einstein.) Bowers had once explained the phenomenon.

"It was too much of an effort to put them on. He could slip into his loafer shoes, but when he tried to put on socks, his belly kept getting in the way."

Puzo apologized for the sudden display of sartorial splendor, blaming it on Carol Gino, his new companion.

"She decided to doll me up."

Mario had lost his beloved wife, Erika. I have a memory of her in the Bay Shore kitchen, preparing the beef braciola of my dreams. In the background, Mario, in his undershirt, gently and patiently stirs a bowl of spaghetti. I understood that night why he had a low opinion of French cuisine.

In her last days, Carol had been Erika's nurse

I'd met her once before at – where else? – Elaine's.

"I'm really surprised," she had said to me. "I thought you'd be a much younger man. You look so much older than Mario."

For all of the convivial atmosphere, it was wise to watch your back at the restaurant. I was annoyed by the comment. Puzo was ten years my senior. I was tan and tennis-fit – or so I thought. Still, Puzo had chosen this woman who had a tough neighborhood style, as if she'd grown up with Mario on the streets of Hell's Kitchen. (In fairness – she also wrote bestselling paperback books.)

I smiled – or at least I think I smiled – and took on the lordly style of the Godfather himself.

"Mario, you will never have cause to doubt the loyalty of this woman."

Heller joined us at Barrister's. As he entered the busy restaurant, a waiter accidentally jostled him.

"For God's sakes," he said. "Watch what you're doing. Can't you see I'm a cripple?"

Recovering quickly, he headed for our table, pinching a few waitresses along the way. He didn't exactly grope women. He was the only one I knew who still "copped feels," as if he was back on the streets of Coney Island.

Puzo shook his head.

"Joe does not realize that he's old."

Heller had just been to the gym. Though no man hated exercise more than he did, he still showed up for an occasional workout. I'd seen him in action at the East Hampton Athletic Club, startling women who were on treadmills by puffing up his cheeks and blowing up his belly to balloon size. And that was his workout.

He vacuumed up a few courses – he had a ferocious appetite – took half of Speed Vogel's sandwich, then began in the needling style that was his trademark.

Pat and I had given a lawn party the night before – the first in the ten years since we had moved to the area. We had gone to great lengths to set out a sumptuous buffet table, with a particular emphasis on smoked fish, a Heller favorite.

"It was a nice party," he said, "but I notice you didn't serve sturgeon."

And, of course, with that unerring instinct, he'd hit a nerve. When the cost of the affair began to get out of hand, we'd cancelled sturgeon, (the caviar of smoked fish, and the most expensive).

Heller moved on to congratulate me for a particularly strong review I'd gotten on a short story collection. Then he struck.

"I know that reviewer. He loves everything. . . ."

Unlike the character in *Stir Crazy* who has only one speed, I had two: either violence or silence. When it came to a Heller attack, I chose the latter. For one thing, I was cowed by his literary eminence. Then, too, Heller was a Brooklyn person, which accounted, or so I felt, for a certain crassness. I thought, in my snobbery, that those of us in the Bronx, were more reserved – cut from finer cloth. This, of course, was absurd. There were more hit men born in the Bronx than in all the other boroughs combined. The fathers of my friends were loan sharks and Broadway ticket-scalpers; some freelanced for Murder, Incorporated.

In his *Dance to the Music of Time* series, an Anthony Powell character observes that "writers coexist uneasily." I'd never found that to be especially true, but Heller and I were an exception, "uneasy" being the operative word.

At Barrister's that day, it turned around.

A neighbor's daughter approached the table and asked if I was free later in the day for a tennis date.

When she'd gone off, Goodman asked Heller:

"How come he knows such pretty girls?"

"It is because he gives them cocaine," Heller announced, to everyone in the restaurant within hearing distance.

Then he took a bite of Vogel's tuna salad sandwich and threw back his head in a horse-laugh. It made for an unlovely sight.

Once again, he had hit on a sore spot. I'd written a short story about cocaine called "Lady" which appeared in *Esquire* and was much-noticed. So much so that I began to be quoted as an expert on the substance. Though my use of the drug was fleeting and negligible I was concerned enough to consult Jack Richardson on the subject. After listening patiently, he said:

"You expect me to be impressed by a gram-a-year habit?"

Still, Heller had yet another bit between his teeth. Whenever he saw me at some social event, he would cry out:

"He's probably got a shitload of cocaine in his pocket."

Followed of course by his trademark horse-laugh.

It took me some time to see that he was more than intrigued by the drug. He was anxious to try it. And I could tell that it would have no effect on him. There are certain people who are immmune to pleasure. And I'd noticed that he was always a decade late on trends – divorce, jogging, affairs – and he'd become interested in the drug when it had already become passé. (There would be comebacks.) Still, there was that interest.

I said: "Joe, if you're so interested in cocaine, go out on the street like everyone else and buy some. I can tell you where to go."

"How much does it cost?" he asked.

"About a hundred and fifty a gram, if it's any good."

The figure was daunting. It was no secret that Heller was, to put it gently, a bit close with a dollar.

"I didn't know that," he said weakly.

After thought, he said: "At least you had fun."

Implied in the comment was that I had turned my back on literature in favor of the movies. (The truth is, I tortured myself by moving back and forth, from one to the other.) He felt the same about Mario. Whenever Puzo told a Hollywood story, Heller took on a bemused and slightly judgmental expression. Though he never said so, he felt that Mario, for all of his achievement, had betrayed his gift and was writing "down." He could have been a great (and starving) novelist. Instead, he had "sold out."

In all of this, Joe conveniently forgot his own film background – partial credits on the movies *Sex and the Single Girl* and *Dirty Dingus Magee*, as well as his work on episodes of the television show, *McHale's Navy*.

And for all of his lack of interest, if not contempt for film, Heller continually badgered me for information about the agency that represented me in Hollywood.

"Who gets you the work?" he would ask.

"It isn't any one person. You deal with a committee."

"Yeah, but there's got to be one individual."

"No. They have a different way of doing things."

He didn't buy it.

"There's one," he said.

"How do you know I had fun?" I asked him.

"I read your books," he said.

And that's when it turned. An end to needling. Growing affection. An easy rapport. I'm always surprised when someone reads my books. But to have Joseph Heller as a reader amazed and touched me. He'd read more of my work than I had of his – at the time. We became the best of friends. As simple as that. A demonstration of how easy (and sluttish?) I can be.

Still, Heller continued to be one of the few people who could embarrass me. Asked his feelings about Kurt Vonnegut, who had lavishly praised *Something Happened* in the *Times*, he said: "I can't stand sci-fi."

"What about Shakespeare?"

"Hate it."

It was one thing to hate Shakespeare in private, but to say it out loud, in public, took something beyond chutzpah.

Now that Heller and I had settled our differences, the mood at the table was tranquil. I immediately muddied the waters, as if in answer to a question Nelson Algren had once put to me:

"Why do men destroy themselves?"

Several days before, I'd been offered a part in the Woody Allen movie *Another Woman*. I'm not an actor, but I do enjoy trying something different – as long as it's not bungee jumping. Anything to escape writing. Allen had asked me to audition. I said I would give it a try. However befuddled I was, I got through a page or two of dialogue. Whatever I did seemed to please him. It's common knowledge in the acting community that Allen only gives the individual auditioning his or her "sides," and never the entire script. I had no idea of what I was reading or where my character fit in the story. It was only later that I realized he'd been auditioning me for the lead role. Happily, he came to his senses and cast the Academy Award-winning actor Ian Holm. I had a small part, which was fine with me.

I mentioned this at the Southampton lunch and instantly saw that I'd made a mistake. There was an awful silence. And I had learned something. Writers will accept and even share in the joy of a colleague's literary triumph – or film sale. With a certain permissible envy. But an acting role is different. *Why him?* is the question that is asked in silence. *"I'm so much better-looking. I just don't get it."* David Newman, a co-writer of *Bonnie and Clyde*, and someone who lived and breathed movies, virtually gnashed his teeth in frustration when he got the news.

"It makes no sense," he said. "Doesn't Woody know I would kill to be in one of his movies?"

Puzo broke the silence at the restaurant.

"Maybe he wants to humiliate you."

It was true that Allen had shown some irritation with the success of *Stir Crazy*. He'd been quoted, revealingly, in the press as saying: "You can't keep audiences away from that movie."

"But what if he does?" I said to Puzo. "I don't mind playing the fool. And it beats the hell out of writing."

Additionally, I'd found that seeing yourself on the screen is the world's best diet. You immediately want to run out and lose twenty pounds. And in most cases, including mine, more people will see a writer on screen, in a minor film, than will have read all of the author's books combined.

There were several other roles that followed, two more in Woody Allen films. A woman was later to run up to me at the entrance of the Beverly Hills Hotel and tell me how much she enjoyed my work.

"That's very kind," I said. "Which of my books have you read?"

"I didn't know you were a writer," she said. "But I loved your acting in *Husbands and Wives.*"

Thom Jones became the subject of conversation. Every now and then a writer – in this case a short story writer – comes out of nowhere and astonishes the literary world with a blaze of originality. Most show up in *The New Yorker.* Salinger, of course, had been one. Roald Dahl another. Lorrie Moore and Alice Munro – to an extent. And now there was Thom Jones. All of us went on and on about the power of his Vietnam stories.

And then Puzo said, quietly: "We do not know if he can write a novel."

That was true enough and the discussion tapered off. But I wondered why it was essential for Jones to write a novel. The standard progression – more or less insisted on by publishers – was that a writer "move up" from the short story to the novel. The short story had become the stepchild of American literature. As if someone who excelled at the 100-yard dash was less of an athlete than an individual who runs the mile. A publisher "indulged" an author by publishing the short stories in order to get at the coming novel. Yet wasn't the short story, with its clean and unrelenting focus, an art form in itself? "The jeweler's art" is what Norman Mailer had called it. And wasn't it true that many of our major writers were at their best in the short story? Or at least I thought so.

Irwin Shaw comes to mind, as does Joyce Carol Oates. None of this can be proven, but John Cheever's stories were far superior to his novels. Chekhov never wrote a novel, nor has – to the best of my knowledge – Thom Jones.

Puzo may have had a minor axe to grind with Jones.

Candida Donadio, beloved by each of us, was known to have turned Jones' career around and helped to get his stories published in *The New Yorker*.

"He praised her as a saint." said Puzo, "and then he fired her."

(And went over to Andrew Wylie who got him a huge advance, for a novel, of course.)

"A novelist," Puzo said, "must have meat on his bones."

Thereby closing out the subject.

On another front, he did have some news. For years he had been collecting books and research on the Borgias, with an eye toward writing a novel about the notorious Renaissance family. In many ways, there were parallels to the Corleones.

"I had all this research stacked up in front of me and I was ready to begin. Then I realized that if I wrote this novel I would have to say 'm'lord' a thousand times. So I shoved aside ten years worth of research and went back to writing about the Mafia."

The book he returned to was *The Last Don*. He fought tooth and nail to have it called *The Clericuzzios*, but the publishers won out. Sometimes they know what they're doing.

We had all made plans to scatter. Heller was off on an all-expenses paid luxury cruise. Typically, he refused to divulge the name of his sponsor. Puzo was headed west to write a movie for a producer who was well set up financially, but whose past success rate was shaky.

"The man is responsible for ten straight flops. Yet he will instruct me on how to write this movie. At no point will he ask me if I have thoughts of my own. And he will do all of this without shame."

I had a meeting scheduled with Martin Scorcese.

"Be wary of him," said Mario. "He will ask you to do things that you do not want to do."

Puzo, of course, was close to Francis Ford Coppola. You were either "with" Coppola or Scorcese – much the way it worked in the underworld.

Before we left, a young man approached the table and asked Heller if he had any advice to give to the youth of America.

"Frankly," he said, "I don't give a shit about the youth of America."

That was his shock-tactic in action. Anyone who has read *Something Happened* would know his true feelings, which were tender.

Then, as if delivering a benediction, Speed Vogel said: "Gentlemen, I hope we all have the good fortune to die in our sleep."

27

"You have a crazy head."
The agent Candida Donadio's reaction to the author's first stories.

I lost two key people in my life soon afterward. Donald Fine, whose cantankerous style was a façade, died. He'd published several of my books and could not have been more loyal. If he was tightfisted, I never noticed it. The last book of mine he published was *A Father's Kisses*. What I had in mind was a suspense/adventure novel. Everyone else was doing them; it was high time I tried one. But I never could believe in people furtively looking over their shoulders, being chased down dark alleys and finding bodies in their hotel rooms. Drawing on a magazine piece I'd written on Bill Clinton, I ended up with the most absurd of hit men – an unemployed poultry worker in Hope, Arkansas. The novel turned out to be an absurdist piece, not what I'd been shooting for. Still, I liked it. The reviews were as good as we wanted them to be. But Fine died soon afterward, as did his publishing house – and my (poor) novel. His last words to me were: "They could have caught it" – a reference to the colon cancer that had killed him, and the test he never took. Candida Donadio retired to the country soon afterward, causing me to reflect on how important she was to me. (And to so many others.)

Her voice wasn't everything, but it had a great deal to do with it. On reflection, it was the most beautiful voice I had ever heard. Rich, deep, womanly, reassuring, and then oddly hesitant and girl-ish. I didn't realize it at the time, but the sound of it was highly seductive. The content of course was formidable, but sometimes it was just gasps, faint sighs, a struggle to express wonderment or disbelief. An eavesdropper might have thought he had been listen-ing to a woman making love.

It was the novelist Alex Austin who first told me about Candida. Though his books were not widely read, he was famed throughout Manhattan for his handsome and majestic book-shelves. And he had fixed ideas on how a writer should look and behave. Before responding to a question, he would furrow his brow and make quizzical novelistic faces. He had great misgivings about the way I dressed, feeling I wasn't half rumpled enough to make my way in literary society. His own look was that of a race-track tout – checkered shirts, plaid jackets, a crushed fedora – which he felt was closer to the mark. Despite his unhappiness with my dress code (off-the-rack suit, striped tie) and my overall appearance, he was anxious for me to meet a young secretary at the McIntosh and McKee literary agency. The appointment was made. Soon after I arrived, I was led into the office of Elizabeth McKee, a handsome woman with a good voice, which seemed to be a requisite for working at the agency. She said she had met my kind before.

"You'll wander off from time to time – like Styron – but you will always come back to your base."

William Styron was one of her clients.

I was then passed along to Candida Donadio, a small, plumpish woman with large black eyes, who seemed almost to be hiding behind her desk and melting away with shyness. But then the voice took over, carried by the enthusiasm for the few stories I'd sent on ahead.

"I like them, Bruce. They're good. You have a crazy head."

Others have said that, after a brief period in her company, she became beautiful. I needed very little time for that to happen.

Not long afterward, she left to form her own agency. I followed her without hesitation. We had a few tentative victories, a story here, a story there, often with a fallow year in between. For her to give up on a piece she admired was unthinkable. I worried about the cost to the agency in postage, as one of my efforts struggled through twenty rejections, in the hope that some poor soul at an obscure journal would snap it up for fifty dollars. (This is not, incidentally, the saga of an impoverished young man, scratching along in a cold-water flat. I was the editor of four adventure magazines at the time. Astonishingly, I had some skills as an administrator, hired good people and did very little work myself. My family of five lived comfortably. But the stories I wrote at midnight and on commuter trains and sent along to Candida Donadio were my hope and my anchor and all that mattered to me.)

The news that there was a call from Candida would make my heart leap, as if it had come from a lover, which in a sense it had. *Candida*. The very name (with apologies to Steven Sondheim) was like music. A letter from her (always handwritten) was cause for celebration – before I knew its contents. When I sent her a story, she never failed, over decades, to respond before twenty-four hours had gone by. The ones she liked became hers, the pleasure in having them published was ours. When my first novel was sold, she luxuriated in the experience.

"Isn't it wonderful," she would say, getting more passion into those few words than would have been thought possible. "Isn't it just grand."

When she read a story and said: "It's good, Bruce." I walked with angels. When she asked: "Do you want it straight?" I went directly to bed.

In the later years, she would say:

"You haven't lost it. Is that what you're worried about? Well, you haven't."

Actually, I never felt that I'd "lost it." Whatever "it" was. But it was nice to have the reassurance. I thought of a once prominent advertising man I'd seen staggering around on the street, with a dazed look in his eyes.

"What happened?" I asked him.

"I've lost it," he said.

"Your advertising touch?"

"Yes."

"You mean to tell me that the fellow, for example, who wrote 'Coke is it' can *lose* it?"

"That's what happened to me."

When I first saw the Geico commercials – which had no connection to anything that had come before them – I understood why my friend might have felt he'd lost his way.

I felt that Candida was provably brilliant. She disagreed.

"That's not it at all," she said. "I'm attuned."

She would often match up writers and editors on the basis of physical appearance.

"He's wrong for you," she might say. "He's too short."

Despite my height advantage, she put me together, happily, with the feisty and passionate – and diminutive – Donald I. Fine.

When asked in an interview to describe the writers she represented, Candida said that I was the most "disciplined." This not only puzzled me, but also called to mind a woman I had misguidedly asked how I compared to her other lovers. "You're the most thorough" was the unromantic verdict. Actually, for a time, I didn't realize Candida represented anyone else. (And when someone in Hollywood claimed to know "Candy" you could assume they didn't.) She had that capability of making you feel you were her only client. Charles De Gaulle might be on the other line, but there would be no indication of it. It was only after time that I realized she was, treacherously, carrying on "romances" with Philip Roth,

Saul Bellow, Joseph Heller, Robert Stone and Thomas Pynchon, to name a few. No doubt she spoke to them all in that same tone of seductive encouragement that I assumed was reserved for me.

I'm afraid I wasn't much of a friend to her. I knew of her brief marriage to the writer "Shag" Donohue, his jealousy of her clients, forcing her, like a schoolgirl, to duck beneath the blankets at night and read manuscripts by flashlight. Or so I'd been told. Mine was never a shoulder to cry on. Much as I admired her – loved her – she existed only to advance my case. Only in recent years have I discovered that other people have lives that are as fascinating and important to them as my life is to me. The lack of this insight can obviously be a handicap to a writer.

Halfway along in her career, she combined her agency with that of Robert ("Robby") Lantz, a Central European charmer, primarily from the worlds of film and theater, who brought along substantial bonafides of his own.

However formidable they appeared to be as a team, the mix (like that of Elizabeth Taylor and Richard Burton, two Lantz clients) proved to be an explosive one; the marriage soon dissolved. A product of the divorce, I ended up somehow in the Lantz camp. Not too long afterward, I began looking for a third and neutral agency. My wife Pat, whose judgment is usually sound, suggested that I get in touch with Candida.

"She's a friend. Ask her what to do. She'll know someone who would be good for you."

It was no secret that she had begun to drink heavily at this time. Who hadn't? Yet when I walked into her office, I was confronted with a monument of sobriety. I don't believe I had ever seen anyone that sober.

"Would I take you back?" were her first words. "Is that why you're here? The answer is 'yes.' I would take you back."

I had walked into a velvet trap. There went my dream of some wonderful and neutral party in the sky.

*

An agent is an agent is an agent.

Illness began to plague her. She retired in stages – coming in to her office a few days a week from her home in Connecticut – then not at all. Others tried to emulate her cheerfully melancholy style, getting the second component right, not the essential first. I refused to accept her retirement, calling her out when a situation demanded her touch – and of course she never refused me.

A week before she died in 2001, I sent her a collection of essays I had written (*Even The Rhinos Were Nymphos*), not so much for her to read, but just to have. I did think she might want to look at some thoughts I'd recorded about another one of her clients, Mario Puzo, who *did* have a shoulder for her to cry on. She wrote and told me – in handwriting that was a scrawl now – that she didn't have much time left. She had an illness that might "bite her in the ass at any moment." Her eyesight was failing, but she swore she would read the book while she could. I hope she didn't. It wasn't that kind of book. Knowing her . . . she did.

She was my youth. My books were hers. It was easy to be brave with someone fearless clearing out the path ahead. We had a love affair, professional, but in many ways richer, deeper than the other.

28

"I came to the brink of quitting."

A director's response when he learned that the author, who had fought to have him hired – was himself fired.

The idea that writers have "fans" always seemed inappropriate to me. Or incongruous. One of the two. Rock stars have fans. As do actors. It ought to be enough for writers to have readers. Yet, in going through the memoirs of Anthony Powell, I discovered that this novelist, who was virtually a deity to me, did, indeed, have fans. From time to time, his wife would call up to his study:

"Darling, you have a young person who is a fan waiting at the front door."

Claire Townsend, an executive at United Artists, called one day and introduced herself as a fan. That was fine. If the magisterial Powell was comfortable having fans, who was I to back away from the thought?

Townsend said she was a slavish admirer of *The Lonely Guy*, in particular.

"What if one of your Lonely Guys were to meet and fall in love with a mermaid? Does that sound like a movie?"

I thought it sounded feasible. And here again was that "what if?" component that was so often the bedrock of a good story.

"Why don't you think about it and maybe you can fly out and kick it around."

I did think about it. Mermaids. Poseidon. Legends of the Deep. And the purest of love stories, something I'd never tried.

A week later, in Los Angeles, I met Townsend, who, incidentally, was the daughter of Robert Townsend, a founder of Avis.

A young man who I took to be an office boy of some kind joined us. I had no idea of what he was doing there. Perhaps taking notes. At one point, as I sketched out a story, he interrupted me with a question. I patted him on the head and told him he had committed the most egregious of offenses.

"Never interrupt a storyteller in mid-story. It's like cutting off his oxygen."

I had no idea that this was Brian Grazer, the producer of the film I was to call *Splash*. Nor did I realize that this "child" was my new boss.

This was at a time when I still clung to the preposterous notion that a writer was a meaningful participant in the film-making process. I was soon to be disabused of that notion.

Once we'd been properly introduced, my youthful employer offered me a ride back to my hotel. Referring to himself as "Bry-Guy," he took me on a hair-raising trip around Cold Water Canyon in a battered BMW. I still haven't entirely recovered from it. But I did sense that anyone who could drive so recklessly – and skillfully – was destined to become one of the most powerful men in Hollywood. (And would, before long, be throwing around the term "Zeitgeist" at meetings.)

Off I went to research Poseidon and his kingdom and Legends of the Deep, none of which made it into the movie. This was before the digital revolution, which would have put such scenes within financial reach. Or perhaps the film-makers decided they weren't necessary.

What I had in mind was a love story, which was, of course,

what I had been hired to write. I'd had more than one romantic skirmish, but the only love affair that ever meant anything to me began when I met my wife Pat. I didn't see any harm in borrowing freely from it. Since the lead character was to fall in love with a mermaid, I thought it fitting that he work in the smoked fish business. I spent weeks researching a smoker in Green Point, Brooklyn, one that sold whitefish and smoked salmon directly to Zabar's in Manhattan. Cats followed me home. All for nothing. Apparently, the smoked fish occupation was felt to be "too Jewish." This remains a touchy area for Hollywood, which is strange since the industry, as it is now called, is thickly populated with Jews. There is an exception now and then when a film goes "Full-Out-Jewish," as the Coen brothers did in the glorious *A Serious Man*. With the stroke of a computer key, my centeral character Adam (also too Jewish?) became Allen and was transferred to the fruit and vegetable business. (Clearly less Jewish than having him work with lox and whitefish chubs.)

I did the obligatory first and second drafts, then a polish, a shine, a gloss and, for good measure, and free of charge, a light buffing. Half-a-dozen scripts in all. Grazer had some difficulty getting a studio interested in *Splash*. The producer Ray Stark was developing a mermaid film with Warren Beatty and suggested "merging" the two projects. (How does one do that?) Grazer rejected the offer and went on to United Artists, which granted the two of us a quick interview.

"Poseidon comes off as being too Jewish," was the only comment I can recall. "Think John Gielgud." (Actually I had modeled the character on Zero Mostel.)

The excutives dismissed us, then rushed off to pour their energies into *Heaven's Gate*, convinced it would save the studio. It buried United Artists and almost took all Hollywood down with it. Disney, with a new division called Buena Vista, agreed to do the film if the budget could be kept modest, which it was. I saw a screening of the vampire comedy *Love At First Bite* and felt it was in exactly the spirit that I had in mind for our (Grazer's) movie. I lobbied hard to have the director, Stan ("Drag") Dragoti hired to do the same for *Splash*. Astonishingly, someone listened to me and he was taken on – at least for a time.

I returned to Water Mill (and Manhattan) to pick up my life as "a real writer." At Elaine's one night a waiter told me that I'd been let go (canned) and that a comedy team, led by someone named Hulabaloo, was "punching up" *Splash*. It turned out the waiter, who had just arrived from Italy, was off a bit on the name, which was Babaloo, although I didn't see that it made much of a difference.

Thrown off stride – one doesn't usually get such news from a waiter – I finished my veal piccata and called Dragoti when I got home.

"Stan, I fought to get you hired. You were down and out. Remember? What did you do when you heard that I was fired?"

He thought for a moment and then made one of my favorite Hollywood remarks.

"I came to the brink of quitting."

I took little comfort in it when Dragoti was fired soon afterward. I saw the movie. There was much to like in it. The cast was fresh, it had a handsome look to it – but I'd made the mistake of becoming personally attached to my screenplay. It began, after all, as my love story. I felt it had been cheapened. Still, there was no arguing with the result: a Writer's Guild Award for Best Movie. A nomination for the Academy Award. Huge commercial success. I made some money. Little girls kept telling me how much they loved it. When I mentioned my disappointment to John Eskow, a very good screenwriter, he said: "Hey, it's a living."

I received two credits on the film – one for something called "screen story" and a screenplay credit that I shared with the Babaloo team. There were the predictable offers. Typically, I retreated to my cottage in Water Mill and returned to what I continued to think of as my "serious" work. Not too long afterward, I fired the powerful CAA agency. I'd been fired. I thought I might as well do some firing of my own. When asked why I had done something so foolhardy, I said the agency was doing "too good a job." This is true. They were bombarding me with work that I didn't care for. Agreeing to realize someone else's notion (dream, in some cases) was like signing on to do a nine-month stretch at Riker's Island. The gifted screenwriter (and novelist) Richard Price once shrugged and said to to me:

"What are you going to do with all that Hollywood money, buy another Lacoste t-shirt?"

My income suffered, although I did sleep better. Or at least theoretically I was supposed to. At one point, I found myself without an agent (for film) and asked Robert Lantz to have lunch at The Century Association, an Elaine's for Seriously Older Guys. Elaine's was now a long and expensive cab ride away. Many of my friends had shuffled off the coil or never now left their apartments. The new club was within walking distance, on a good day. I'd seen Henry Kissinger dozing in a chair at the Century and thought: "This is the club for me."

Lantz was knocking on the door of ninety. He had targeted one hundred, his great friend, the illustrator Harry Hershfield, having missed that goal by a whisker.

He told me that after many years and with great regret, he'd had to part company with his client, Elizabeth Taylor.

"She sits by the phone and waits to be offered leading roles. I told her 'Liz, save your energy and take some cameos. Take the money.' But she refused to listen. Life is short. It was too much for me."

Then he reflected.

"But when I walked into a room with Liz on my arm – or we entered a theater – and I saw the effect she had on others – I said to myself: 'Now *this* is the definition of a star.'"

I gathered up my courage. This was going to be difficult.

"Robby, I left you twenty years ago," I said, over Waldorf salad, a favorite of his. "Would you consider taking me back?"

His answer was unbearably moving.

"Dear boy," he said," "I hadn't realized you'd left."

29

"America will dance again."

> Pete Hamill, writing in the *N.Y. Daily News*, in response to the 9/11 attack.

Pat and I woke up one morning and realized we'd spent close to two decades in *Water Mill*, for God's sakes. What could we have been thinking? It was if we'd checked into the Betty Ford Center and forgotten to leave. How much clean living could two people survive? Molly was off to school in Connecticut. Pat was anxious to pick up a degree at N.Y.U. in therapy. I noticed, with some disquiet, that the men who lived on our street (Holly Lane) were passing on, one by one. My closest neighbor had been telling me that he enjoyed living in the country because he could walk out of his house and take a pee on the lawn. And then he died, as he was taking one. There had been yet another neighbor, a British colonial, who kept soliciting me for funds to preserve the local windmill.

"People like us can't afford to let these old landmarks rot, now can we, Friedman?"

It was that 'people like us' phrase that got me every time – and cost me an extra hundred. He expired, pressed against his wife, the two octogenarians wearing a single pair of pyjamas called "funzies" and watching lesbian porn movies.

Holly Lane was becoming The Street of Widows. Chilling. I thought it best to start packing before it was too late.

Still, I had a fear of change. (My mother again – *don't move a show, don't get divorced, don't do anything. Let other people do things. Our family does nothing.*) And I was uneasy about returning to Manhattan. We had to move me in, virtually house by house, until we arrived in beloved Greenwich Village, the last one of my literary generation to land there. Embarrassingly, I was sixty-five when I made my first visit to The White Horse, as if it might still be possible to catch a glimpse of a long-vanished Dylan Thomas.

My first night in the Village, I'd walked out on Seventh Avenue with a cane, as a weapon, actually – my knees were still holding up admirably. For a boy from the wild streets of the Bronx (they weren't that wild) to be fearful of the city was absurd. By the second night, I'd settled in comfortably and had rediscovered a gay-and-lesbian hangout that now had a piano bar, one that featured the music of Kurt Weill, Cole Porter and other favorites. Before long, I was singing along with the regulars, and listening with pride to an eleven P.M. announcement by my new friend, the lesbian manager.

"All straights have to leave now – except for Bruce."

I'd like to report that we took advantage of the wonders of this great city and kept running around to museums and concerts. We didn't. It was enough to just *be* in Manhattan and to know that the Stuttgart Ballet was in town in case we got a sudden urge to take it in. (It was in other cities, St. Louis, for example, that I would immediately dash out to see exhibitions.) I did tour the city on a bike each day, sick at heart that I couldn't investigate every street, sample every restaurant, talk to every new arrival and, in a sense, save myself a trip to Bangladesh. I generally parked my bike beneath the World Trade Center and, for lunch, bought an incredibly crisp and delicious panini, which was, at that time, new to the city.

One morning, I took poor blind Freddie, our Tibetan terrier, out for his ten-in-the-morning walk and saw an an army of stunned and seemingly sightless executives, each of them holding a jacket over the shoulder with one finger, staggering up Seventh Avenue. Traffic had disappeared. They were headed uptown on a downtown street. I thought there might have been an exhibition at the Fashion Institute, which was close by. I stopped a middle-aged woman who said that something awful had happened at the Twin Towers and she had no idea if she'd be able to get the subway back to her apartment in Queens. Somehow, this seemed to embarrass her. This, of course, was the day of horror. I watched events unfold on my rooftop as if I were looking at a giant TV screen. My daughter called from her college dorm in Pennsylvania and was distraught – she had seen the TV images and thought the entire city had gone up in flames, along with her parents.

"What do you plan to *do*?" she asked.

I said that for a start I thought I'd warm up my coffee in the microwave, which seemed to calm her.

Later in the day, I needed some help with a laptop and realized that my computer person had his office in the bowels of one tower and had, as it turned out, been incinerated. And here I'd been upset about his fees. Calls kept coming in from my three sons, telling me how upset their mother was in Toronto. I suggested that I was a little upset myself, but they indicated that I couldn't possibly be as upset as their mother was. Apparently, you had to be in Toronto to be really upset.

Each day that followed, I rushed over to a Relief Facility with a basket of food, mostly so that I could feel virtuous. You had to do something. Maybe canned peas would be helpful.

My address in lower Manhattan must have thrown up a flag. E-mails from around the country started to pile up. A former Hollywood agent unaccountably began to address me as "baby-doll." PBS got in touch and asked if I would be part of a writer's round table discussion of the event. With the ashes still in my nose, I said I hadn't had time to develop any Higher Thought. Pete Hamill, in the *N.Y. Daily News*, informed the Taliban stiffly that America would dance again. This was heartening, especially for those among us who were dancers.

A friend in London e-mailed his support.

"Be assured that we here in Britain stand beside you."

I felt for a moment as if we were France and had fallen to the Wehrmacht.

I did not feel the heart and soul of America had been reached until a bachelor friend on Bank Street called and said that after shopping at Balducci's he had found dust in his stringbeans.

I'm not the first to report that it was as if there had been a genetic (tectonic?) change in the culture, that life could no longer be lived in the same way. And there *was* this change, but from what I could see, most of it took place below Thirty-Fourth Street in Manhattan.

Shortly afterward, I wrote the following in a notebook:

It was difficult to separate the depressive effect of all this news from the generally depressive feelings I'd experienced before the event. Philip Roth was quoted on one of the cable networks as saying he spends eight hours a day, seven days a week, 365 days a year writing. "It's the only way." And here I was taking time out to gauge the level of support we were getting from the Saudis. Somehow this disturbed me more than the attack itself.

For diversion I lost myself in the mammoth Richard Reeves book about the deceitful and backstabbing Nixon White House. Dean, Liddy, Haldeman, The Plumbers, Egil "Bud" Krogh – with the saturnine – and oddly satisfying – Nixon in the lead role. Nixon as a great "character." The awful Watergate days, with the presidency in peril, had seemed a sunnier time. Somehow, weirdly, I felt I was back among friends. What had once seemed cataclysmic was much easier to manage than the horror down the street.

Down the street. Just down the road. *With each day that passed, I kept pushing myself closer to the center of it. Making myself more of a "player." When friends called and said they felt the full force of it in Los Angeles, I answered, with no small touch of smugness, "It's just down the*

*street from us." Actually, it was a mile away, which was close enough.
One of the greatest disasters the country had ever suffered, and here I was
scoring points for how close we were to it.*

Comedy slowly came out of the bushes. The New Yorker *declared
an end to official gloom, and the Friar's Club tried to follow along. At a
Hugh Hefner roast, a performer tried a few tentative jokes that were topi-
cal and there were shaming calls from the Gallery. "Too early. Too early."
Still, I began to feel less uncomfortable about an earlier thought – that we
ought to retaliate with our own group of suicide bombers. I knew a few
writers who generally felt awful and might jump at the chance to
volunteer.*

*The name Bin Laden reverbertated in my head, replacing Manolo
Blahnik. I continued to puzzle over why – following the attack – George
W. Bush had dashed over to congratulate the CIA. And was the doorman
in our building a "sleeper"?*

*I was cheered when the historian Francis Fukuyama weighed in with
the assurance that history was on our side. But an analyst had said it
would feel much worse a month later, when the full extent of the attack
sunk in – and it did, possibly because the analyst had said so.*

*For a writer, there is always a ray of hope in the worst of circum-
stances – a chance to avoid writing. . . .*

30

"Thank God I won't have to deal with the internet."
Mario Puzo's last words to the author.

Before leaving Water Mill, I had lunch with my friends at Barrister's. It turned out to be the last time we would all get together.

Puzo had seen this coming.

"Once you're in the city, you will never again have lunch with us."

I said that was absurd. I'd always thought of the trip from Manhattan to Water Mill as a two-cigar drive. But I was no longer smoking cigars, which made the trip unendurable.

The mood was elegiacal.

Puzo had learned for the first time that the publisher Donald Fine had passed away.

"How old was he?" he wanted to know.

"Seventy-seven."

"That ain't bad. After seventy-five, you are playing on the casino's money."

Though Pat and I had already made arrangements to leave the area, Heller, in a surprisingly dramatic move, gripped me by the shoulders and said: "You can do it."

It was as if he and the others were imprisoned on Devil's Island and too old to make a break for it. But at a youthful sixty-five, I had a chance to escape – and carry the flag – on their behalf.

Puzo seemed frail. He could hardly walk. No longer could he smoke his beloved Dunhill cigars; he was reduced to chewing them or so he claimed. I was convinced he took a surreptitious puff now and then.

Nonetheless, he found some pleasures in old age.

"For the first time in my life, I can be with a beautiful woman – with the knowledge that she has no power over me."

(I've reached his age. I've been waiting in vain for this phenomenon to take place.)

I had shut the door on Hollywood, but I continued to feel uneasy about it. There was Puzo's fictional advisory, which was unsettling:

"A man's first responsibility is to put bread on the table."

When I first read this I had teased him:

"Does that include croissants?"

This was a not so veiled reference to the dozens of family and friends he supported lavishly. Still, his words nagged at me. I wasn't putting quite as much bread on the table. Impulsively, I'd fired the most powerful agent in Hollywood; it may not have been the wisest career move.

Heller took a different view.

"Do you sleep better?" he asked.

"Yes."

"So?"

Hearing that, I slept more soundly.

When the Barrister's check came, I made a grab for it. Having fallen, or thrown myself, on hard times, I was all the more determined not to come off as a poor relation.

Heller had read my mind. A prankster to the last, he grinned and said: "I took care of it." (True to form, he had handed it to Puzo.)

The streets were icy. Puzo and Heller both asked for help in getting to their cars. I walked to the parking lot with an icon on each arm. Neither had the least bit of shame in asking for assistance. Years before, when I had tried to help my aging father cross the Grand Concourse in the Bronx, he snatched his arm away in anger. Following suit, I rejected my eldest son when he tried to help me negotiate a busy highway. At one point, it would have been thought I lacked a "feminine" gene. I felt, at the time, that it was this reluctance to admit to weakness or frailty that kept me from being a better writer.

Some years back, Irwin Shaw insisted I meet the producer Sam Spiegel (*The Bridge on the River Kwai*) and his mogul friends.

"They live like emperors," he said.

I met them and they did live like emperors and it was all very nice for them and I continued about my business. I visited Mario at his home in Bay Shore several times before he died. He had taken a simple house on a street that was less than grand, and then added wings and guest houses and tennis courts until he too lived like an emperor. And yet, in terms of location, he remained in a (comforting) blue-collar neighborhood.

Somehow I could never find the house on my own. Two of his sons had to come and pick me up at a nearby gas station. He had been held up at gunpoint in his bedroom once and had installed an elaborate security system.

"What infuriated me," he said, "was not the fear of death so much as the power this person held over me."

It had always been about power. The (Godfather) Corleones' ability to correct injustice on behalf of the powerless (at a price of course.) The poor boy in Hell's Kitchen who gained power through literature. Carol Gino's family had given a banquet in his honor, the lavishness of which had never before been seen on Long Island. Like handmaidens in the court of a king, women, who were relations, lined up for what seemed like a mile, each passing before Mario with a platter of delicacies, designed to make a strong man swoon. Uncles knelt beside Puzo, whispering flatteries into the ears of a suitor and a man they saw as a prospective groom.

"But I had no interest in marriage," he said later. "I didn't want nobody telling me what to do with my money."

Translation: *My power.*

Size was important, too. The home that stretched on forever. The huge cigars. The great bowls of pasta when his health was sound. The astronomical gambling debts. The mountain of books.

One of the most beautiful women in Hollywood lusted after him.

"But she only gives blowjobs," he said, dismissively. (This created an image of the woman at a stand, passing out oral treats like party favors.)

It didn't seem the most unpleasant arrangement to me, but he needed to have it all.

There were just the two of us on my last visit. And I was now in awe of him. He picked up on this.

"Don't worry," he said. "You're still the boss."

And indeed, each of his novels that he gave to me had the same inscription:

"Still trying to keep up with The Boss."

A table was set with enough food (Italian delicacies) to feed all of Bay Shore. I wondered what would happen to it after I left. The most I could manage was a good-sized sandwich. And a slice of the mozzarella that had been rushed over to the house only minutes before, warm and dripping with flavor. There was no question in my mind he would have traded all this opulence for another year . . . another month at his beloved blackjack tables.

He watched me eat the sandwich. He ate nothing.

The Sopranos dominated television at the time. The series was religion in my family. I asked Mario, tentatively, what he thought of it. Perhaps the show had been too "heavily influenced" by his novel.

At a Book Fair, Puzo had once run into Lee Iaccoca, who had written a popular memoir. He told the chairman of Chrysler:

"Stay out of my racket."

It was said jokingly, of course, but I have a theory about jokes. There are usually dozens to choose from. The one that is selected has significance.

"I *love* that *Sopranos* show," he said. "The very idea of naming a character 'Uncle Junior.' That alone makes it a work of genius."

It was a treat to report this to Dominick Chianese who plays the part in the series. He was, of course, enormously pleased.

"It's amazing," he said. "David Chase, who created the show, had to fight the network tooth and nail to make sure the character was named 'Uncle Junior.'"

We wandered into Puzo's sitting room. His *Godfather* Oscars were displayed prominently on bookshelves. Leaning back in the biggest couch I'd ever seen, he slowly began to disappear into the cushions. As he flailed about, throwing out his arms like a drowning man, I reached in and hauled him back to safety. If he had expired then and there, the metaphor would have been too obvious – being sucked up and losing his life to all that opulence. As a novelist, he would have appreciated the scene. (In a Puzo novel, a rival family would have arranged for a special couch to pull him down, and have him sleep with the upholstery.)

He gave me some books I *had* to read – Larry McMurtry's *Lonesome Dove* and a huge novel about Brazil which still stares guiltily at me on my night table. Out of loyalty, I'll get around to it. In truth, I've had all I can take of Montezuma.

"Books," he said, "are the only thing that has never let me down."

He took pleasure in every phase of his life and never once complained about his health. The very process of losing his life amused him.

"This dying business is really something," he said, as if he was trying to sell it to me. "It's terrific fun to fall asleep and then wake up and there are six pairs of eyes staring at you to see if you're still in the game."

Two nurse/assistants came over to help him prepare for bed. Each was a walking centerfold, exploding out of her uniform. I'm not sure if they were hired to give him pleasure or to torture him.

We shook hands a final time. His grip was firm.

"Don't worry about me. I'm not going anywhere."

The nubiles in their white coats began to lead him off.

He whispered to me: "Women are crazy . . . and thank God I won't have to deal with the Internet."

He died several days later.

Carol told me about his last moments. Their final exchange was vintage Puzo.

He awakened at four in the morning, surprised he was alive.

"You said you'd knock me off, Carol."

"I am not knocking you off, Mario."

And then he passed away on his own.

Several hundred people attended his memorial on Long Island. The novelist George Mandel asked me if I would drive him out from Manhattan. At one time, as the author of *Flee the Angry Strangers*, it was thought in the fifties that Mandel was on a path to be the Next Great American Novelist. A small and feisty man, he had been a highly decorated WWII hero and came away from Normandy with a steel plate in his head and a one hundred percent disability pension. Forty years before, I had bought a story of his for *Male* magazine and been forced to cut a few paragraphs for length.

On the drive out to Long Island, he reminded me of this act of what he felt was editorial treachery. Apparently, he'd been brooding about it for years.

"You should have run the entire story," he said, with mounting anger. "You cut the heart out of it."

He kept at it for miles, until I stopped the car and asked him if he would like to get out and walk the rest of the way. He quieted down, but on the drive back, he picked up the theme again.

"A beautiful story like that," he said. "And you had to piss on it."

Speed Vogel came out to greet us at the memorial.

"What happened to Joe?" I asked.

"Joe does not go to funerals," he said, as if this was common knowledge.

Many of the mourners were handsome young men, running their fingers through ink-black hair, as if they were there to audition. At least a dozen women had flown in from different parts of the world, each claiming to have tended to Puzo in his final weeks. Shortly before he died, a competition had started up over who was the last to visit him. I had mentioned to Heller that I'd driven out to Bay Shore just before his final moments. Heller said: "Speed and I heard you were there."

The minister was a woman with a New Age style. She assured the mourners that Mario hadn't really died.

"Each time the clouds pass over and the birds fly by, Mario will be there, among them. He is in transition."

I imagined my old friend saying, with the boyish delight that had never deserted him:

"Hey, that's great. I'm in transition. And all I thought I did was drop dead."

Several weeks later, I ran into Jospeh Heller at Elaine's. We were both alone, casting about for a dinner partner, delighted by this chance meeting. He was surprisingly robust. Though he hadn't moved back from East Hampton, he was in love with the city.

We became old-fashioned literary drinkers, exchanging confidences. He made a confession that was touching.

"I'd like to fall in love."

A pillar of propriety, I reminded him that he had forgotten about his wife.

"I know, I know," he said. "I'm talking about something else."

He was seventy-six at the time.

Toward the end of the evening, I felt I'd never had a better friend.

As we were leaving, Elaine pulled me aside.

"Did Joe have a good time?"

"He had a great time," I assured her.

"Thank God," she said and smacked the table, as if she'd gotten a good result on a medical test.

Some weeks later, I was casting about for a dinner companion. I was generally indoors all day. My wife, who taught long hours, preferred to stay at home in the evening. She suggested that I call Heller.

"I don't think so."

"You might regret that one day."

Soon afterward, he had an "episode" in Europe. It was thought to be overexposure to the sun. He returned home and died in Southampton Hospital.

I imagined a Joseph Heller character saying. "Why Southampton Hospital? They only know how to treat clamming injuries."

Puzo, then Heller. Thus ended a tradition. At no time did I think of myself as having been more than a junior partner. Nor do I forget that I'd been in the company of (unlikely) giants, men who had made a lasting imprint on the culture – and on literature.

Some months later, in the West Village, I ran into an old friend, David Markson. His novel, *Reader's Block*, is one that I kept on my night table and returned to again and again. We chatted, and along came James Lincoln Collier, a Newbury prize winner for his children's books and a distinguished authority on jazz. Both had worked for my old company, The Magazine Management Company. We decided to have lunch. It worked out nicely. We made plans to do it again. It wasn't Barrister's. But it wasn't half-bad.

31

"Do you know of any good Chinese restaurants in Toronto?"
A question the author can't resist asking the distinguished novelist, Ha Jin.

Woody Allen was puzzled when he learned that I had moved to Water Mill, a full two hour drive from his beloved Manhattan.

"What do you *do* out there?"

"Read, write, throw logs on the fire. Run along the beach."

"Oh, great," he said, with a shudder. "Then all of a sudden you're eighty."

I discovered, that it's possible to become eighty "all of a sudden," even in vibrant Manhattan.

From time to time, as I approached that unimaginable age, I would say to Pat:

"I am knocking on the door of eighty."

"You've been saying that all year," she would answer. "Can we at least wait till you get there?"

I thought of eighty as being a location, rather than an age, much like a high and wintry city of ice I thought I saw in the distance on the outskirts of Reykjavík. Several friends had quietly slipped past the ghostly marker and gone beyond. I asked each one what it was like "up there." One had settled into a cozy apartment and kicked back, ready to enjoy his hard-earned prize, when a young (70-year-old) Shanghai pepperpot had scooped him up to accompany her on trips around the globe. Suddenly he was calling in from Lebanon and landed estates in Cornwall. When I saw him he was exhausted. A childhood friend, who was eighty-two, kept searching about for a philosophy, phoning me from time to time to ask if I knew of a serviceable one. I didn't, though Pat assured me I would get one when I needed it. ("Shouldn't I hurry up?" I wondered.)

I decided, after considerable thought, that I didn't actually need a philosophy. The solution to the question is to remove the question. Wittgenstein?

I shied away from yet another octogenarian who stretched and yawned and began each conversation by saying "Well . . . it won't be long now."

Fifteen years in Manhattan flew by irritatingly on the wings of every cliché. Gather ye rosebuds? I hadn't gathered half-enough. Had anyone? Had Trollope, with his fifty novels?

Stories, quite a few of them, got written and published. If they lacked energy (were less frantic?) I assured myself they were more "dimensional." Once I discovered that comforting description, I clung to it like life itself. There were a few books, some plays that still need attention. And quite a few pieces about me in the literary journals, wondering what had happened to me. Where had I gone? I began to feel like the most (fondly) remembered forgotten writer in America. And there had been a mistake or two. The wrong turn, a misstep in the literary jungle, can be costly. A producer takes an oath that he will produce a play. He does only one a year. He loves this particular play. All of his energies will be poured into producing it. There are readings, auditions, directors come and go. Years pass. Finally, a theater is selected. Casting begins. An opening date is pencilled in. He drives down to the playwright's apartment in a limousine, hands him a check that can cover a week's worth of groceries and says:

"I can't produce a play unless my heart is in it."

Anthony Powell reports in his memoir that Binkie Beaumont, London's leading producer at the time, told the author that his first play would be produced in a grand manner, and would star Olivier and Gielgud, the leading lights in the British theater. And then Powell never heard from the producer again.

But no sad stories. Plays that should be produced will be produced. The same is true of novels and short stories. Or so I have to feel. There are few masterpieces languishing in the trunks of writers. But the "The Saul Bellow Lesson" can be instructive.

The one play he had written was going poorly. The leading man (Zero Mostel) was having a temperamental fit. The director threatened to quit. The sets were falling apart. All was chaos. Yet the novelist sat there calmly, taking it all in. Clearly a disaster was in the making. The stage manager wondered why he wasn't in a lather.

"Simple," he said. "I have another iron in the fire."

The iron was *Herzog*, a novel that was about to become his greatest triumph.

When it comes to the theater, it's important to have that iron.

Though I barely noticed it, I found myself being gently nudged a bit further into the academic world. For a brief time, I held what was called The Leila Hadley Luce chair at Marymount College in Manhattan. It was useful in that I was able to work it into conversations.

"And incidentally, I hold the Leila Hadley Luce chair at Marymount College."

When Leila Hadley Luce died, the chair was snatched away. There I was, a man without a chair, although I did have my own (academic) iron in the fire. Some years before, a group of remarkable Canadians had turned up in my life, and asked me to teach an intensive – and it turned out to be intensive – course in short fiction in Toronto. They showered me with money and a promise (kept) of handsome accomodations. Thus began, each July, an eighteen-year romance with Humber College on the banks of the Humber River. The fun of it was in the variety of students who turned up in my class: a man who trained race horses; a fellow whose job it was to invent ice-cream flavors; a woman who had won an award for giving the best phone sex in North America. And there were my colleagues, among them D.M. ("Don") Thomas, who was in the habit of marrying his students and who had written two of my favorite books, the acclaimed *White Hotel*, of course, and the lesser known but hysterically funny *Bleak Hotel* about the twenty-five years of almost but not quite getting the *White Hotel* movie made. (The first to show interest was Barbra Streisand, who met with the director Bernardo Bertolucci and asked him how he planned to film the sex scenes.

"I thought perhaps fiber optics up the vagina."

That ended the meeting.)

Another appeal of Humber was the list of distinguished guests who came up each year. The playwright Edward Albee was one. I told him that I'd once taught a playwriting course at York College, using his play *The Zoo Story* as a workshop piece. For the two leads, I cast a 75-year-old retired black postal worker and a comic book fanatic who was seventeen. He thought a moment and said:

"That would work." (It did, actually. It was mesmerizing.)

The novelist Martin Amis was another visitor. He kept me enthralled with tales of the lunches he'd had with his father, Kingsley, author of the comic masterpiece, *Lucky Jim*, and with the revered Anthony Powell.

One year, it was Ha Jin, who had written brilliant books about Mao and the Red Guard, a group that had always fascinated me. Someone failed to tell him that he would have to teach a course – in addition to delivering a lecture and being lionized. There were some bruised feelings. As a neutral party, and someone who had devoured his early books, I was dispatched to sit beside him at the annual banquet. His English was limited; we ran out of conversational topics quickly. They became generically bookish . . .

Faulkner, Doctorow, Updike. All fine, all gifted. . . . And that about covered it. We sat there uncomfortably, my low-grade Tourette's Syndrome beginning to kick in. I felt a (burning) need to ask him a question, though inner voices told me not to. Finally, I could resist no longer.

"Ha," I said, "I wonder if you know of any good Chinese restaurants in the area."

He hissed at me. It was as if he'd asked me where he could get a good bowl of matzoh ball soup.

Always, and right from the start, there was what may have been a genetic need to tell stories. They were a bond. A friend could not be a friend unless there was the ability to tell a good story. Some feel that storytelling is a writer's bid for immortality. For me, it's a need to stave off The Inevitable. If Mr. Scheherazade can just keep spinning tales, perhaps he'll be granted an exemption and not be spirited off to the Next World.

At one time, it seemed a miracle to know enough to tell an entire story. Now, there is so little time to tell the ones that are lined up, waiting to be told. If only it were an assembly line, with all the parts fitting neatly into place. Time. I envied Philip Roth when he said in an interview not that long ago that he had "all the time in the world." For me, there has never been enough time. It's been a race – against what? – from childhood on. You'd think I'd been diagnosed with a rare malady, like Irving Thalberg, the revered Hollywood executive who was the first to "spearhead" films. Some five hundred of them. There are now studio people who have as an epitaph:

"He was one of the producers who spearheaded *Tootsie*."

Regrets? A story that seemed to be within my grasp and slipped away . . . The abandoned book or play. If only I'd been brave enough to push on. In truth, and in most cases, I didn't know *how* to push on, until a decade or so had passed. And *abandoned*. What a sad word. In the collected stories of Bernard Malamud, the word "abandoned" sits beside a handful of stories. I felt that some were superior to those that had been . . . what? . . . adopted?

There have been few regrets in life itself. But there was the Sinatra episode.

The crooner was sitting at a table at Elaine's having dinner with George Plimpton, who had apparently, and unimaginably, run out of anecdotes. I was at the bar, ten feet away, trying to shake off the worst hangover I'd ever experienced. Plimpton approached me, put an arm around my shoulders and said:

"Francis would be delighted if you could join us."

I barely had the strength to apologize and wave him off.

It troubles me that I didn't stumble over to say hello. Who knows, I might have been the most sober person he'd met that week.

But that was it. A few financial catastrophes, the Sinatra episode. It would have been nice to be a student at Harvard and to get a jump-start on Suetonius. And I had once seen a canvas behind a sink at an art dealer's warehouse. Two young men in a bistro. Painted with what seemed like flourishes of gold. It continues to haunt me. The price: $20,000. The artist? Matisse. I had the (screenwriter) money. But I'd befriended the notorious "Society Thief" Albie Baker, who had visited my flat and taken a quick look around at the doors and windows. No sooner had I hung the Matisse, than Baker, always the consummate professional, would have figured out a way to break in and waltz off with my one valuable painting. Nothing personal. Just business. So I left the warehouse without it.

That's about it: Harvard, Sinatra, the Matisse. Other than that, it's been a highly decent life.

And always – no matter how weak the knees and frail the bank account – there has been the pleasure at Customs of filling in the blank for Occupation with the single word that has always felt treasured and benighted: *writer.*

Acknowledgements

The author wishes to thank the following individuals for their help of one kind or another along the way: David McCormick, Patricia J. O'Donohue, John Metcalf, Daniel Wells, Robert Fogarty, John Bowers, Dan Wakefield, Joe Kertes, Antanas Sileika, Lewis B. Frumkes, Terry McDonell. Lawrence Dukore, Dennis Aspland, Jack Richardson, Lou Anne Walker, Geoff Huck, Josh, Drew, Kipp and Molly Friedman.

Some material, often in different form, appeared in the following publications: *Southampton Review, Antioch Review, Esquire, Playboy, New York Magazine*, Nextbook(website).

Novelist, playwright, short story writer and Oscar-nominated screenwriter **Bruce Jay Friedman** was born in New York City. Friedman published his first novel *Stern* in 1962 and established himself as a writer and playwright, most famously known for his off-Broadway hit *Steambath* (1973) (TV) and his 1978 novel *The Lonely Guy's Book of Life*. In addition to short stories and plays, Friedman has also published another seven novels, and has written numerous screenplays, including the Oscar-nominated *Splash* (1984). He resides in New York City with his wife, educator Patricia J. O'Donohue.